THE WAY OF PERFECTION AND CONCEPTIONS OF DIVINE LOVE
BY

St. Teresa of Avila

FOREWORD

Saint Teresa of Avila (also known as Saint Teresa of Jesus) (1515-1582), was a Spanish nun and mystic, and is recognized as a Doctor of the Church. *The Way of Perfection* and *Conceptions of Divine Love* are two of Saint Teresa's most famous works.

TO THE REVEREND SUPERIORESS
OF THE
CONVENT OF THE INFANT JESUS,
NORTHAMPTON.

MADAM,

I HAVE long known how tenderly you love St. Teresa, and how much you admire and strive to imitate her heroic virtues.

It is, then, with the greatest pleasure that I dedicate the "Way of Perfection" to you; for it is a truly golden book, the sublime lessons of which it is your unceasing desire and endeavour to impress on the hearts of the sisters, who live under your wise and gentle rule.

Like St. Teresa, you and another Religious (whom but to name is to praise), left your own convent in Belgium, to found a new house in Northampton. And you came amongst us, resolved to suffer every privation and trial with calm resignation and fortitude, for the good of those precious souls whom Providence might commit to your tender care.

Numerous and various were the difficulties you met with, just as St. Teresa did in the foundation of her convents in Spain. But your courage and confidence in God supported you amidst all your troubles; and you were encouraged patiently to endure them, by the kind exhortations and assistance given to you by his Lordship and other friends.

As time went on, you found what great things often come from small beginnings. Now you have a large and commodious house and a fervent community, whose sole desire is to serve Him whom they have chosen for "the God of their heart, and the portion of their inheritance for ever."

May Saint Teresa intercede for you, Madam, that grace and strength may be given you, to fulfil the high duties of your office with fruit a hundred-fold. May she intercede, too, for your beloved Sisters, that they may practise every virtue, even as she did, which can adorn the religious life and beautify their own soul, and so prepare them and you for the joys of another and a better land.

I have the honour to be,
MADAM,
Your very respectful Servant in Christ,

JOHN DALTON.

PREFACE.

THE translation of St. Teresa's wondrous "Life" has met with such general approbation, that I am induced to present to the public a translation of the "Way of Perfection," and the "Conceptions of Divine Love," both written by the same glorious Saint.

Those who have read her "Life," will remember the account she gives us of the foundation of the Monastery of St. Joseph's, at Avila.1 It is wonderful to contemplate the innumerable trials, labours, and difficulties of all kinds which the Saint had to endure in founding this new House. But it is still more wonderful to consider the admirable fortitude, and undaunted courage, and heroic perseverance, joined with a most unbounded confidence in the divine assistance, by which she conquered every obstacle that men and the devil raised up against her. On one occasion, when all her hopes seemed to be lost, she went to our Lord and said to Him, "This house is not mine; it is to be established for you, and since there is no one to conduct the case, do you undertake it."

Having spoken these words, the Saint tells us, "That she felt as great repose, and as free from care as if she had the whole world to plead for her; and immediately she considered the business as completed."2

The new monastery was established on the Feast of St. Bartholomew, in the year 1572. The day on which the Saint entered the new house must indeed have been a day of great joy and consolation to her. All her troubles were now at an end. The raging tempest had passed away, and she saw herself in a peaceful harbour, for which she had so long sighed. She and her beloved nuns lived together, as if they had but one heart and one soul. They were entirely disengaged from earthly things. Their whole study was to advance in the Way of Perfection. Solitude was their delight; and to hold converse with their heavenly Spouse, was their only recreation. When the nuns were one day at prayer, in the choir, St. Teresa saw our Blessed Lady in great glory, and she seemed to be protecting them all under a very white robe, which she had on. By this vision the Saint understood what a high degree of glory our Lord would bestow on the Religious of the new house.

When the Holy Mother left the monastery of the Incarnation, she took with her four Religious, who were willing to embrace the "reform" our Saint wished to introduce. Others were afterwards admitted. She chose Anna de Sancto Joanne to be prioress, simply because it was her own sincere desire to obey, rather than command. But the Provincial and the Bishop of Avila, knowing well how fit she was to govern, soon after commanded her to undertake the office herself

It is unnecessary for me to mention here with what heavenly prudence, judgment, and sweetness she fulfilled all the duties of prioress. The reformation of the Order dates from the year 1563, when the "Constitutions" were drawn up by the Saint, and approved by Pope Pius IV., in 1565.3 To understand more clearly the nature of the "reform "introduced by the Saint with so much labour and difficulty, it is necessary to mention that, in the year 1205 (some say 1209), Albert, Patriarch of Jerusalem, who had been a Religious of Mount Carmel, gave to the Carmelites, who then lived on that holy mountain, a rule taken from another which had been given to the same Order, by John, Patriarch of Jerusalem. This rule was confirmed by Pope Innocent IV., in the year 1248, and was called the "Primitive Rule." For many years it was observed in all its strictness. But gradually, as the fervour of the Order declined, many relaxations and abuses crept in: it also seemed so austere, that several persons considered it impossible to be observed. The Order was accordingly induced to request Pope Eugenius IV. to mitigate some of the rules, which petition his Holiness complied with.4 Great evils, however, arose from this relaxation, especially in the monasteries of the women. St. Teresa was determined to apply a remedy; and we have already seen how gloriously she executed her project. Let her speak of the result in her own words: – "Methinks that all the troubles which have been endured for the monastery have been well bestowed. For though the rule is somewhat rigorous, because flesh meat is never eaten, except in case of necessity, and we fast eight months in the year; yet the Sisters consider it not to be severe enough, and therefore they observe additional mortifications, which seem to be necessary in order to keep the rules with greater perfection. I hope in our Lord, that what has been begun, will prosper and increase, as His Majesty has promised me." (Chapter xxxvi p. 347.) 5

The Saint tells us, in the Book of her Foundations, 6 that she lived five years in the Monastery of St. Joseph, and that those years seemed to be the happiest of her whole life, because they afforded her that repose and tranquillity the loss of which her soul so often felt. She also mentions how several young ladies entered the house, and became religious, our Lord having delivered them from the pomps and vanities of the world, and endowed them with many virtues. Their number did not exceed thirteen. St. Teresa assures us what delight she experienced in conversing with such pure and holy souls, whose only desire was to serve and praise our Lord.7

They, too, knew well what encouragement their Holy Mother gave them, to serve with fidelity and perseverance the beloved Spouse of their heart, and what a glorious example she was of every virtue that can adorn the religious life. Sweet and pleasant was her rule, and sweeter far the heavenly lessons of wisdom which she delivered to them. Never did she inculcate any duty which she herself did not practise first. Though superioress, she often chose the greatest humiliations: the smallest fault she confessed in chapter with surprising humility; and it was her delight to steal unknown into the choir, and fold up the cloaks of the sisters, to sweep the most filthy places in the yard, to wait at table, to serve in the kitchen, to spin, or to assist any of the Sisters in their work. The "Acts and Bull of her Canonization" testify the many virtues which shone so pre-eminently in her soul. Indeed, when we consider on what familiar terms (so to speak), she was with our Lord, and how lovingly He caressed her, and spoke to her, and consoled her, and assisted her in all her troubles, and this, too, in a way so different from that which He employed towards other Saints, we must come to the conclusion that the soul of Teresa was "all fair, without spot or stain."

These remarks bring me to the direct subject of the preface. As the nuns had such a high idea of the sanctity of their Holy Mother, they besought her to give them some instructions on prayer; and with this request she lovingly complied, having previously asked permission from her confessor, F. Domingo Bañez. These instructions are comprised in the "Way of Perfection."8 This beautiful book the Saint composed in 1563. Yepez mentions, that she sent the manuscript to Don Teutonio de Verganza, Archbishop of Evora, who ordered it to be printed at Evora, while the Saint was still living. The precious manuscript is preserved to the present day in the Royal library of the Escurial.

To speak of the merits of this work seems superfluous. It abounds in noble and sublime thoughts, heroic sentiments of love, praise, and gratitude to God, and is full of the most practical lessons of humility, obedience, poverty, and self-denial;9 &c. Her explanation of the Lord's Prayer is very admirable. The three first chapters are particularly interesting and valuable, as she there mentions the motives by which she was especially induced to compose the work. The style is everywhere simple and pure, yet always rich in illustrations. The interior life of the Saint is drawn to the very letter, in words which really seem to have been inspired. All the hidden secrets of "mental prayer," are communicated to us, in which the soul buries herself, and is consumed with burning transports of love; and though we are unable to understand all that the Saint says on this sublime subject, yet we cannot but rise up from the perusal of her words, better men than we were before, more determined to aim at perfection, and to implore the divine assistance and that of our glorious Saint for so important an object.

I have given in Appendix No. 1 a translation of the Saint's "Admonitions" to her nuns. They are full of sound sense, and contain maxims well worth remembering.

In Appendix No. 2 are given certain "Relations " of the Saint, which contain some things not mentioned in her life.

In Appendix No. 3 is a list of all the works of St. Teresa, with some remarks on each of them, which I hope will be acceptable to the reader.

Appendix No. 4 contains some interesting details connected with the personal appearance of the Saint, as described by Ribera, and also some particulars regarding her authentic likenesses.

These additions will not, I trust, be considered as matter introduced, merely to swell the size of the book. No; far from it. My only object is, to give the reader all the particulars I can respecting so admirable a Saint, inasmuch as everything connected with her is valuable, edifying, and interesting.10

JOHN DALTON.

Bishop's House, Northampton, 1852.

PREFACE OF ST. TERESA.

THE Sisters of this Monastery of St. Joseph, in Avila, having heard that I had leave from my present Confessor, Father Domingo Bañez, of the Order of the glorious St. Dominic, to write certain instructions on prayer, in which I seemed likely to succeed well, because I have spoken on the subject with many spiritual and holy persons, have begged of me to say something on prayer with such importunity, that I have resolved to obey them. I see that the great affection they bear me will make my imperfect discourse more acceptable (however bad my style may be) than some books, which have been more correctly written by men, from whom I have learnt what I know. I rely on their prayers, that so our Lord may perhaps be pleased to enable me to say something respecting what is suitable to the manner of living in this House, and that He may allow me to communicate it to the Sisters.

But if I should say anything incorrectly, Father Bañez, who is to see what I have written first, will either correct the manuscript or burn it; and thus I shall have lost nothing in agreeing to the request of these servants of God, and they will see what I am in myself, when His divine Majesty does not assist me.

I intend to mention certain remedies for small temptations (which, perhaps, are slighted because they are little), that the devil employs; and other matters, just as our Lord shall give me understanding, and as the subjects shall occur to my mind. As I know not what I am to say, I cannot proceed with any order or method: and this way I think is the best, because it is unusual with me to proceed thus.

May our Lord assist me in everything that I shall do, that all things may be done according to His will, for such have always been my desires, though my actions are as imperfect as myself. I know I am not wanting in love and a desire to advance, to the best of my power, the souls of these, my sisters, in the service of our Lord.

And this love, together with my years and the experience which I have had of some Monasteries, may possibly be useful in enabling me to succeed better in these small matters, than learned men would, who, having other more important affairs to manage, and being men of perfection, do not pay much attention to things which in themselves seem nothing. But every object may injure such weak creatures as we women are; for numerous are the snares of the devil against persons who live in strict enclosure, because he sees he stands in need of some new arms to attack them.

Being so very wicked myself, I have been able to make but a poor defence, and, therefore, I desire my sisters should take warning by me. I shall say nothing but what I have either experienced in myself, or have seen in others. Only a short time ago, I was commanded to write an account of my Life, in which I have said something about prayer; and perhaps my Confessor does not wish you to see this at present. I shall, therefore, repeat here something of what I said there, adding other matters also, which I may consider necessary.

May our Lord direct all that I shall say (as I have requested of Him), and make it conduce to His greater glory. Amen.

TERESA DE JESU

THE WAY OF PERFECTION.

CHAPTER I.

THE SAINT MENTIONS THE REASON WHICH INDUCED HER TO FOUND THIS MONASTERY IN SUCH GREAT AUSTERITY.

WHEN this monastery was first founded, for the reasons mentioned in the book11 I have already written, and on account of certain great favours I received from our Lord, whereby He gave me to understand how much He would be served in this house, it was not my intention to use such great rigour in exterior things, or to be without rent: nay, I wished the house to be so established as not to want anything. But this I did as a weak and wicked creature, though certain good intentions influenced me more than my own pleasure.

About this time I heard of the miseries of France, and of the disorders and havoc those Lutherans had committed there, and how rapidly this miserable sect went on increasing. This afflicted me exceedingly; and as if I could have done something, or had been something, I cried to our Lord, and implored Him to remedy so great an evil. It seemed as if I could have laid down a thousand lives, to recover only one of those innumerable souls who are lost in that heresy. But seeing myself only a woman, and so wicked too, and prevented from promoting as I desired the glory of God (and all my care was, and is still, that as He has so many enemies and so few friends – these last at least might continue good), I resolved to do the little which lay in my power, viz. to follow the evangelical counsels with all the perfection I could, and to induce the few nuns who are here to do the same, confiding in the great goodness of God, who never fails to assist those that are determined to leave all things for Him; and hoping (these nuns being such as I had represented them in my desires) that, in the midst of their virtues, my faults and imperfections might have no. force, and that thus I might be able in something to please our Lord; and that, all of us being engaged in prayer for the champions of the Church, the preachers and doctors who defend her, we might, to the utmost of our power, assist my Lord, who has been so much insulted by those for whom He has done so much good, that the traitors seem now to wish to crucify Him again, and not to leave Him a place whereon to lay His head.

O my Redeemer! my heart cannot think of this without feeling excessive grief. What a crime is this for Christians to commit! Must they who owe you the most, be always the persons who afflict you the most? They for whom you do the highest favours, – whom you choose for your friends, – among whom you converse, and to whom you communicate yourself in the Sacraments? – Are not the torments enough which you have already endured for them? Certainly, O my Lord! he does nothing who now separates himself from the world; for if men show such disloyalty to You, what can we expect? Do we deserve perhaps better from them? Have we conferred on them greater favours, that they should keep friends with us? What is this? What do we hope more concerning them, – we who, through the goodness of our Lord, are not infected with this pestilential scab? They already belong to the devil. By their own hands they have received a just punishment, and with their worldly delights have purchased eternal fire. There ruined they must be, though my heart cannot help breaking to see the destruction of so many souls. O, that the evil were not so great! I wish not to see more ruined every day.

O my sisters in Christ! help me to entreat our Lord herein, since for this object He has assembled you here: this is your vocation; these are to be your employments – these your desires; hither your tears, hither your petitions must tend. You are not here, sisters, for worldly concerns; I laugh, and at the same time I grieve, at the things which people come here to recommend to our prayers to God in their behalf; I wish such persons would rather beg of God that He might enable them to trample such foolery under their feet; their intentions, however, are good, and beholding their devotion, we satisfy their desires, though I am persuaded our Lord never heard me in these matters, – for persons even request of us to ask His Majesty for money and revenues. The world is on fire. Men wish to pass sentence on our Lord again, as it were, since they bring a thousand false witnesses against Him: they wish to overturn the Church;12 and shall we lose time in praying for things which, if God should grant, we should have one soul less in Heaven? No, my sisters; this is not the time for praying to God about things of little importance. Truly, did I not consider human infirmity, which loves to be helped in everything (and it would be well if we could assist it in some way), I should be glad if it were understood that these are not the things which we beg of God at St. Joseph's, with so much earnestness.

CHAPTER II.

THE SAINT TELLS HER SISTERS THAT THEY MUST BE INDIFFERENT ABOUT CORPORAL NECESSITIES: SHE SHOWS WHAT GOOD THERE IS IN POVERTY.
THINK not, my sisters, that because you must not seek to please secular persons, you shall therefore want support. I assure you this will not be the case. Never strive, by human artifices, to maintain yourselves, for then you will die of hunger, and that with reason. Fix your eyes on your Spouse, for He will maintain you. If He please, those who are least affected towards you will, even against their wish, provide you with food, as you have seen by experience; and if thus you died of hunger, O! happy would be the Nuns of St. Joseph! Forget not this, for love of our Lord; and as you have given up revenues, give up also all care about food – otherwise all is lost. Let those whom our Lord wishes to receive revenues, attend to such cares in good time, since it is very proper – because it is their vocation; but for us, sisters, it is improper. To be solicitous about an income from others, seems to me to be thinking on what others enjoy. In spite of all your care, another does not alter his mind, nor does he intend the more to bestow an alms. This care leave to Him, who knows how to move all men; who is the Lord of revenues and of their possessors. By His command we have come here: His words are true; they cannot fail; heaven and earth shall pass away first; let us not forsake Him, and we shall have no reason to fear He will forsake us; and if at any time He should leave us, it will be for our greater good; just as the saints lost their lives, when put to death for our Lord; their martyrdom only augmented their glory. And what a good exchange was this – immediately to have done with all the world, and to enjoy eternal happiness!

Mind this, sisters; for it will concern you much when I am dead, and therefore I leave it to you in writing; though as long as I live I shall remind you of it, because I know by experience the great gain (you may derive therefrom).13 When I have least, I am the most free from care. And our Lord knows that, to the best of my opinion, our superabundance afflicts me more than our wanting necessaries. I know not whether this arises from my having seen our Lord presently assist us. It would otherwise be deceiving the world – to make ourselves poor, when we are not so in spirit, but in appearance. My conscience would blame me, so to speak; and, in my opinion, this would be as if the rich asked for alms: may God grant this may not be so. Where these immoderate desires exist about others giving something to us, we may some time or other beg this through custom; or some may ask what they do not want, perhaps from those who need it more than we do; and though the donors lose nothing, but gain; yet we may lose thereby.

God forbid this, my daughters; if such a case as this should happen, I had much rather you had revenues. In no way let this thought occupy your mind; I beg this of you, as an alms for the love of God. And let the lowest of you, whenever she perceives such a practice in this house, cry out unto His Majesty, and in humility acquaint the superioress therewith, telling her that she is going wrong; this is so important, that by little and little true poverty might easily be lost. I trust in our Lord it may never be so; that He will never forsake his servants, and that what you have made me write, if it be of no other advantage, may at least serve to awaken you. And believe me, my daughters; since for your good our Lord has given me to understand a little the advantages that are to be found in holy poverty; and those who try it will find it so, though perhaps not so much as I, because I was not only not poor in spirit (notwithstanding that I professed to be such) – but in spirit a fool. It is a good which includes within itself all the goods of this world: it is a large property.14 I repeat; it is to rule over all the riches of this life; and he does so who despises them. What do I care for kings and lords, if I desire none of their estates, nor strive to please them, and if I am obliged ever so little to offend God on their account? What care I for their honours, if I understand in what a poor man's chief honour consists – viz., in being really poor? I consider, that honours and riches almost always go together, and that whoever desires honour does not abhor and detest riches; so likewise, whoever hates money has little regard for honour.

Understand this rightly; for methinks this point of honour always carries with it some interest about revenues and money, because it is a wonder to see a person honoured in the world if he be poor: on the contrary, though he may deserve honour, men will esteem him but little. True poverty has with it a certain dignity, so that none suffer by it (I speak of poverty undertaken only for God's sake): it need not please any one but Him: it is very certain that one acquires many friends, by not being dependent on any one. This I have seen proved by experience; and because so much has been written concerning this virtue, which I cannot understand, much less express, I will say no more about it, that I may not injure it by praising it. I have spoken only of what I have seen by experience; and I confess I have been so absorpt in it, as not to observe it myself till now. But, as it is said, let it go for the love of God. Since then holy poverty is our badge; and since that which, at the first foundation of our Order, was so highly esteemed and so strictly observed by our holy fathers (for one told me who knew it – that they never kept anything for the next day), is not now practised exteriorly with so much perfection, let us at least endeavour to keep it in our interior.15 We have but a short time to live:16 the reward is exceeding great; and even if there were no other, but that of accomplishing what our Lord has advised us to do, the mere fact of our imitating His Majesty in anything would be an abundant recompense.

These are the arms that must be inscribed on our banners: these things must we faithfully observe in the house, in apparel, in words, and much more in our thoughts. As long as these points are observed, have no fear about the decay of the discipline of this house, through the divine assistance; for, as St. Clare once said, "The walls of poverty are strong." With these united with those of humility, she used to say, "that she desired her monasteries to be enclosed." I am confident, that if this be truly observed, both chastity and everything else will be much better fortified, than by very sumptuous buildings, against which I beseech you to be on your guard, for the love of God, and of His precious blood; and if with a safe conscience I could wish, that on the same day that you build a fine house, it may tumble down again and kill you all, I do wish it, and pray God it may happen (supposing I could say it with a good conscience). It looks very bad, my daughters, to erect stately houses out of the property of the poor. God forbid this should be done; let our houses be poor and mean in every way. Let us somewhat resemble our King, Who had no house save the stable at Bethlehem, wherein He was born, and the cross on which He died. These were houses from which little pleasure could be received.

As for those who build large houses, they have their reasons, and other pious intentions. But any little corner is large enough for thirteen poor women. I tell you (since strict enclosure is necessary, and also conduces to prayer and devotion), that if they possess a piece of ground, with some small hermitages, to retire to prayer, well and good; but from stately buildings, large houses, and everything fine and beautiful, may God deliver us. Ever remember that all such places must fall at the day of judgment; and who knows how soon that may be? And for a house of thirteen poor women to make a great noise with its fall is not proper, since the really poor are not to make any noise. They must be persons without noise, in order to excite compassion.

O! how would you rejoice to see some one delivered from hell, on account of an alms bestowed upon you. All this is possible; and, therefore, you are strictly bound to pray continually for those who give you support. It is our Lord's will also, that though all good things come from Him, we should show our gratitude to those persons likewise, by whose means He supports us. Do not neglect this duty. I have so wandered from the subject, that I know not what I began to speak about. I think, however, it was our Lord's pleasure, for I never intended to write what I have said here. May His Majesty always protect us, that none of us may ever neglect our duty. Amen.

CHAPTER III.

SHE CONTINUES THE SUBJECT OF THE FIRST CHAPTER, EXHORTS THE SISTERS CONTINUALLY TO PRAY TO GOD, THAT HE MAY PROTECT THOSE WHO LABOUR FOR THE CHURCH.

RETURNING, then, to that for which especially our Lord has assembled us together in this house (and for this object, I desire that we may likewise contribute something, in order to please His Majesty); I say, that seeing the evils of the age are so numerous and great, human strength is not sufficient to stop, much less to quench the fire enkindled by these heretics, which still burns so furiously. I think, then, it is necessary to do what is done in time of war; for when the enemy has overrun the whole country, the king thereof, seeing himself pressed on all sides, retires into some town, which he ordered to be well fortified; and from thence he sometimes assaults the enemy; and those within the town, being select warriors, are able to do more singly than many faint-hearted soldiers altogether, so that oftentimes a victory is gained by this means; at least, if not gained, it is not lost; for as there is no traitor among them, they cannot be taken except by famine. Now, here there can be no famine, so as to make us surrender. Die we may, but never can we be vanquished. But why have I said this? That you may understand, my sisters, that what we are to beg of God is, that none of us who are to-day within the castle of good Christians, may go over to the enemy, and that God may make the Captains of this castle or city (that is, the preachers and doctors), completely victorious in the way of our Lord. And since most of them are in religious Orders, pray that these may advance more and more in perfection, and in their vocation – a point very necessary; since now, as I have said, the ecclesiastical, and not the secular power, must help us. And since we women are unable to assist our king, either in one or the other, let us endeavour to be such – that our prayers may aid these servants of God, who with so much labour have fortified themselves with learning and virtue, and are now striving to help our Lord.

You may perhaps ask, why I press this point so much, and tell you to help those who are much better than ourselves? I will tell you the reason: because I do not think you sufficiently understand how much you owe to our Lord, for having brought you to a place where you are so free from cares, from occasions of sin, and conversation with the world. This is a very great favour, which they have not received, of whom I am speaking; nor is it fit they should in these times less than in others, because they are to be the persons who must strengthen the weak and encourage the faint-hearted. Can soldiers remain well without their captains? These must live among men, and converse with men, and live in courts, and sometimes even exteriorly conform to them.

Think you, my daughters, that little is required for conversing with the world, and living in the world, and carrying on the business of the world, and (as I said) conforming ourselves to the conversation of the world; and at the same time to be in our interior strangers to the world, and enemies of it, and to live as one in exile; yea, in a word, to live not as men, but as angels? If they be not so, they deserve not the names of captains; and may our Lord never allow them to leave their cells, for they will do more harm than good, because it is not now the time to notice imperfections in those who are to instruct others; and if these be not interiorly strengthened, by understanding how important it is to trample all things under foot, to be disengaged from transitory affairs, and to fix our attention only on what is eternal, however much they may desire to conceal such imperfections, they are sure to be known. With whom have they to deal, but with the world? Never have any fear about their being pardoned, or that any imperfection can escape being discovered. Many good actions will pass unobserved, and perhaps not be considered as such; but for one bad action – for one imperfection, let them not hope for such an indulgence.

I wonder who it is that shows the world such perfection, and yet not practise it, except to condemn others (to the practical part they seem to consider themselves not at all obliged, thinking they do a great deal, if they tolerably observe the Commandments): and sometimes what in reality is virtue, to them seems a mere gratification. Think not, then, that this great battle in which they are engaged requires little assistance from God: no, it requires a very great deal. I entreat you to endeavour to be such, that we may be worthy to obtain these two things from God. The first is, that among the many learned and religious whom we have, many may be found possessed of the abilities necessary for this object, as I have before mentioned; and that our Lord would make those better who are not so well prepared, since only one perfect man will be able to do more than many imperfect ones. The second is, that after engaging in this contest (which, as I have said, is no insignificant one), our Lord may protect them; that so they may escape the many dangers of the world, and stop their ears, in this dangerous ocean, against the songs of the Syrens. And if we can obtain anything from God in this respect, we fight for Him, even though we are enclosed here: and I shall consider the pains well bestowed, which I have taken in erecting this house, where I likewise intended that this rule of our Lady and Empress should be observed with the same perfection as it began. Do not consider it useless continually to make this petition; for there are some people who consider it hard, not to pray much for their own souls; and what prayer is better than this? If you be troubled lest the punishment of purgatory should not be diminished, be assured that it will be lessened by this kind of prayer. And what does it matter, even though I should stay in purgatory till the day of judgment, if only one be saved by my prayers? How much more, if many should be benefited, and God's honour promoted? Make no account of pains which end, when some service may be done for Him who suffered so much for us. Always learn what is the most perfect, since you will always have to deal with learned persons, as I shall earnestly request you to do so, and shall give you the reasons for it. I, therefore, entreat you, for the love of our Lord, to beseech His Majesty to hear this our prayer. I, though so miserable a wretch, beg this favour of His Majesty, since it is for His glory, and for the welfare of His Church, for my desires tend to this object.

It seems presumptuous to think that I shall in any way obtain this favour. Still, I trust, O my Lord! in these your servants who are here, and who, I know, neither desire nor aim at anything else but to please you. For you they have given up the little they had; and more they would wish to have possessed, wherewith to serve you. And Thou, O my Creator! art not ungrateful – that I should think that Thou wilt refuse to grant what they request of You. When You lived in this world, You did not, O Lord! repulse women from You; but rather, you always favoured them with great compassion. When we ask You for honours, revenues, money, or anything that savours of the world, do not hear us: but for the honour of Your Son, why should You not, O Eternal Father! hear one who would lose a thousand honours and a thousand lives for You? Not for our sakes grant this favour, O Lord! since we do not deserve it: but hear us, through the merits of the blood of Your Son. O Eternal Father, behold, so many scourgings, so many injuries, and such grievous torments are never to be forgotten. O my Creator! how can such tender bowels as Yours endure, that what was instituted by Your Son, through such burning love, and the more to please You (for You commanded Him to love us) should be so undervalued by these heretics, who now at this very time despise the Most Holy Sacrament, for by destroying the churches they deprive that Most Blessed Victim of a habitation? It would indeed be something to complain of, if Thy Son had neglected doing any thing: which might please you: but He fulfilled everything most perfectly. Was it not enough, Eternal Father! that while He lived, He had no place whereon to lay His head; that He was always in the midst of labours? Must they now take away those places also, which He made use of for entertaining His friends, because he saw we were weak, and knew that they who are to labour must of necessity be supported by such food? Has He not most abundantly over-paid for Adam's sin? Every time that we commit sin again, must this most loving Lamb pay for it? Do not suffer this, O my Emperor! May your Majesty be appeased: look not on our sins, but on your Most Holy Son who redeemed us, and on His merits, and on those of His glorious Mother, and of so many Saints and Martyrs who suffered death for you. But, alas! O my Lord, who am I that have presumed to offer up this petition, in the name of all? What a bad advocate you have, my daughters, to be heard and to have your petition presented by me? What if the Supreme Judge, seeing me so bold, should rather be the more incensed? He might deservedly and justly be so. But, behold, O Lord! Thou art now a God of Mercy. Show it to this miserable sinner – this poor worm, who is thus so bold with Thee."17 Behold, my God, my desires, and the tears with which I beg this favour of Thee: forget my works, through Thy infinite goodness – have compassion on so many souls that perish, and defend Thy Church. No longer permit any more destruction in Christendom; illuminate now this darkness.

I beseech you, my sisters, recommend also to His Majesty this poor sinner, and beg of Him to give her humility, for this is a duty to which you are bound. I do not command it particularly for kings and prelates of the Church – especially our own bishop: I see you are at present so very careful in this respect, that I think there is no necessity to enjoin this obligation. But come who may afterwards, if they have a holy superior, such will be his subjects. 18 As this, therefore, is so very important, always recommend it to our Lord. But when your prayers, and desires, and disciplines, and fastings, are not directed to this object, which I have mentioned, remember that you do not aim at, nor accomplish that end, for which our Lord assembled you here together.

CHAPTER IV.

SHE SPEAKS ON OBSERVING THEIR RULE, AND ON THREE THINGS WHICH CONDUCE TO A SPIRITUAL LIFE.
NOW, daughters, you have seen the great design we undertake to perform. How perfect then ought we to be, so that in the eyes of God and of the world we may not be considered very presumptuous? It is evident we must labour hard; and for this object, to have noble thoughts is of great assistance, that we may force ourselves to make our works correspond with them. Now if we endeavour, with great diligence, to observe our Rule and Constitutions punctually, I hope in our Lord that He will hear our prayers. I request no new thing of you, my daughters, but only to observe our profession – since it is our vocation, and we are obliged thereto, though in the observance of it there is a great difference.

Our first rule tells us "to pray without ceasing." Now if we observe this with all possible care, it being a matter of the greatest consequence, we shall not neglect to observe the fasts, disciplines, and silence commanded by the Order: for you know well, that our prayers must be assisted by these, in order to be proper prayers, since delicacy and prayer cannot agree with each other. You have desired me to say something to you on the subject of prayer; and I desire you, in return for what I shall say, to practise, and very willingly often to read over what I have hitherto said. But before I speak of the interior, which is prayer, I will mention some things necessary to be observed by those who intend to walk along the road of prayer; and so necessary are they that should they observe them, they may advance very far in the service of our Lord, even though the persons should not be very contemplative – but without them, it is impossible to be very contemplative: and if they should fancy they are so, they are greatly mistaken. May our Lord assist me herein, and teach me what I should say, that it may be for His glory. Amen.

Think not, my friends and sisters, that I will lay many things upon you: our Lord grant, that we may perform those duties which our holy fathers commanded and observed, who thereby merited this name; it would be an error to seek it by any other way. Three things only I will explain at large, which belong to the same Constitution, because it is of the utmost importance for us to understand how highly we are concerned in observing them, if we wish to obtain, both interiorly and exteriorly, that peace which our Lord recommended to us so much. The first is, love one for another; secondly, a disengagement from every creature; thirdly, true humility; which, though I name it last, is the most important of all, and includes all the rest.

With regard to the first, it is very important to love one another tenderly, for there is no grievance which is not easily borne, among those who mutually love each other, and that must be something extraordinary which displeases them. Hence, were this commandment observed in the world, as it ought to be, I believe it would conduce much towards enabling us to observe the rest: but because we offend against it, either by excess or by the contrary, we never come to practise it with perfection.

It may seem, that amongst us an excess herein can do no harm; whereas it brings with it so much mischief, and so many imperfections, that I am confident people will not believe it, those only excepted who have been witnesses thereof. Here the devil spreads many nets, which, in consciences that strive to please God imperfectly,19 are scarcely discerned – nay, they think it to be virtue. But they who aim at perfection clearly perceive it, since by degrees it deprives the will of its strength, lest it should be totally employed in loving God. This, I think, happens to women oftener than to men, and it does very considerable injury to the community. Hence proceeds our not loving all the rest so much – resenting an injury done to one's friend – desiring to have something to treat her with20 – watching an opportunity of discoursing with her, and often rather to express her affection for her, together with other acts of foolishness, than to show her love for God. These close friendships seldom conduce in helping us to love God more; rather, I believe, the devil is the cause of them, in order to raise factions in religious Orders; for when it is to serve His Majesty, it seems immediately that our will is not influenced with passion, but only procures assistance for subduing the other passions. Of these friendships I would have many, where the convent is large: but in this house, where there are not – and must not be – more than thirteen sisters, all should be friends alike; all should mutually love each other, wish well to all, help one another. For the love of God, let them avoid these particular friendships, however holy they may be; for this poison is accustomed to creep in even among brothers, and if they be relations, it is much worse – it is a pestilence. Believe me, sisters, for though what I say may appear extreme, in it consist great perfection and great peace; and many occasions of sin are removed from those who are not very strong. But if our will incline more to one than to another, (and it cannot be otherwise, for it is natural; and often we are induced to love what is base, if we possess more gifts of nature), let us stop the evil carefully, and not suffer ourselves to be overcome by that affection.

Let us love virtue and a good interior, and use all care and diligence to prevent ourselves from making any account of the exterior. Let us not consent, O sisters! for our will to become a slave to any one, but to Him who has purchased it with His own blood: otherwise consider, that without knowing how, you will find yourselves tied fast, and you will not be able to escape. Good God! the fooleries that spring hence are innumerable. Now, that so many imperfections of women may not be divulged, and that those who do not know them may not hear of them, I forbear mentioning them in detail (but I am indeed sometimes astonished to see them), since, through the goodness of God, I was never much entangled in them. But, as I have said, I have often seen this, and I fear it happens in most monasteries, for in some I have observed it; and I know that it prevents strict discipline and perfection, and is an evil most dangerous in all persons: but in superiors it would be a very plague – this I have already mentioned. But in cutting off these partialities, great care is required in the first beginnings of such friendship, and it is to be done rather by industry and love, than by severity. And as a remedy, it is highly important not to be together, except at the times appointed; nor to talk, conformably to the custom now observed by us; which is, not to be together (as the rule enjoins), but for every one to be apart in her cell. Let them be cautious in St. Joseph's, of having a common work-room; since though it be a laudable custom, yet silence is observed better by each one being alone. Being accustomed to solitude is a great help to prayer; and since this is to be the foundation of the house, and we are assembled here more for this object than for anything else, it is necessary we should carefully love that which conduces the most thereto.

To return then to the mutual love we ought to have one for another, it seems almost useless to recommend it; for who can be so foolish and mad as not to love one another, when they are always conversing with each other, living in society together, not allowed to have any intercourse, or conversations, or recreations with persons out of the house, and believing that God loves them, and they Him, since for His Majesty they have left all things, and they see especially that virtue always attracts love? Now this, through God's mercy, I hope in His Majesty, will always continue in this house; hence, in my opinion, there is not much need of recommending this mutual charity. But how this love is to proceed; what the virtuous love is which I desire should be found here, by what signs we may discover whether we possess this great virtue (and it is very great indeed, since our Lord has so strongly recommended it to us) – on these points I will now say a little, according to my dulness. But if you find the subject better expressed in other books, you need not take any notice of mine, for I do not perhaps understand what I say.

There are two kinds of love of which I speak: one is purely spiritual, so that neither sensuality, nor any tenderness of our nature, seem in any way to mingle therewith, so as to take away its purity. The other is spiritual: but with it, sensuality and weakness show themselves. Now this love is good, and seems lawful – the same as that of friends and kindred; of this something has already been said. I will speak at present of that which is purely spiritual, without the intervention of any passion. If passion once creep in, this harmony will soon be destroyed: but if we exercise the love I speak of with moderation and discretion, all will be meritorious; for that which may seem to us sensuality, changes into virtue; though it is so intermixed, that sometimes we can scarcely discern it, especially if we like some confessor: for if persons given to prayer see that he is a holy man who understands their ways, they have a great affection for him. And here the devil raises a great battery of scruples, that quite distract the soul: this is his aim, especially if the confessor guide her to greater perfection; he harasses her so much, that through such scruples she leaves her confessor, and she has no repose either with one or another.

In such a case, that which they can do is, to endeavour not to think about their loving or not loving: but if they love – let them do so; for if we love any one that does some good to our body, why may we not have an affection for one who is always endeavouring and labouring to benefit our soul? I rather consider it a good beginning for great advancement to love one's confessor, if he be a holy and spiritual person, and I see that he takes pains to do good to my soul; because such is our weakness, that sometimes he assists us much in enabling us to perform very great things in the service of God.

If the confessor be not such a one as I have mentioned, here lies the danger, viz., that as he perceives they bear an affection to him, this may do very great harm, and the more so in houses of strict enclosure than in others. And because it is difficult to know who is so good, great care and prudence are required. It would be the best plan, to prevent his knowing that they love him, and not to tell him of it. But the devil so artfully entangles their soul – that he does not give them this power, for all imagine this is the chief thing to be confessed, and that they are bound to confess it. For this reason, I had much rather they would believe it to be nothing, and take no notice of it. Let them follow this advice; if they perceive in the confessor that all his discourses tend to the improvement of their souls; and if they observe no vanity in him (which is soon discovered by one who is not willing to be stupid) but find that he fears God, let them not trouble themselves about any temptation they may have respecting any immoderate affection; but let them despise it and turn away their eyes from it; for when the devil is weary he will leave them. But if they discover the confessor to be addicted to any vanity, let them suspect everything; and though his discourse may be good, let them on no account hold any with him; but confess in few words and then depart. The best way would be to acquaint the superioress that her soul does not get on well with him, and so he might be changed for another. This would be the most prudent course, could it be done without injuring his reputation. In such cases, and others like them, which the devil by his intrigues can entangle in difficult occasions, and where one knows not what advice to adopt, the surest course will be to consult some learned person (and when there is a necessity, this liberty is granted), and to confess to him, and to do what he directs in the case; because since some remedy must of necessity be used, a great error might otherwise be committed. How many errors happen in the world, through things not being done with advice, especially in what relates to our not injuring another? We must not neglect, therefore, to apply some remedy, because when the devil begins here, it is for no small object – unless he be stopped immediately. Thus what I have said about consulting another confessor is the safest course, if there be an opportunity (as I trust in God there will), and to use every exertion to have nothing to do with the other, though we should even die for it.

Consider how important this is; for it is a very dangerous thing – it is a hell – and ruin to all. I wish them not to wait till they discover so much evil, but to stop it in the beginning by all possible ways they know of; they may do so with a safe conscience. But I hope in God, that He will not suffer persons who are always to be employed in prayer to be able to have any affection, save for one who is a great servant of God; or else that they exercise not prayer, nor aim at perfection, conformably to what is here intended; because if they see that he does not understand their language, nor is delighted with discoursing of God, they cannot love him, because he is so unlike them. If he be such a one, on account of the very few occasions he will meet with here, either he will prove very simple, or not desire to trouble himself, or the servants of God. Since I have begun to speak on this subject, know that this is all, or the greatest harm which the devil can bring on monasteries enclosed, and it is very late before the discovery can be made: and thus perfection goes to ruin, without our knowing how; for if the confessor give way to vanity, through being vain himself, he will consider it but a slight matter in others. May God, by the goodness of His Majesty, deliver us from such things. They are enough to disturb all the nuns, for their conscience tells them differently from what their confessor does; and if they be tied to have only one, they know not what to do, nor how to rest, since he who should free them from trouble and relieve them is the very person that causes it. These misplaced affections are, no doubt, found in some places, and on this account I have great pity for the persons; and hence you need not wonder that I employ so much care in making you understand this danger.

CHAPTER V.

SHE CONTINUES HER DISCOURSE ABOUT CONFESSORS, AND SHOWS HOW IMPORTANT IT IS THAT THEY SHOULD BE LEARNED.

MAY our Lord, in His infinite goodness, never suffer any one in this house to experience the above-mentioned affliction, of seeing herself reduced to such distress both of soul and body: or that the superioress should take the part of the confessor so much, that the sisters dare not complain of her to him, nor of him to her. Here will come a temptation upon them, to conceal in confession very grievous sins, lest the wretched creatures should fall into trouble and disquiet. Good God! what mischief may the devil do hereby! How dear do this miserable restraint and honour cost them! And because they have only one confessor, they think the credit and discipline of the monastery are greatly promoted; and so in this way the devil entraps souls, when he cannot do so in any other way. If the poor sisters desire another confessor, the observance of discipline immediately seems to be destroyed; or if he do not belong to the Order, merely consulting with him, even though he be a saint, is considered to be an insult upon the whole Order. Praise our Lord exceedingly, my daughters, for the liberty you enjoy at present; since, though it does not extend to many, you may confer with some, besides the ordinary confessors, and these may enlighten you on every point. And, for the love of God, I beg of her who shall be the superioress, always to obtain from the bishop or provincial this same holy liberty, that so, beside the usual confessors, she and the other sisters may sometimes confer with learned persons, and give them an account of their souls, especially if their own confessors be not learned, however good they may be in other respects. May God deliver the sisters from being directed in everything by one confessor, whatever spirit he may seem to them to have21 (and may in reality possess), if he be not learned.

You know the first stone to be laid is a good conscience; endeavour, therefore, with all your strength, to free yourselves from even venial sins, and follow that which is the most perfect. One would think any confessor knew this; but it is a mistake. I happened to consult one about matters of conscience, who had finished his whole course of divinity, and he did me great harm in things which he told me were of little or no consequence. I know he did not intend to deceive me, because he had no reason, but he knew no better. The same happened to me with two or three others besides. All our good consists in having true light to observe the law of God with perfection: on this foundation prayer is securely fixed; but without a firm foundation, the whole building will fall; thus the sisters must of necessity confer with confessors of learning, and who understand spiritual things.22 If the confessor cannot claim all these requisites, then at certain times procure others; and if they should unfortunately be commanded not to confess to others, let them without going to confession discover the state of their souls to such persons as I have mentioned. I dare say even more, viz., that though the confessor may have all this, yet what I have mentioned must sometimes be done; for it will happen he may be mistaken, and it is proper that all should not be deceived through his means, provided always that nothing be done against obedience; there are means for doing everything, and even one soul exceedingly deserves that her welfare should be attended to in every possible way, how much more, then, many!

All that I have said relates to the superioress. I again, therefore, entreat her, that since no other consolation is intended hereby, except that of the soul to procure its consolation in this way; for there are different ways whereby God conducts souls, and it is not necessary for one confessor to know them all. I assure you, you will not want holy persons who will be glad to give you advice, and comfort your souls, if you be such as you should be, though you be poor; for He who supports your body will excite and inspire some with a desire of enlightening your souls, and of remedying this evil, which is what I fear the most; for when the devil seeks to deceive the confessor in some point, if he sees there are others to whom you may confess, he will proceed with caution, and consider more carefully what he does. If the devil be stopped at this point, I trust in God he will find no other way to enter this house. I therefore entreat the bishop or superior, whoever he may then be, to allow the sisters this liberty; and where there are confessors who have both virtue and learning (which is soon discovered in a little town like this), 23 not to deny them leave to confess to them sometimes, though there may be other confessors, because I know this is necessary for many things, and the harm which may arise is nothing in comparison with the great, hidden, and almost irremediable evil that is in the other course. It is usual with monasteries, that the good therein, unless preserved with great care, soon falls away; and the evil, when once it has begun to creep in, is removed with very great difficulty; and by being accustomed to imperfections, we very quickly contract a habit.

What I have here said, I have both seen and heard, and discoursed with holy and learned persons, who have considered what is most convenient for this house, towards advancing it in perfection. Now, among all the dangers (which happen in everything, while we live), we shall find this to be the least, that there is no bishop who has the power of coining in, and commanding, and going forth, nor has any confessor this liberty; but these persons have only to take care of the recollection and piety of the house, and its improvement, both interior and exterior, and to tell the superior when there is any fault, but not to be the superiors themselves. And this is observed at the present day, and not by my advice alone; for the bishop we now have, under whose obedience we live (since, for many reasons, we are not subject to the Order), being a lover of discipline and holiness, and a great servant of God, called Don Alvarez de Mendoza, of very noble extraction, and exceedingly inclined to favour this house in every way, called together persons of learning, of spiritual knowledge and experience, to consider this point; and after so many persons, including my own miserable self, had prayed much and earnestly, they came to this determination. It is, therefore, but reasonable that succeeding generations should comply with this resolution, because it has been agreed upon by such good men, and so many prayers have been addressed to our Lord for this object, to discover what was the best; and as far as can be discovered hitherto, this is certainly the case. May our Lord be pleased always to promote it more and more, that so it may tend to His greater glory. Amen.

CHAPTER VI.

SHE RETURNS TO HER DISCOURSE ON PERFECT LOVE.

I HAVE made a long digression; but what I have said is of such consequence, that whoever understands it will not blame me. Let us now return to that love which is good and lawful for us to have. Respecting that which I call purely spiritual, I know not whether I understand what I say; at least, it seems to me needless to speak much of it, for I fear but few possess it: let those to whom our Lord has given it praise Him exceedingly. I wish, however, to say something about it; perhaps it may do some good, for by placing virtue before our eyes, he that desires it, and endeavours to obtain it, becomes enamoured of it. God grant I may be able to understand it, and yet more to explain it, for I hardly know what "spiritual love" is, nor when sensual is mixed with it, nor do I know how to begin to speak of it. I am like one who hears words spoken at a great distance off, and who understands not what is said; for it is certain that sometimes I do not understand well what I say, and yet our Lord is pleased it shall be well said: if at other times I speak nonsense, it is only natural to me; in nothing am I correct.

It now seems to me, that when God brings a person to understand clearly what the world is; that there is another world, and what the difference is between one and the other; that the one is eternal, and the other a mere dream; what it is to love the Creator, and not the creature"24, (this is seen by experience, which is entirely another matter, from only thinking and believing it); and to see and to try what is gained by the one, and what is lost by the other, and what the Creator is, and what the creature is, together with many other things which our Lord truly and clearly teaches him who desires to be instructed by Him in prayer, and whom His Majesty is pleased to teach in this way; it seems, I say, that such persons love in a manner different from those who have not got so far.

You may, sisters, think it useless to insist on these points; and you may say: "We all know the things you have mentioned." God grant it may be so – that you may know them in a way which may be useful, and that you may imprint them deeply on your heart. If you know them, you will see that I do not lie in saying, that he whom our Lord conducts so far has this love. Those whom God raises to this state are noble – royal souls. They are not content with loving such vile objects as our bodies are, whatever beauty or gifts they may have; the sight thereof may please them, and they praise the Creator for it; but they do not rest there. I mean, they do not dwell upon them in such a way as to be affected towards them; for this they would consider to be loving a thing without substance, and embracing a shadow; and this would make them so ashamed of themselves, that they would not have the face, without being exceedingly ashamed, to tell God that they love Him.

You will reply: – "Such persons as these know not, either how to desire, or to requite the love which is shown them. "I answer, at least they have little regard for others' love; and though sometimes nature suddenly makes them feel delighted in being loved, yet when they return to themselves again, they see it is foolishness, except they be persons who may do good to their souls by their learning or prayers. Not that they cease to be thankful to such persons, and to requite them, by recommending them to God: but they consider our Lord to be the Person most concerned among those who love them, for they know the love comes from Him. As they find in themselves nothing deserving of love, they immediately think others love them because God loves them, and they leave the payment to His Majesty, beseeching Him to discharge it, and thereby they are in a manner acquitted of the obligation. Considering the matter attentively, I sometimes think what great blindness it is to desire others should love us, except they be persons who (as I have said) might be of use to us in acquiring solid goods.

Now observe, that as in desiring any one's love, we always have some interest or advantage in view, or pleasure to ourselves; so these perfect souls have already under their feet all the goods which the world can bestow upon them – all its delights – all its pleasures: and they are so disposed, that though they wished (so to speak), yet they cannot find pleasure in anything but God, and in discoursing of God. They cannot find what benefit they can derive from being loved, and so they care not for it. When they behold this truth lively represented to them, they laugh at themselves for the trouble it has sometimes caused them, to know whether their affections were appreciated or no; for though the love be good, it is very natural to desire to be requited. But when payment is made, it is made in straws: everything is empty air, and without substance, which the wind blows away. Granting that we are greatly beloved, what do we gain thereby? Hence, these persons no more care for being loved than not loved, except by the persons I have mentioned above – for the good of their souls, and because they see our nature to be such, that if there be no love, it presently gets weary. You may think that such as these neither know how, nor can love any one but God. Yes! they love more, and with a truer, more profitable, and more ardent affection; in a word, theirs only is true love. And such souls are always much more willing to give than to receive, and this even to the Creator Himself. This, I repeat, deserves the name of love; for those other mean affections have but usurped this name.

We may also ask, "If these persons do not love the things they see, what do they love?" It is true, they love what they see, and are taken with what they hear: but the things which they see are permanent; if such persons love, they quickly look beyond the body, and fix their eyes on souls; observing whether there be anything worth loving, and if not, they see some beginning or disposition thereto, that so in digging the mine they may at last find gold: if they love souls, the labour of digging does not trouble them; nothing presents itself to them, which they would not willingly do for the love of that soul; because they desire to continue to love it: but they know well this is impossible, except that soul have virtues, and love God much. I say "impossible," though the person showed so many favours to such a soul, and even die for love of it, and perform for it every possible good office, and were possessed of every natural endowment; yet the will cannot acquire strength enough to love such an one, nor can this love be made to continue firm. Such an one now understands and knows by experience what all things are, without being cheated: he sees their judgments do not agree, and that it is impossible they should always continue to love one another, for it is a love which must end with life, if the other do not observe the Law of God, and he knows he does not love Him, and that they must part and go different ways. And this love (which lasts only here in this world) a soul, into which God has infused true wisdom, values not above its worth, nay, even under it; since among those who delight to take pleasure in the things of this world – viz., pleasures, honours, and riches, – it may pass for something, if one be rich, or have opportunities to enjoy some recreation with him; but whoever detests all this, regards the other as little or nothing. If therefore such have any love, it is an affection to cause this soul to love God, that so she may be loved by them; (because, as I said, they know if they love in any other manner, it will not last, and that such love costs them very dearly) – they neglect not to do all they can to benefit it, and would lose a thousand lives to do it the least good. O! precious love, which imitates Jesus, the Captain of love, and our highest good.

CHAPTER VII.

SHE CONTINUES THE SAME DISCOURSE ON SPIRITUAL LOVE, AND GIVES SOME DIRECTIONS FOR OBTAINING IT.

IT is strange to see how vehement this love is: what beads, what penances, and prayers it costs! What care to recommend to all what it thinks may benefit such a soul with God, and that they may recommend it to God. What continual desiring to advance, and uneasiness if he sees there is no improvement! Then if he thinks he is much improved, and sees that he afterwards goes back a little, the lover seems to take no pleasure in his life – he neither eats nor sleeps, but he has this care upon him, always fearful whether the soul he loves so much may perish, and whether they must be eternally separated (for the death of the body in this world, such persons pay no regard to), since he does not wish to rely on an object, which in an instant escapes through our hands, without our being able to retain it. It is, as I have said, a love without any self-interest, great or small – all it seeks and desires is, to see that soul rich in heavenly goods. This, indeed, is love, and not those unhappy affections here below; but I do not mean "vicious and inordinate ones" – from these may God deliver us. We need not tire ourselves in speaking against an evil which is a very hell itself, the least of its effects cannot be sufficiently exaggerated. We ought not, sisters, even to mention the name of this love, nor imagine it is in the world; nor should we hear it named, either in jest or in serious conversation; nor should we allow persons to speak of it in our presence, nor mention such affections. It is good for nothing, and merely hearing it may hurt us. But I speak here (as I have said) of those other lawful loves, which we have one for another, and which exist between friends and relations. All the desire is, that the person beloved may not die: if his head ache, our souls seem to ache; if we see him in affliction, we lose our patience, as the saying is; and so with regard to everything else.

But this other love is not so; for though, through natural infirmity, we quickly feel something for the misery of others, yet reason immediately considers whether it be good for the soul, whether she grows richer in virtue, and how she bears it: then she begs of God to grant her patience, and to gain merit by these sufferings. If she sees that she is patient, then no trouble is felt, but rather joy and consolation, though such a lover would more willingly endure trouble, rather than see her endure it, could the merit and gain which are to be found in suffering be given over entirely to her, but not so as to trouble or disquiet herself thereat.

I say again, this love seems to imitate that love which Jesus – our good lover – bore us; and hence it proves so profitable, for it embraces all kinds of afflictions, that so others without any pain may reap the benefit thereof. Thus do they gain much, who are on terms of friendship with them; and believe me, they will either give up such intimate friendship, or obtain of our Lord that they may go along the same way, since they are travelling towards one and the same country. Thus did St. Monica pray for her son Austin. Their heart does not allow them to use double-dealing with their friends, or to see them in fault, if they think they can be of any service to them by their reproofs; and this they do not at any time forget to tell them of, through the desire they have to see them exceeding rich. What arts do they use for this purpose, though they care not for the whole world besides! They cannot prevail on themselves to act otherwise – they cannot flatter them, nor pass over any fault at all. They will therefore either correct themselves, or break friendship with them, since they cannot endure it, nor is it to be endured. There is a continual war between them; and though the one cares not for the whole world, nor heeds whether others serve God or not, because they mind only themselves, yet they cannot be so to their friends. Nothing is concealed from them – they discover there the least mote. I tell you, they carry a heavy cross. O happy souls, who are loved by such persons! Happy the day wherein they came to know them!

O my Lord! will you not do me the favour, that I may have many such to love me? Truly, O my Lord! I would more willingly obtain this, than be loved by all the kings and lords of the world; and with great reason, since these labour, by all possible ways, to make us such, that we may command the world itself, and make all things herein subject to us. When you are acquainted, sisters, with such persons as these, let the mother-prioress endeavour, with all diligence, that you may have an opportunity of consulting them. Love such as much as you like, as long as they continue such. They are few in number, but our Lord will not fail to make it known, when there is one who has arrived at such perfection. People may say to you, "There is no need of this; it is enough for us to possess God." But I reply, it is a good means of enjoying God, to be able to converse with his friends – great benefit is always obtained thereby: this I know by experience; and, next to God, I owe it to such persons as these, that I am not in hell – for I was very desirous for them to recommend me to God, and I likewise endeavoured to do so myself. But let us return to what we were speaking about.

This is the kind of love which I wish we had. Though at first it be not very perfect, our Lord will go on improving it. Let us begin by what is suitable to our means, for though we may meet with a little tenderness, it will do us no harm, as it is general. It is sometimes necessary and good to show some tenderness in affection, and even to have it, and to sympathize with some of the afflictions and weaknesses of the sisters, though the afflictions may be trifling. For it happens sometimes, that a very little thing troubles one quite as much as a great cross would do another; and persons of a timorous nature, are much afflicted at small things. If you have more courage, you must not fail to sympathize with others, and not wonder at their troubles; for perhaps the devil has employed his utmost power and strength therein, and this more so than he does to make you feel great torments and afflictions. And perhaps our Lord will be pleased to exempt us from these troubles, and we may find them in other things, and those trials which seem grievous to us, and that are so in themselves, will prove light to others.

Thus we must not judge in these matters by ourselves, nor esteem ourselves at a time when God has perhaps made us stronger – without any labour on our part; but let us estimate ourselves by the time when we were much weaker. Observe, that this advice is very useful towards making us know how to compassionate the miseries of others, however slight they may be, especially for those souls mentioned above; for as these desire crosses, they consider all but little; yet it is very necessary to be careful in reflecting on the time when they were weak, and to know that if still they be not such, it proceeds from themselves; for by this means the devil may be able to cool our charity for our neighbour, and make us take a fault for a perfection. In all things there is need of care and vigilance, since the devil slumbers not: and greater is required in those who aspire to higher perfection, because his temptations against them are much more concealed, for he dare not act otherwise; hence the mischief seems not to be discovered till it be done, unless (as I have said) care be used. In a word, it is necessary to watch and pray continually, for there is no better remedy for discovering those hidden snares of the devil, and for forcing him to a disclosure of them, than prayer.

Endeavour likewise to recreate yourselves with the sisters, when they find it necessary to use recreation, and this during the usual time, though you may have no inclination for it: if you act with discretion, all becomes perfect love. And so it is, that desiring to speak of that love which is not so perfect, I find no grounds whereby it seems proper for us to allow it an entrance amongst us in this house; for, granting it to be good, as I said, yet all must be referred to its original, which is the perfect love mentioned above. I thought of saying much about the other; but when I came to examine it deeply, 25 it seemed I could not endure it here, considering our manner of living, and therefore I will not speak any more about it; for I trust in God, there will never be any occasion in this house for your loving in any other manner, though it may not be with all perfection possible. Thus, it is very proper you should compassionate the necessities of one another; but take care you do not fail in discretion or in obedience. Though what the superioress enjoins some, may seem in itself severe, do not discover this to any one but to the prioress herself, and this do with humility, otherwise you may cause much harm. And learn to know what those things are which deserve our pity, and have compassion on the sisters. Any imperfection that you observe in a sister, if it be known, should always affect you much. Here love is best discovered and exercised, in knowing how to bear it, and not to be astonished at it, 26 (for so will others act with regard to those faults which you show in yourselves, and even to those which you do not see, which must doubtless be more numerous); and in recommending the sister earnestly to God, and by endeavouring yourselves to practise with great perfection the virtue which is contrary to the imperfection which you notice in another: force yourselves thereto, that you may teach by actions what perhaps she will not understand by speaking, or derive any profit from, even by punishment. But the method of practising the virtues which we see shine in others, does great good. This is good advice, and let it not be forgotten.

O! what excellent and sincere love has that sister, who can benefit all, and gives up her own profit for that of others, to advance them still higher in every virtue, and observe the rule with greater perfection. Better is this friendship than all the expressions of tenderness which can be uttered, and which are neither used, nor can be used, in this house; such as "My life, my soul, my good," &c., and other like expressions; for they call some by one name, and others by another. Let them reserve these endearing terms for their Spouse, seeing they are to be so much with Him, and so much alone; and it will be necessary to make use of all of them, since His Majesty allows it. If these words are often used in other ways, they will not soften the heart when we converse with our Lord; and except for this, they are useless. It is usual with women; but I do not wish you, my daughters, to be, or seem to be, women, but stout men,27 since if you do what lies in you, our Lord will make you so manly, that even men will wonder at you. And how easy is this for His Majesty, since He created us out of nothing.

It is likewise a very good sign of love, to endeavour to ease others of their labour, and to take it upon one's self, in the different duties of the house; and also to rejoice and to praise God exceedingly for the increase of their virtues. All these things (omitting the great benefit they bring with them) conduce much to the peace and mutual comfort of the sisters, as we now see by experience, through the goodness of God. His Majesty grant they may always increase; since were it otherwise, it would be a terrible thing, and very intolerable for you, who are few in number, to disagree; may God forbid this evil. But all the good, already begun by means of our Lord, must either be lost, or such great evil will not arise. If any be displeased, on account of some words hastily spoken, let the matter be speedily remedied, and let them pray much. And with regard to factions, or desires of superiority, or some punctilio of honour (and it seems my blood congeals when I write these words, to think that hereafter such evils may happen, since I see they are the principal evil of monasteries); when I say any such things shall happen, let them give themselves up for lost; let them imagine and believe that they have turned their Spouse out of doors, and that, in some degree, they for Him do go and seek another lodging, since they expel Him from His own house. Let them cry to His Majesty: let them procure a remedy, for unless frequent confession and communion obtain one, they may fear lest there be some Judas. For the love of God, let the prioress be extremely careful lest she give any occasion to this evil: let her be very diligent in stopping the beginnings, for therein lies all the mischief, or thereby a remedy may be applied. If she see any of the sisters is factious, 28 let her be sent to some other monastery, for God will provide a dowry for her. Let this plague be driven away from them: let them cut off the branches as much as they can; or if this be not sufficient, let the root be pulled up; and when they cannot do this, let them keep her a close prisoner who shall attempt such things. To do this is much better, than that such an incurable pestilence should infect the whole house. O! how great an evil this is! May God deliver us from the monastery where it enters. I had rather a fire should seize the place, and burn us all up. But as I think I shall speak more on this matter elsewhere, because it is so important for us, I will not enter here into any further details. I would much rather the sisters should love one another tenderly, and with some fondness, though such love might not be so perfect (taken generally) as that mentioned before, than that there should be the least disunion. May our Lord, through His infinite Majesty, never allow this evil to happen. Amen. I beseech our Lord, and let all the sisters beseech Him, to deliver us from this disquiet, since this favour must come from His hand alone.

CHAPTER VIII.

SHE TREATS OF THE GREAT ADVANTAGE OF BEING DISENGAGED, BOTH INTERIORLY AND EXTERIORLY, PROM ALL CREATURES.

WE now come to the disengagement we ought to have [with regard to created objects;29] for in this everything consists, if it be perfect. Herein I say "everything" consists, because when we adhere only to the Creator, and heed not any creature at all, His Majesty infuses virtues into souls, so that doing by little and little what we can, we shall have much less to encounter, for our Lord will take our part against the devils and against all the world in our defence. Think ye, sisters, it is a slight benefit to obtain this great favour of giving ourselves up entirely to Him, and not by parts and parcels, since, as I have said, all good things are comprised in Him? Let us praise Him exceedingly, my sisters, that He has assembled us in this place, where no other discourse, save this, is held. But I know not why I mention this, since all of you who are here may teach me; for I acknowledge that, in so important a matter, I have not the perfection I could wish, and which I know to be necessary. Of all the virtues, and of what I am here speaking about, I say the same, viz., that it is much easier to write about them than practise them; and even in this respect I may not succeed well; for sometimes the skill of writing consists in experience; so that if in anything I speak properly and correctly, it must be by guessing from what I have experienced myself in the opposite to these virtues.

As to the exterior, people already see how disengaged we are here from all things. It seems our Lord wishes that we, whom He has brought here, should separate ourselves from everything, that so His Majesty may draw us nearer to Himself without any impediment. O! my Creator and

Lord, when did I deserve so great an honour? It seems you have gone about, seeking by what means to approach nearer to us. May it please your Goodness, that by our own fault we lose not this favour. O! my sisters, for the love of God, understand the great honour our Lord has done those whom He has brought here; and let each one consider it well within herself, since among only twelve, His Majesty chose her to be one. And how many better than myself do I know, who would joyfully take this place, but which our Lord bestowed upon me, who so little deserve it! Blessed be thou, my God, and may all the angels praise Thee, and every creature also; for this favour can as little be merited as many others which Thou hast bestowed upon me: my being called to be a nun was a very great favour; since, as I have been so wicked. Thou wouldst not, O Lord! put any trust in me; for where so many good persons were assembled, my wickedness would not have been so evident, until the end of my life; and I should have concealed it, as I did in reality for many years. But Thou, O Lord! hast brought me to a place where, as there are so few, it seems impossible that my wickedness should not be known; and that I may proceed with more care, Thou takest away from me all occasions. I have now no excuse left; O Lord, I acknowledge it, and therefore I stand more in need of Your mercy to pardon my offences.

What I earnestly request of you is, that whoever perceives herself to observe what is practised in this house would mention it before she is "professed." There are other monasteries wherein our Lord is served: let such persons not disturb these few sisters whom His Majesty has gathered together here. In other places, liberty is allowed of consoling themselves with their relations: but here, if any relations be admitted, it is done for their consolation. Let the nun, who desires to see her friends for her own comfort, and is not weary with a second visit (unless they be spiritual persons), consider herself imperfect; let her understand, that she is not disengaged from creatures; that she is not well; that she will not enjoy liberty of spirit, nor true peace, but that she stands in need of a physician. I say, that unless she be freed from it and be healed, she is not fit for this house. The best remedy I know of is, not to see her friends till she perceive that she is free from all attachment, and has obtained this favour from our Lord by frequent prayer. When she finds herself affected in such a manner that she takes it for a cross, I am willing for her to see them sometimes, in order that she may do them some good; for she will certainly be of some profit to them, and will not hurt herself. But if she have any affection for them; if their troubles afflict her greatly; if she willingly listen to their worldly prosperity, let her know that she will both hurt herself and not benefit them at all.

CHAPTER IX.

SHE SPEAKS ON THE GREAT ADVANTAGE THOSE ENJOY WHO, HAVING ABANDONED THE WORLD, HAVE ABANDONED THEIR RELATIVES ALSO, AND WHAT TRUE FRIENDS THEY FIND THEREBY.

IF we Religious did but understand what harm we receive by frequently conversing with our relatives, how should we shun them! I do not understand what consolation that is which they give – (even independent of what relates to God), if it be merely to promote our quiet and repose. In their pleasures we neither can, nor is it lawful for us to participate, but we may feel for their miseries – let none of them pass without deploring them, and this sometimes more than we feel for themselves.30 I dare say, if those friends refresh the body a little, the soul pays dear for it. But this you are quite free from, for as all things are in common, so that no one can have any particular comfort, hence the alms which are given become general, and she on whom it is bestowed is not obliged to gratify her relations by it, for she knows that our Lord provides for us altogether.

I am astonished at the harm we receive from conversing with them. I am certain no one could imagine it, but he who has experienced it, nor suppose how this perfection seems now-a-days to be forgotten in religious houses, or at least, in the greater part of them. I know not what it is we leave belonging to the world – we who say "we have left everything for God" – if we do not disengage ourselves from the principal obstacle, viz., our kindred. Things have come to such a state, that people consider we are wanting in virtue, if Religious do not love and converse often with their friends, and this they freely declare, and allege their reasons for it. In this house, my daughters, our great care should be to recommend them to God (after what has been said regarding the wants of the Church), and it is only proper we should do so: as to the rest, we should blot them out of our memory as much as possible, because it is natural to place our affections upon them, more than upon other persons. I was (they say) exceedingly beloved by my relations, and I loved them so much, that I did not suffer them to forget me. But yet I found by experience, both in myself and in others, that except parents, who scarcely ever omit providing for their children – (and it is proper, when they need comfort, if we see it does not, on the whole, prejudice us, that we should not show ourselves strangers to them, since this is consistent with perfect abnegation, nor to our brothers) – my kindred have given me the least assistance when I was in trouble; nay, they who have helped me therein, have been the servants of God.31

Believe me, sisters, that in serving Him as you ought, you will find no better relations than those servants of His, whom His Majesty will send you. I know this to be the case; and if you be diligent in this way, as you already understand (for in doing otherwise, you will be wanting to your true Friend and Spouse), believe me, you will in a very short time attain this liberty; and you may put more trust in those who love you merely for His sake, than in any of your kindred; for they will not desert you, and those you will find to be fathers and brothers to you, who you did not imagine could ever be so. As these expect their reward from God, they relieve us; while the others who expect some reward from us, seeing that we are poor and unable to benefit them in any way, soon grow weary. And though this may not be the general practice in the world, yet it is very common, because it is, in fact, the world itself. Whoever tells you differently, and that it is a virtue to do so, believe them not; for should I mention all the evils which this love for our friends brings with it, I should be obliged to make a very long discourse; but because others have written on this subject, who know what they say better than I do, let what I have said be sufficient. Since I, who am so imperfect, have understood this matter so well, what will those say who are perfect? It is quite clear, that what the saints tell us about flying from the world, is very good and proper. Now (as I have said before), believe me, that what adheres to us the most are our relations, and most difficult is it to part from them. They do well, therefore, who leave their country: I mean, if this serve to disengage them from their relations, which, I think, does not consist in the body flying away, but in the soul resolutely embracing Jesus, our good Lord; for as she finds all things in Him, she soon forgets everything else. Still it is a great help to go into retirement, till we perfectly understand this truth; for afterwards it may be, our Lord will have us converse with our friends, in order to give us a cross, in that wherein we used to take delight.

CHAPTER X.

SHE TELLS THE SISTERS THAT THE ABOVE-MENTIONED DISENGAGEMENT IS NOT SUFFICIENT, UNLESS THEY FORSAKE THEMSELVES ALSO.

HAVING abandoned the world and our kindred, and living hence enclosed under the rules above mentioned, it seems now that we have done everything, and have nothing left to contend with. O! my sisters, be not too secure, nor allow yourselves to sleep, or else you will be like to him who lies down very quietly in bed, having bolted his door fast for fear of thieves, while at the same time he had them in his house. You know there is no thief worse than a domestic one. Since, therefore, we are always ourselves,32 if great care be not used (as is used in important affairs), and every one do not diligently use all her endeavours to be continually denying her will, there are many things which may deprive us of this holy liberty of the spirit which we seek after, that it may fly to its Creator, without being burdened with earth and lead.

The great remedy against this evil is, continually to remember the vanity of all things, and how soon they come to an end. Thus we shall take off our affections from things so vile, and place them on that which never ends. This may seem a weak remedy, but it strengthens the soul exceedingly. And with regard to very small matters, it is useful to take great care, when we have an affection for any object, to turn our thoughts away from it, and to fix them on God – herein His Majesty assists us, and does us a great favour, because in this house the greatest difficulty has already been overcome. But because this separating from ourselves, and denying and renouncing ourselves is very difficult, since we are so closely united to ourselves and love ourselves so excessively, here true humility may enter; for this virtue and that of mortification, seem always to go together, and they are like two sisters who cannot be separated from each other. These are not the relations from whom I advise you to keep; rather embrace and love them, and never be seen without them.

O sovereign virtues! mistresses of all creatures, empresses of the world, our deliverers from all the snares and toils which the devil lays for us, and so much beloved by our Master Jesus Christ!33 whoever possesses you may go forth boldly and fight with all the powers of hell united together, and with the whole world and its dangers. Let them not fear anything, for the kingdom of heaven is theirs: they have nothing to fear, for they care not about losing everything, nor do they consider it lost – their only fear is to displease their God; and they beseech Him to strengthen them in these virtues, that so they may not lose them through their own fault. It is true these virtues have this property of hiding themselves from her who possesses them, so that she never sees them, nor does she think she has one of them, though others tell her so. Yet she values them so much, that she still goes on endeavouring to possess them, and to perfect them in herself, although those who do possess them are soon known; for those who converse with them soon notice those virtues, without the individuals themselves wishing it should be so.

But how foolish is it for me to attempt to praise humility and mortification, which have been so highly commended by the King of Glory, and so strongly confirmed by His sufferings! You must labour then, my daughters, to leave the land of Egypt; for if you obtain these virtues, you will find manna. All things will be sweet to you, and however unsavoury they may be to the taste of worldlings, to you they will be pleasant. The first thing we must aim at, is to banish from ourselves the love of this body of ours, for some of us are so delicate in our constitution, that no little pains are to be taken herein; and we are so careful of our health, that it is wonderful to see the war these two things raise, especially among nuns, and even among those who are not Religious. But some nuns amongst us seem to have come to the monastery, for no other object but to endeavour not to die:34 this each one endeavours to do as far as she can. To speak the truth, there is little convenience in the house for accomplishing this object, and I do not wish you to entertain so much as a desire for such a thing. Remember, sisters, you have come here to die for Christ, and not to regale yourselves for Christ: this, the devil suggests, is necessary, in order to endure and observe the rule the better; and some so much desire to keep the rule by taking care of their health, that they die without even observing it for a month, or perhaps for a day!

I know not, then, why we come here; never fear that we shall want discretion in this respect. This would indeed be wonderful, for the confessors would immediately fear, lest we might kill ourselves with penances; and this want of discretion is so hateful to us, that I wish we observed all the rest as punctually. I know that those who practise the contrary will not agree with what I say; nor need I mind what they say, for I judge of others by myself, that they speak the truth. But I believe, and indeed I know, that I have more companions than I have persons displeased with me, who act differently. I am confident our Lord allows us, therefore, to be more unwell and sickly; at least God has shown me great mercy in being so; for since I was to pamper myself (as I did), He would have it done for some reason; it is pleasant to see the torments with which some afflict themselves, of their own accord. Sometimes a frenzy seizes them of doing penance, without using any moderation or discretion, and this lasts for two days, so to speak. The devil afterwards suggests to their imagination, that such mortifications do them harm, and hence they never do any more penance; no, not even what the rules of the order command, having already found the mortifications hurt them. Then they do not observe even the meanest injunctions of the rule, such as silence, which cannot do us any harm; and no sooner do we fancy that we have the headache, but we refrain from going to choir, which is not likely to kill us either. One day we omit going because our head aches, the next because it did ache, and three more days we keep away, lest it should ache!35 We love to invent penances of our own, that we may be able to do neither the one nor the other; and even at times when we are not so ill, we think ourselves obliged to do nothing, but that we satisfy for everything by asking leave.

You may ask, "Why does the prioress grant leave?" I answer, did she know your interior, perhaps she would not do so; but as you inform her of your wants, and the doctor does not fail to support the account you give, and as there may be some friend or relation of yours who stands weeping by her side, what is the poor prioress to do, though she sometimes sees you go too far? She is scrupulous lest she might be wanting in charity. She would much rather you would fail therein than she herself, and she does not think it just to judge evil of you. O my God! can such complaint be found among nuns? May He pardon me, for I fear it has already become a custom. These things, it may be, happen sometimes; and I mention them here that you may be on your guard against them; for if the devil once begin to terrify us with the idea, that we have not good health, we shall never do anything. May God give us light to be right in everything. Amen.

CHAPTER XI.

SHE CONTINUES THE SUBJECT OF MORTIFICATION, ETC.

IT seems to me, my sisters, a very great imperfection to be always complaining of light evils: if you can bear it, do not do so. When the evil is great, it complains of itself: this is another kind of complaint, and it soon appears. Consider, you are few; and if any one among you have such a custom, it is enough to afflict the rest, if you would observe love and charity. But she who is ill – really and truly ill, should mention the case at once, and take what is necessary; for if you have no self-love, you will so dislike all kind of delicacy, that you need not fear using any without necessity, or complaining without cause. When there is cause, it is very good to mention it, and much better than to use any delicacy, 36 without mentioning it, and it would be very wrong if none were to pity you. But of this I am confident, that where there are prayer and charity, and as you are so few that you see one another's necessities, you will never want proper nourishment, nor care in being attended to. But do not complain of certain weaknesses and little indispositions belonging to women; for sometimes the devil fills the imagination with these pains, which go and come, and unless you entirely break off the habit of speaking and complaining of them (except to God), you will never have rest.

I lay great stress on this point, because I consider it very important, and one of the things by which the discipline of monasteries is greatly relaxed: and our body has the fault, – that the more it is honoured, the more necessities it discovers. It is strange to see how it loves to be well treated; and when it has some good excuse, however trifling may be the necessity, it deceives the poor soul, and hinders her improvement. Think, how many poor sick people there are, who have no friend to complain to: now being poor and dainty do not agree together. Think also on the many married persons – even of quality (and some such I know) – who, though they have grievous maladies and suffer great afflictions, dare not complain for fear of displeasing their husbands. Alas! wretched sinner that I am, I know we came not here to be more caressed than they are. Since then you are free from the great troubles of the world, O! learn to endure a little for the love of God, without letting every one know it. Suppose a woman has not married well, who, in order that her husband may know nothing, says nothing nor complains, though she is very unhappy, without unburdening her mind to any one; and shall we not conceal, between God and ourselves, something of those evils which He sends us for our sins? This we should do the more, since the evil is not lessened thereby. In all that I have said, I do not include violent maladies; as for instance, when one has a burning fever, though even then I wish moderation and patience might always be observed: but I speak only of certain indispositions, which one may go about with, and not disturb all the world by our complaints. But what shall I do, if what I have been writing should be seen out of the house? What will all the nuns say of me? O! how willingly would I bear this, if I knew any one would thereby correct her faults! For when there is one of this character, 37 things come to such a pass, that for the most part no one is believed, however grievous her infirmities may be.

Let us call to mind our holy fathers – the ancient hermits, whose life we pretend to imitate. What pains did they endure, and this too all alone! What extreme cold, and hunger, and heat, having no one to complain to – but God! Think you, they were made of iron? No, they had the same flesh as we ourselves have. Believe me, daughters, when once we begin to subdue these our wretched bodies, they do not trouble us so much: there will be enough to observe what you stand in need of: take no care of yourselves, except there be a manifest necessity. Unless we resolve at once to undervalue death and the want of health, we shall never do anything. Endeavour not to fear death, and give yourselves up entirely to God – come what may. What matter should we die? Since our body has so often mocked us, may we not mock it once? Believe me, this resolution is more important than we imagine. If we often practise it, we shall by little and little, with God's assistance, become masters of our body. Now to conquer such an enemy helps us greatly to triumph in the battle of this life. May God grant this favour, since He is able. I am confident that no one knows the gain but he who already enjoys the victory; and this, in my opinion, is so great – that no one would regret the labour which would be required, in order to obtain this repose and dominion.

CHAPTER XII.

SHE SHOWS HOW THE TRUE LOVER OF GOD MUST DESPISE LIFE AND HONOUR.
I WILL now speak on other subjects, which are also very important, though they may seem of little consequence. All appears to be great labour, and justly so, because it is a war against ourselves; but when we begin to act, God works so powerfully in the soul, and grants her so many favours – that all which can be done in this life seems but little. Now since we nuns do the most, such as giving away our liberty for the love of God, subjecting to another's power, and enduring so much labour, fasting, silence, enclosure, and frequenting the choir, so that were we ever so desirous of regaling ourselves, this could be done but seldom; and perhaps I am the only person that does it, in all the monasteries which I have seen; why then, I ask, must we be so slow in mortifying the interior, since without this practice we cannot properly perform all the rest, which thereby becomes much more perfect and meritorious, and we are afterwards able to go through those duties with great ease and delight? This is acquired if we accustom ourselves by little and little – not to do our own will and follow our own appetite, even in very trifling things, until we have completely made the body subject to the spirit. I say again, that all, or the greatest part, consists in throwing off all care of ourselves and of our own pleasure; for the least which he can offer, who begins to serve God in earnest – is his life, after he has already given up his will to Him. And in giving Him this, what are you afraid of? If he be a true Religious, or one truly given to prayer, and wishes to enjoy Divine consolations, I know he will not refuse desiring to die for Him, and to suffer crosses.38 Do you not know, sisters, that the life of a good Religious, of one who wishes to be numbered among the intimate friends of God, is a long martyrdom? I call it "long," because it may be called so in comparison with those who are beheaded in an instant: but our whole life is short, and some lives are extremely short. And is it not uncertain whether our life may be so short as to end an hour hence, or in the very moment that we have resolved to serve God with all our strength? It is possible; and after all, we have no reason to make any account of that which has an end, and much less of life, since one day of it is not certain. And who is there that, remembering every hour may be his last, will not spend it in labour?

Believe me then, these thoughts give the most security; let us therefore learn to contradict our own will in everything; for though we cannot do this all at once, yet by using diligence with prayer (as I have said) – you will by little and little attain this object, without knowing how. It may indeed seem very severe to say, that we must not please ourselves in anything, because the delights which this denial brings with it, and likewise the benefits which we obtain therefrom, even in this life, are not also mentioned. But as you practise all this here, the chief difficulty is got over: excite, therefore, and help one another forward, and let each one endeavour to outstrip the rest.

Let your interior motions be strictly observed, especially if they concern desires of superiority. May the merits of Christ's passion deliver us from saying, or dwelling on the thought, that I am the senior in the order, or the oldest, or that I have laboured more (than others), or that another is better treated. If these thoughts come, they must be smothered immediately; for if you dwell upon them, or discourse about them, they will become a very plague, and from this arise great evils in monasteries. If you have a superioress who will allow such things, however trifling they may be, believe that God has permitted you, on account of your sins, to have such an one, and that by her your ruin will commence: cry, therefore, to God, and let all your prayers have this end, that you may obtain a remedy for such great danger.

You may ask, why I insist so much on this, and you may think it is too severe, since God caresses even those who are not thus disengaged. I believe this also, because in His infinite wisdom He sees it expedient, to induce them thereby to abandon all things for His sake. If one enters into religion, I do not call that forsaking all things, because even there a person may have attachments; while on the other hand, in every state of life, a perfect soul may be disengaged, and be humble; yet she will have more difficulty, because order and retirement are great helps. But in one point believe me, that if there be any hankering after honours or riches (and this may happen in monasteries as well as in the world, though Religious by being removed from the occasions are more to be blamed), although they may have spent many years in prayer, or to speak more correctly, in speculation (for perfect prayer takes away all these defects), they will never make any great progress, nor be able to enjoy the true fruit of prayer.

Consider, sisters, if you are in any way concerned in these apparent trifles, for you are here for nothing else [but to conduct yourselves as Religious]. 39 You are not more honoured by seeking honour, and the opportunity is lost whereby you might gain much more; thus loss and dishonour are here united. Let each one observe how much humility she has, and she will discover how much she has improved. I think the devil will never dare to tempt one who is truly humble, even with the first motions to desire superiority, because being very crafty, he fears a blow might be given him. If one be humble, it is impossible not to gain more strength and improvement in this virtue, if the devil should attack her on this point; for it is evident she will reflect on her whole life, and consider what little service she has done, together with her great obligations to our Lord, and what wonderful love it was in Him to abase Himself, that so He might leave us an example of humility; and she will also consider her sins, and where she has deserved to be for them. By these considerations the soul becomes so victorious, that the enemy dare not return the next day for fear of a broken head.

Take this advice from me, and do not forget it; endeavour that not only in the interior, where it would be a great evil not to come off with victory, but in the exterior also, the sisters may derive some benefit from the temptation; and if you wish to be revenged on the devil, as soon as the temptation comes, discover it to the superioress, and beg and entreat of her to command you to perform some mean employment, or else perform it yourself as well as you can, and be thinking how to subdue your will in things to which it is averse, and which our Lord will discover to you; you might also make use of public mortifications, since they are practised in this house. By these means, the temptation will last but a short time, and do you endeavour that this may be the case. May God deliver us from those persons who wish to serve Him, from motives of honour, or through fear of dishonour. Consider that it is a poor wretched gain; and as I said, honour itself is lost by seeking it, especially in desiring high posts of honour, for there is no poison in the world which so effectually destroys perfection as these things do.

You will say, "These are very trifling things, which are natural to every one." Do not deceive yourselves by such a pretext, for it increases like froth in monasteries, and nothing is trifling in such imminent danger, such as these points of honour, and noticing when we are injured. Do you wish to know the reason? Without mentioning many other reasons, there is this: perhaps the devil begins by a little affront offered to one, which is almost nothing; then he immediately persuades another to think it is a great offence, so that she will consider it a charity to tell her of it, and to ask how she can possibly endure such an injury? She hopes God will give her patience, that she should offer it up to Him, and that a saint could not suffer more.

In a word, the devil so poisons the tongue of the other, that though you may be resolved to suffer, yet you are still tempted with vain glory on account of that which you have not borne with such perfection as you ought. And our nature is so weak, that even when we have cut off the occasion of a temptation by saying, "This does not deserve the name of suffering;" yet we think we have done something, and feel this: how much more when we see others have a like feeling in our regard! It makes our pain increase, and persuades us we have reason, and the soul loses all the opportunities she had of meriting, and becomes weaker; and we give the devil an entrance to come and attack us another time with some worse temptation. It may even happen that, when you are most willing to bear it, persons may come and ask you, whether you are a beast, and that it is proper to feel wrongs and insults. O! for the love of God, my sisters, let no indiscreet charity move any one to show compassion for another, in matters relating to these imaginary injuries; for it is like that charity which holy Job received from his wife and friends.

CHAPTER XIII.

SHE SPEAKS ON TRUE HUMILITY AND MORTIFICATION, AND SHOWS HOW RELIGIOUS OUGHT TO AVOID HONOURS AND ALL THE MAXIMS OF THE WORLD.
I OFTEN tell you, sisters, and now I wish to leave it here in writing, lest you might forget it, that not only those belonging to this house, but even every one who wishes to be perfect must fly a thousand leagues from saying, 40 "I had reason – I was injured – he who thus treated me had no reason for what he did:" may God deliver us from such miserable reasoning. Do you think it was reasonable, that our good Jesus should suffer so many injuries, and that these should be committed so much against reason? She who is unwilling to bear any cross, but that for which they who impose it have very good reasons, had better leave the house, for I cannot understand why she should remain in the monastery – let her return to the world again, where none of these "reasons" are observed. Can you suffer so much, that you ought not to suffer more? What reason is there in this? I do not indeed understand it. When people show us any honour, or do us any favour, or treat us kindly, let us produce these reasons – for it is really against reason that we should be made much of in this life – but when we receive injuries or wrongs (for so we call them without any injury being done), I know not why they should be mentioned. Either we are

spouses of so great a king, or we are not; if we are, what respectable lady is there, who does not share in the disgrace and affronts which are cast upon her husband, though she herself may not desire it. In a word, both of them share in honour or dishonour. For us to desire, then, to share in the kingdom of our Lord, and yet refuse to take any part in labours and affronts, is unreasonable. May God preserve us from desiring such a thing. But let her who thinks she is esteemed the meanest of all, account herself the happiest of all the sisters, and truly she is so, if she bear it as she ought, for honour will not be wanting to her, either in this life or in the next – let them believe in this case. But what a foolish thing have I uttered in saying, "let them believe me," when true Wisdom itself has said the same thing.

Let us, my daughters, imitate the great humility of the most Sacred Virgin, whose habit we wear; for it is a shame we should be numbered among her nuns, since however much we may seem to humble ourselves, we fall far short of being daughters of such a mother, and spouses of such a Spouse. Hence, if what I have mentioned above be not carefully prevented, that which today seems nothing, will to-morrow prove a venial sin; and it is so difficult to digest, that if you neglect it, it will not remain alone, since it is an evil very dangerous to communities. We who live in communities must carefully attend to this point, viz., that we do no harm to those who labour to benefit us, and to give us good example.

If we knew what great harm is done in beginning a bad custom, we should prefer death rather than be the cause of it; for the one is only a corporal death, but the loss of souls is a great loss; and this in my opinion never has an end, because when some die, others succeed them, and all perhaps retain more of one bad custom which we may have introduced, than of many virtues. The devil also does not allow such customs to die away; but natural infirmity roots out virtue, if a person do not keep a strict watch, and beg assistance from God.

O! what a most precious act of charity, and what a great service to God would that nun perform, who seeing she was unable to observe the rules of this house, would acknowledge it, and depart before she made her profession, and so leave the rest in peace. And even in all monasteries (at least, if they will believe me), they should not retain her, or give her leave to be "professed," till after a trial of many years, in order to see whether she will amend. I speak not of faults relating to penance and fasts, for though they are faults, they are not matters which do so much harm. But I speak of certain humours, 41 peculiar to persons who love to be esteemed and respected; who spy out the defects of others, and never acknowledge their own, and so with regard to other similar things, which certainly arise from want of humility. Unless God be favourable to such a person, by granting her abundance of the gifts of His Holy Spirit, so that after many years her amendment appears, may our Lord deliver you from keeping her in your society. Know that she will neither rest herself, nor let you rest, but she will continue to disturb every one.

On this account I pity those monasteries, which, in order to avoid the repayment of the money or dowry received, oftentimes retain a thief that robs them of their chief treasure. In this house, you have already hazarded and even lost all prospects of worldly honour (for poor people are not honoured); seek not, therefore, other honours, which cost you so much. Our honour, sisters, ought to consist in serving God. Whoever thinks you are to be disturbed in this, let her remain at home with her honour, for this object it was that our Fathers appointed a year's probation, and here it is my wish, that no one might be allowed to make their profession under ten years' probation; for an humble Religious will be little troubled at not being "professed," knowing well that if she be good, she will not be sent away; if she be not good, why should she desire to hurt this community of Christ?42 By not being good, I mean not loving vanity, which, by God's grace is far, I hope, from this house, but not being mortified, and being attached to the things of this world, or to one's self in matters which I have mentioned before. And she who finds not in herself great mortification, let her believe me, and not make her profession, if she would not suffer a hell in this world, and God grant there may not be another in the next, for there are many things in her, which tend that way; and perhaps neither she nor the rest will understand this matter so well as I do. Herein let them believe me, otherwise time will convince them of it; for the object we aim at is not only that of being nuns, but hermits also, as were our holy Fathers, our predecessors; and thus must we disengage ourselves from all created things – and whomsoever our Lord has chosen for this house, we see in a special manner that He confers this favour upon her; and though as yet it be not in all perfection, it is evident that she already tends to perfection, by the great pleasure and satisfaction she takes, in seeing that she is to have no more to do with the concerns of this life, and also by the delight she finds in all the exercises of religion.

I say again, if any one feels an inclination for the things of this world, and perceives that she does not go on improving, she is not fit for this house; she may go to some other, if she wish to be a nun; or if not, let her mark what follows. And let her not complain of me (who began this) – for not having warned her. This house is a heaven, if such can be on earth, to one whose sole delight is to please God, and who regards not her own pleasure; here, she may lead a very good life; if she grasp at any anything more she will lose all, because she cannot keep it. And a discontented soul is like one who has a great loathing; for however good the food may be, she casts it up; and that which persons in health can eat, with great delight, makes her stomach loathe. In another place, she may have better opportunities of being saved; and by little and little she may possibly attain to that perfection, which here cannot be reached – because it is to be acquired all at once; for though as to the interior, time is to be allowed for entirely disengaging and mortifying one's self, yet as to the exterior, it should be done speedily, on account of the harm it may do to others. And if here one does not make any progress in a year, though she sees all the others do, and though she is in such good company, I fear that such a person will not improve even during many years. I say not, that the improvement must be so complete in her – as in the others: but it is to be understood she goes on still recovering her health; and this is soon discerned, if the malady be not mortal.

CHAPTER XIV.

HOW IMPORTANT IT IS NOT TO ALLOW ANY TO MAKE THEIR PROFESSION, WHOSE DISPOSITION IS THE CONTRARY OF WHAT HAS BEEN MENTIONED BEFORE.

I BELIEVE that God highly favours him who has made good resolutions, and therefore we must, examine – what intention she has who is admitted; it must not be for her own convenience only, as is the case with many now-a-days, though our Lord can perfect this intention if the person have a good understanding; otherwise, on no account let her be admitted; for she will neither understand herself – how she comes into religion, nor will others afterwards, who would direct her better: generally speaking, they who have this defect, always think that they understand what is best for them – better than the wisest superior. This is a disease which I consider incurable, for it is very seldom without carrying malice with it. Where there are many Religious, it may be tolerated; but among so few (as we are) – it cannot be endured. When a strong understanding begins to like what is good, it adheres firmly to it, because it sees that this is its most secure course; and should it be of no use towards advancing much in virtue, it may be useful for giving good advice and for43 many other things, without tiring any one. But when a person has no understanding, I know not in what she can be useful in a community, and one may do much harm. This defect is not soon discovered, for many speak well and understand little; others again speak little and not very elegantly, yet they have a good understanding. But there are others also, who living in holy simplicity,44 know little of the business and customs of the world, but they are skilful in discoursing of God. There is great need, therefore, of strict examination before they are admitted, and a long trial before they are professed. Let the world once know, that you have power to reject them; that in monasteries where austerities are practised, there are many occasions in which this must be done; and then, when this power is made use of, they will not consider it an injury done to them.

I speak thus, because these times in which we live are so miserable; and so great is our weakness that though we have the command of our predecessors for it, this is not sufficient to make us neglect observing what the world at present has taken for an honour, viz., not to grieve our friends: but we allow virtuous customs to be forgotten, in order to avoid giving a slight offence, or to prevent any ill rumours – which indeed are a mere nothing. God grant, that those who admit such, may not have to pay for their fault in the next life: for we always have some pretence or other, by which we persuade ourselves – that the persons may be admitted. This is a matter which each one ought to consider for herself, and recommend to God; it should also animate the superioress, hence it is so very important for all; I therefore beg of God to give you light therein. For my part I consider, that when the superioress, without affection or passion, aims at the good of the house, God will never allow her to fall into error; but if she pay attention to this false tenderness and foolish punctilios, I am persuaded there will always be some errors.

CHAPTER XV.

ON THE GREAT BENEFIT WE DERIVE FROM NOT EXCUSING OURSELVES, THOUGH WE MAY BE CONVINCED WE HAVE BEEN BLAMED WITHOUT CAUSE.
WHAT I am now about to induce you to do (viz. – not to excuse ourselves) – produces great confusion in me, for it is a very excellent practice and of great merit, because I ought to practise what I tell you concerning this virtue. Thus I acknowledge that I have made very little advancement in it; for methinks I never want a reason to imagine, that to make an excuse – shows more virtue in me. Now as it is sometimes lawful to make an excuse, and it would even be wrong to omit it, I have not the discretion, or to speak more properly – the humility to make it, when it is proper to do so. It is indeed a proof of great humility, to see one's self condemned without any reason, and at the same time to say nothing; this is a noble imitation of our Lord, who blotted out all our offences. I therefore earnestly entreat you, to use all possible care in this respect, because it brings great advantages with it; and I see no benefit in endeavouring to excuse ourselves, except it be (as I said) in certain cases which may cause offence, by not speaking the

truth. She who has more discretion than myself, will easily understand this. I am persuaded it is very important to accustom one's self to this virtue, or to endeavour to obtain true humility from our Lord; from Him it must come, for one who is truly humble must sincerely desire not to be esteemed, but to be persecuted and condemned, though she may have given no cause. If we wish to imitate our Lord, wherein can we do better – than by imitating Him in this way? Here no corporeal strength is necessary, nor any one's assistance – except only God's.

These great virtues, my sisters, I wish to become our study and our penance: as to other severe and excessive penances, you already know that I keep you from them, because they may injure your health, if performed without discretion. In those others you need not fear, because the interior virtues, however great they may be, do not destroy the strength of the body, which is required for observing the rules, but fortify the soul; and (as I have said), persons may accustom themselves, in very small things, to gain a victory in great things. But how well have I spoken on the subject, and yet how careless in practising what I say! Indeed, I could never yet make this trial in matters of consequence, because I never heard any one speak ill of me; but I saw clearly it was far from being true; for though I may not have offended God in these particular cases, yet I have offended Him in many others, and I thought they favoured me greatly in omitting them, for I am always more delighted that people should say what is not true of me, than what is.

It helps us greatly if every one would consider how much is gained every way, for in my opinion nothing is lost. The principal gain is to imitate our Lord in something. I say "in something," for we may clearly see, that we are never blamed without having faults, of which we are quite full, since the just man falls seven times a day, and it would be a lie to say, "we have no sin." Thus, though it be not the same thing which they accuse us of, yet we are never altogether without fault.

O my Lord! when I consider in how many ways Thou didst suffer, and yet didst not at all deserve it, I know not what to say for myself, nor where my senses were, when I did not desire sufferings, nor where I am when I excuse myself. You know, O my God! that if I have any good, it has been bestowed by no one but You. And how are You restrained in giving me much rather than little? If it be because I do not deserve it, I deserve as little the favours You have bestowed on me. Is it possible I should wish any one to think well of a creature so bad as I am, when so many evil things have been spoken against You, who are the supreme Good above all goods? Do not suffer it, do not suffer it, O my God! nor let me desire that You should endure anything to be in your servant, which is not pleasing to you. See, O Lord! my eyes are blind, and are satisfied with very little. Give me light, and make me really desire, that every one may abhor me, since I have so often forsaken You, though You loved me with so much fidelity. What is this, O my God? What do we imagine we shall obtain by pleasing creatures? Why are we concerned in being falsely accused by all of them, if we are innocent before You, O Lord?

O my sisters! far, far are we from understanding this truth! And thus it is that we shall never arrive at the top of perfection, except we often carefully consider and observe what it is in reality, and not in appearance.45 When, then, there is no other benefit except the confusion which the person receives who accused you, by seeing you suffer yourselves to be condemned without cause, even this is a very great benefit. Such a virtue sometimes elevates a soul more than ten sermons. Now, we must all endeavour to be preachers by our works, since the Apostle and our own incapacity forbid us to be such in words. Never fancy that the good or the bad which you do, will be concealed, however strictly you may be enclosed. And think you, daughters, that though you do not excuse yourselves, you shall want one to defend you? Observe how our Lord answered for Magdalen in the house of the Pharisee, when her sister complained of her. He will not act with such severity towards you, as He did to Himself; for the good thief was not allowed to undertake His defence; till He was hanging on the cross. Thus His majesty will raise some one up to undertake your defence; and if not, there will be no necessity for one. This I have seen, and it is true (though I do not wish you to be influenced by this motive, but that you should rejoice when you are accused); as for the benefit you will perceive in your souls, time will convince you, and be a witness thereto. Then we begin to obtain liberty, and care no more about being ill than being well spoken of: it even appears to be as it were another's business, and is like two persons talking together, whose discourse not being with us, we are unconcerned about making any answer; they seem not to speak to us. This may seem impossible to us, who are so very sensitive, and too unmortified. At first, it is indeed difficult, but I know that by God's assistance, this abnegation and disengagement from ourselves may be acquired.

CHAPTER XVI.

SHE BEGINS TO SPEAK ON MENTAL PRAYER AS COMPARED WITH CONTEMPLATION, ETC.

LET not all that I have been saying appear much to you, for as the saying is, "I am only setting the men for a game at chess."46 You desired me to explain to you the beginning of prayer. I know no other, daughters, though God did not conduct me by this beginning, for I have scarcely the commencement of these virtues. Believe me, then, that whoever does not know how to place the men at chess, will not be able to play well; and if he know not how to give "check," he will not know how to give "checkmate."47 You may blame me for mentioning a game, which neither is, nor can be practised in this house. Here you see what a mother God has given you, skilled even in this vanity! But people say, "This game is lawful sometimes;" and how lawful would it be for us, and useful in some degree, to "checkmate" this Divine King, that so He might neither wish, nor be able to escape out of our hands! The queen puts him to the greatest difficulties in this game, and for this object all the other pieces help. Now no queen makes the king yield so soon as humility. This brought Him down from heaven into the womb of the blessed Virgin, and by means of it, we may with a hair bring Him into our soul. Believe me, that whoever has most humility, will possess Him most, and less he who has less. For I do not, and cannot understand, how there is or can be humility without love, or love without humility. And it is not possible that these two virtues should be in their perfection, without a great disengagement from all created objects.

You may ask me, my daughters, why I speak to you of these virtues, since you have plenty of books to teach you them? and you desire only to hear something on contemplation. I answer, that had you desired some discourse about "meditation," I could have spoken on it, and advised all of you to use it, even though you have not the virtues; for it is a commencement towards obtaining all virtues, and a matter that concerns the souls of all Christians, if they wish to begin a new life; and hence, none, however abandoned they may be, whom God excites to so great a good, ought to neglect meditation, as I have elsewhere mentioned, and so have others who know what they write about, for God knows I do not. But, contemplation, daughters, is another thing. This is the mistake we all make, viz., that if any one accustom herself to think every day for a short time upon her sins (which every one ought to do, if he be a practical Christian), people immediately call her a great "contemplative," and would have her instantly possess as high virtues, as he is bound to have who is eminent for contemplation, and even she herself imagines so too, but she is mistaken. She has not learnt at first to arrange the men; she thinks it is sufficient to know the pieces in order to "checkmate" but this is impossible, for the king will not give Himself up in the way we are speaking of, except to him who surrenders himself entirely into His hands.

Thus you see, daughters, if you wish me to tell you the way to arrive at contemplation, allow me to enlarge a little on things, which though they may not immediately seem to you to be so important, yet in my opinion they are so; and if you will not hear them nor practise them, continue all your life with your mental prayer, for I assure you and all who aspire to this happiness (though I may be mistaken, since I judge by myself, who have been endeavouring to obtain it these twenty years) that you will never attain to true contemplation.

I now wish to explain what mental prayer is, since some of you do not understand it – and God grant that we may practise it as it should be practised – but I fear it will be obtained with great labour, except those virtues be acquired (though not in so high a degree), which are necessary for contemplation. I say, the King of Glory will not come into our soul (I mean, will not be united with her), unless we strive to obtain eminent virtues. I will explain this point, because should you find me telling an untruth in anything, you will believe nothing; and you would have reason, if it were done wilfully. But may God deliver me from any such temptation – it must arise from ignorance, or want of understanding. I wish to mention, that sometimes God is pleased to bestow great favours on persons who are in a bad state, in order to advance them to contemplation, that so by this means He may snatch them from the power of the devil.

O my Lord! how often do we force You still to fight with the devil for us! Was it not sufficient that you allowed yourself to be grasped in his arms, when he carried you to the pinnacle of the temple, in order to teach us how to vanquish him? What a spectacle must it have been, daughters, to behold that Sun surrounded with darkness, and what fear must that wretch have had, without knowing whence it came? God did not allow him to understand it. Blessed be so much goodness and mercy! And how ought we Christians to blush, for making him every day (as I have said) encounter so foul a beast? It was very necessary, O Lord, you should have such strong arms; but did they not become weak by all those torments which you endured on the cross? O! how does all that is endured for love soon heal up again! And so I think, that had you continued alive, the mere love you had for us would have healed your wounds, and there would have been no need of any other medicine. O my God! who will apply such a medicine to me, in all such things as may cause me pain or trouble? how willingly would I bear these, if I were sure to be cured by so saving a remedy! But to return to what I was saying.

There are some souls which God knows He can attract to himself by such means; and though now He sees them quite lost, His majesty desires they may not remain for Him;48 and so though they be in a bad state, and destitute of virtues, He gives them caresses, consolations, and tenderness, which begin to excite desires; and sometimes He brings them even to contemplation, though this is seldom, and of short duration. This He does (as I have said), in order to make a trial of them, whether by that sweetness they will dispose themselves to enjoy him more frequently. But if they do not dispose themselves, let them pardon God for retiring from them; or, rather, do You pardon us, O Lord! for it is not indeed just, that You should come into a soul in this way, and that afterwards she should again have anything to do with creatures, so as to adhere to them. I am persuaded, that there are many of whom God makes a trial in this manner, and few there are who dispose themselves for enjoying such a favour. For when our Lord makes this trial, and we are no hinderance to it, I am certain that He never leaves off giving more favours, till He brings us to the highest degree. When we do not give ourselves up to His majesty, with the same determination that He gives Himself to us, He does enough in leaving us in Mental prayer, and visiting us from time to time, as servants who are working in his vineyard. But those others are His dear children, whom He wishes should be near Him; nor does He part with them, because they do not desire to leave Him. He makes them sit down at His table, and gives them part of his own food, so as to take (as the saying is) the morsel out of His own mouth, to give it to them.

O happy pains, my daughters! O blessed abandonment of things so small, and so base, which leads us to so high a dignity! Consider how little you will regard being blamed by the world, while you rest in the arms of God, who can deliver you from the whole world. He is powerful to free you perfectly, for once He commanded the world to be made, and it was made: His willing is acting. Fear not, then, unless it be for the greater good of those who love Him, that he will not allow you to be defamed: He does not love so imperfectly those who love Him. Why should we not, then, my sisters, show our love for Him as much as we can? Consider, that it is a fair exchange to give our love for His. Remember, He can do all things, and we, who are here, can do nothing at all, except what He enables us to do. Now what is this, O Lord, our Creator! which we do for You? As much as nothing – a poor feeble resolution.49 If then His majesty wishes us to purchase all things, with that which is a mere nothing, let us not become foolish.

O Lord! all our evils come from our not fixing our eyes upon Thee. If we considered only the way, we should soon arrive there; but we fall a thousand times, and stumble and stray from the way, by not fixing our eyes (as I said) on the true way. It seems never to have been trodden, for it looks so new to us. That is truly to be regretted, which sometimes happens; and therefore I say, we seem not to be Christians, nor to have read the passion in our life, since we cannot endure to be despised even in a trifle; nay, it seems impossible to be endured. They reply immediately; "We are not saints." When we do something imperfect, may God deliver us, sisters, from saying – "We are not angels," – "We are not saints." Consider, that though we be not angels or saints, it is a great happiness to think that if we strive, we may be such by God's assistance; and fear not that He will fail, if you fail not.

And since we have come here for no other purpose, let us set to work; let us not think there is anything, whereby our Lord may be served better, which we may not hope to succeed in, by His help. Such presumption I wish to see in this house, for it always makes humility increase, and produces a holy boldness; for God assists the valiant, and is no acceptor of persons. I have wandered much from my subject, and now wish to return to what I was saying. We must know what mental prayer is, and what contemplation is. It may seem foolish in me to speak on these subjects; but you do not mind, and you may, possibly, understand the subject better by my rude style, than by another more elegant. May our Lord grant me His assistance herein. Amen.

CHAPTER XVII.

SHE SHOWS HOW ALL SOULS ARE NOT FIT FOR CONTEMPLATION, ETC.

I AM now about to enter on the subject of prayer; but I must first say something of great importance to you. It is concerning humility, which is so extremely necessary in this house, because it is the principal exercise of prayer; and as I have said, it is very important that you endeavour to understand how to exercise yourselves well in humility: this is very important, and very necessary for all those who give themselves to prayer. How can one who is truly humble, imagine himself to be already as good as those who have become "contemplatives?" God can indeed, by His goodness and mercy, make one to be such; but let him take my advice, and always sit in the lowest place, since our Lord has told us to do so, and has taught us it by his practice. If God wishes to lead any one this way, let her dispose herself for Him; if not, humility serves instead, while she considers herself happy in serving the handmaids of our Lord; and she praises Him, because though she deserved to be a slave to the devils in hell, His majesty has placed her among His servants.

I speak this not without great reason; for (as I have said) it is very important to understand, that God does not conduct all in the same way; and perhaps she who thinks herself the lowest, is the highest in the eyes of God. Hence, because all in this house give themselves to prayer, it does not follow that all must be contemplatives: this is impossible, and it will be a great consolation for her who is not a "contemplative" to know this truth, for God only gives this gift; and since it is not necessary for salvation, nor required for our future reward, let her not think that it is here demanded of her, because without this she is sure to become very perfect, if she does what has been said. It may even be, that she has much more merit, because it costs her more pains; and our Lord treats her as a valiant person, and keeps in reserve for her all that which she does not enjoy here. Let her not therefore be discouraged, nor omit her prayer, or neglect to do what all the rest do; for sometimes our Lord comes very late, and pays one as well and as much together, as He has been giving to others during many years. I was more than fourteen years, during which I could never use even meditation, unless joined with reading. There will be many persons of this kind, and others also, who although they make use of reading, yet cannot practise meditation, but only pray vocally, because that is a little hinderance to them. There are imaginations so volatile, that they cannot remain on one thing, but are always uneasy; and this to such a degree, that should they strive to keep their thoughts on God, they run into a thousand absurdities, scruples, and doubts.

I know a very old person, who has led an exceedingly good life, (God grant mine may be like hers), and has been given to penance, and is moreover a great servant of God, having spent many hours and years in vocal prayer, but mental she could not use: the most she could do, was to continue a short time in her vocal prayers. There are many other persons of this kind, who if they have humility, will not I believe be anything worse in the end; but they will share equally with those who enjoy many consolations, and they will have even more security in some respect, because we know not whether these consolations be from God or from the devil; if they come not from God, there is more danger, because what the devil strives at most here, is to excite them to pride; but if they be from God, there is no reason to fear, because they carry humility along with them, as I have shown at some length in another book.50

Those others who receive no consolations proceed with humility, fearing lest it might be through their own fault, being always anxious to go forward: they do not see others weep, but except they do the same, they imagine they are far behind in the service of God, and yet they are perhaps much more forward, since all heads are not perfect, though they be good. There is always more security in humility, mortification, abnegation and other virtues; there is no reason to fear or doubt; you will not fail to attain perfection, as well as become great contemplatives. Martha was a saint, though she is not said to be a contemplative. Now, what do you desire more, than to be able to resemble this Blessed woman, who deserved so often to entertain Christ our Lord in her House? Had she been like Blessed Magdalen – always absorpt – there would have been no one to provide food for the Divine Guest. Imagine then that this community is the House of St. Martha, which must have something of everything; and let not those who have been led along the "active way" envy those who are engulfed in contemplation, since they know our Lord will undertake their defence, though He may be for the most part silent, in order to make them careful both of themselves and of all things. Let them remember, there must be some to dress His meat, and let them account themselves happy to serve with Martha. Let them remember, that true humility chiefly consists in being very ready to be contented with whatever our Lord shall be pleased to do with them; and let them always consider themselves unworthy to be called His servants.

If then to make use of contemplation, mental and vocal prayer; attending the sick, serving in the house, and working even in the meanest offices, – if all this be not waiting ont his Guest, who comes to stay, and to eat, and to refresh Himself with us, is it not important for us to serve Him in one way, rather than in another?

I do not say, however, that it is in your power to arrive at contemplation, but that you should use all your exertions to attain it; for this does not consist in your choice, but in our Lord's: and if after many years, trial, He should wish each one to serve in her particular office, will it not be a pretty kind of humility to desire to make your own choice?51 Let the master of the house do what he pleases; He is wise and powerful; He understands what is best for you, and best for himself also. Be assured, that if you do what lies in you, and dispose yourselves for contemplation with the perfection mentioned before, even should he not bestow it upon you (though I believe He will not fail to give it to you, if you have true mortification and humility), be assured that he reserves this favour for you, to give it to you altogether in heaven: and as I have said elsewhere, He intends to lead you on like valiant persons, giving you in this world a cross to carry, just as His Majesty carried one. And what stronger proof of friendship can we have, than to choose for you what he chose for Himself? Perhaps you would not have so great a reward in contemplation. These are His judgments, and we must not dive into them. It is a great blessing that we are not at liberty to do this; for thinking there would be more repose in contemplation, we should all be great contemplatives. O! immense gain, not to desire any gain by your own choice, through fear of some loss! God never allows any one, who is truly mortified, to sustain any loss, except it be for his greater gain.

CHAPTER XVIII.

THE SAME SUBJECT IS CONTINUED, IN WHICH THE SAINT SHOWS HOW MUCH GREATER ARE THE SUFFERINGS OF THE CONTEMPLATIVE, THAN OF THE ACTIVE LIFE.

I SAY then, daughters, to those amongst you whom God does not lead in this way, that as far as I have seen and understood from those who walk in it, they do not carry a higher cross than you do; and that you would be surprised at the ways and manner whereby God afflicts them. I am acquainted both with the one and the other, and understand clearly that the afflictions which God gives to contemplative souls are intolerable, and of such a character, that unless He gave them these caresses, they could not be endured. And it is evident (since it is true), that those whom God loves, He leads along the road of afflictions: and the more He loves them, the greater are the afflictions. I cannot believe that He abhors contemplative souls, because with His own mouth He commends them, and considers them His friends. It is foolish, therefore, to imagine that He admits into friendship with Him persons who live delicately and without troubles: nay, I am very confident that God sends them greater crosses. And as he leads them through such a rough and uneven way, that sometimes they think they are lost, and must begin the journey again, so His Majesty thinks it necessary to give them some refreshment – not water, but wine – that so being inebriated with this heavenly wine, they may not consider what they suffer, but may be able to endure it.

Hence it is that I see few contemplatives who are not courageous, and resolved to suffer; for, if they be weak, the first thing our Lord does is to infuse courage into them, and make them not fear afflictions. I believe that those of the active life, when they see how they are caressed for a little while, think there is nothing else but those consolations: but I tell you, that perhaps you could not endure for one day what they do. Thus, as our Lord knows what all are fit for, He gives every one their employment, as He sees it is most expedient for their souls, His own glory, and the good of their neighbour. And since this does not depend upon your having disposed yourselves, be not afraid lest you should lose your labour.

Consider what I say – that we must all aim at this object, since we are here for no other purpose; and that not for one or two years only; no, nor for ten, lest we may seem to act like cowards. It is well if our Lord sees not that we are in fault, like soldiers, who, though they may have been long in the service, must always be ready to perform whatever the captain may command them, or to take whatever post he gives them, since he will pay them very handsomely. But how much better pay will our King give, than any one here on earth! Now, as the captain, when he sees his men present, and thoroughly knows what his men are fit for, distributes their posts according to their abilities: so, my sisters, apply yourselves to mental prayer; and whoever cannot do this, let them use vocal prayer, reading, and colloquies with God; as I shall explain hereafter, let them not leave their hours of prayer (because they know not when the Bridegroom may come), lest they share the same fate as the foolish virgins. Perhaps He will send them more trouble, under the appearance of consolation: but if He give it not, let such know they are unfit for it, that the other course is best for them. Here we have an opportunity of meriting by humility and believing sincerely – that they are not even fit for that which they do; yet they go cheerfully serving Him in what is commanded them, as I have said. And if this humility be sincere, blessed is she who is such a servant in the active life, for she will complain of no one but herself: let her leave others to their war in which they are engaged, and this is no trifling one. For though the ensign does not fight in the battle, yet he is not therefore exempt from being in great danger, and must needs suffer more in his interior than all the rest, because, as he carries the colours, he cannot defend himself, nor let them go out of his hands, though the enemy should cut him to pieces. And so contemplatives are to carry erect the standard of humility, and bear all the blows the enemy gives, and to return none, because their duty is to suffer like Christ, and to carry the cross on high, nor let it go out of their hands on account of any dangers whatever; neither must they show any weariness in suffering; for this purpose it is that they are advanced to so honourable a post.

Let them consider what they do, for if the ensign should desert his colours, the battle is lost; and so, I believe there is great hurt done to those others who are not so advanced (in perfection), if they see that those whom they already consider to be captains and favourites of God, do not act in their works conformably to the post they hold. The common soldiers act as well as they can, and sometimes move from one place to another, when they see themselves in greater danger: no one takes notice of this, nor is any one discouraged thereby: but the ensigns draw all eyes upon them, and cannot stir without being observed. The post is good and very honourable, and the king does a favour to him, on whom he bestows it: hence their obligation is so much the greater, in order to discharge properly the duties of their office.

Thus, sisters, we neither know nor understand what we ask; let our Lord, therefore, do what He pleases, for He knows us better than we do ourselves; and it is humility to be content with what is given us, for it seems there are some who, in justice, wish to ask favours of God! A pretty kind of humility this! The searcher of all men does well, then (in my opinion), by seldom granting favours to such persons: He plainly sees they are unworthy to drink of His chalice.

To know then, daughters, whether you have made any progress, you must judge by this mark, viz. – if every one considers herself the most wicked among you all; and if it appear by her actions that she thinks so, for the good and advantage of the rest; but not if she have more caresses in prayer – more raptures and visions, and favours of this kind, which God may bestow upon her. These we must hope for in the other world, in order to understand their value. This other is current money – a revenue which fails not – an estate in perpetuity, and not an annuity which ceases (for the other goes and comes). I allude to the great virtue of humility, mortification, and entire obedience, by not acting in the least point against the commands of the Superior, knowing for certain that God commands you, since the Superior holds His place.

Obedience is that virtue, on which I should enter more at large: but because I believe if nuns are wanting in this point, they are no nuns at all, I say nothing about it; for I speak to nuns (and I think to good ones – at least they desire to be such); and hence, in a matter so important, and so well understood, I add but one word, lest it be forgotten. I say, then, that whoever is under obedience by vow, and fails therein, not using every exertion to observe her vow with the utmost perfection, I cannot understand why she remains in the monastery. I can assure her at least, that as long as she remains here, she will never become a contemplative, nor even a good nun in the active life. This I consider certain; and though she may not be a person who is obliged thereto. yet if she desire or intend to arrive at contemplation, it will be necessary for her (in order to proceed more securely) to submit her own will, with full determination, to a confessor who is himself a contemplative. It is well known, that in this way she may advance more in a year, than without it in many; but because it does not concern you much, I need not say more about it.

I conclude, that these are the virtues which I desire you, my daughters, should possess, or endeavour to procure, and devoutly envy the possessors of them. As for other devotions, be not solicitous, or troubled at your not having them; they are uncertain things. It may be that in others they come from God; yet in you, His Majesty may permit them to be an illusion of the devil, and that he may deceive you as he has done others. Why do you desire to serve God in a doubtful way, when you have so many secure ways whereby to serve Him. I have dwelt so much on this point, because I know it is necessary, since our nature is weak: and those His Majesty will strengthen, on whom He wishes to bestow contemplation. As to those on whom He does not bestow it, I am glad I have given them directions, whence the contemplatives also may have a means of humbling themselves. May our Lord, by His goodness, give us light to follow His will in everything, and we shall have no cause to fear.

CHAPTER XIX.

ON THE KIND OF PRAYER THOSE PERSONS SHOULD USE WHO CANNOT DISCOURSE WITH THEIR UNDERSTANDING.

IT is so many days since I wrote the preceding discourse, not having an opportunity of resuming it, that unless I read it over again, I know not what I said: but not to lose any time, what I have said must remain written, without order or connection. For solid understandings and souls that are already well trained, and which can continue still within themselves, there are so many excellent books written, and by such eminent persons, that it would be an error in you to pay any attention to what I say with regard to prayer. As I have said, you have these books, wherein the mysteries of our Lord's life are arranged according to the days of the week: you have likewise meditations on the last Day, on hell, on our own nothingness, and how much we owe to God, with excellent instructions in order, respecting the beginning and end of prayer. Whoever is able, and is accustomed to practise this kind of prayer, has no need of anything being said to him, for by so good a way God will bring him to a port52 of light, and the end will correspond with such good beginnings. And all those who can go along such a road, enjoy rest and security, for when the understanding is once restrained, we go on with ease. But that which I desire to treat of, is to lay down some remedy, if it please God that I speak to the purpose; if not, that you at least may understand there are many souls who pass through this affliction, and, therefore, if any of you be in the like distress, do not torment yourselves.

There are some souls so disorderly, like unbroken horses, that no one can stop them; but they run here and there – always restless: such is either their nature, or God permits it. I pity them much, since it seems to me they are like persons extremely thirsty, who see water a great distance off, and when they wish to go there, they meet with others who oppose their journey, both in the beginning, and in the mid-way, and at the end. And so it happens, that after they have overcome the first ranks with very great labour, they are left to subdue the second, and thus they would rather die with thirst, than drink water which is to cost them so dear. They want strength, and so their courage fails; and though some have courage for conquering the second kind of enemies, the third quite disheartens them; and perhaps they were not two steps off from the "Fountain of Living Water," of which our Lord spoke to the Samaritan woman, "of which whoever drinks, shall not thirst." And with how much reason and truth (since the words were spoken by the mouth of Truth itself), shall such an one never thirst after anything in this life, though with regard to the things of the other life, this thirst is greatly increased, far beyond what we can imagine respecting our natural thirst. But with what a thirst is this thirst desired! for the soul understands its great value, and it is also a very painful thirst that afflicts us, and yet it brings with it a satisfaction, whereby our other thirst is cooled: hence it is a thirst which only extinguishes a thirst for earthly things: it affects us also in such a way, that when God satisfies it, one of the greatest favours He can do the soul, is to leave her in this necessity, and she always has a greater desire to drink again of this water.

Water has three properties (as far as I can now remember), which will illustrate my meaning; it may also have many other properties. The first property is, that it cools, so that however hot we may be, when we take water, our heat goes away; and if there be a great fire, water puts it out, except wildfire, for then it burns the more. O my God! what wonders there are in this fire, which burns the more when water is poured on it, since it is a strong and mighty fire, and is not subject to the other elements! Though water is the opposite element to it, yet this does not extinguish, but rather increases it the more! If I understood philosophy, I could explain this phenomenon, because knowing the properties of things, I should be able to express my meaning better; but now I amuse myself in speaking of it, and I know not how to speak about the matter, and perhaps cannot even understand it. When God shall bring you, sisters, to drink of this water, you will delight in it (as those know who now drink of it), and you will understand how the true love of God is master of all the elements of the world, if it be in its strength and entirely free from all earthly things, and soar above them all. And as water comes from the earth, fear not that it will quench this fire of the love of God: it is not under its jurisdiction; and though they are contrary to each other, this love is now absolute master; it is not subject to the water; and so, sisters, wonder not that I have said so much in this book; for I wish you to obtain this liberty.

Is it not an excellent thing, that a poor nun of St. Joseph's may obtain dominion over the whole earth and the elements? And what wonder that the saints do with them what they please, by the help of God? Fire and water obeyed St. Martin; the fowls and fishes obeyed St. Francis; and so with regard to other saints, who it clearly appears were such absolute lords of all earthly things, because they laboured so well to undervalue them, and so truly subjected themselves with all their strength to the Lord of the universe. Hence, as I have said, the water which rises from the earth has no power against this fire, the flames of which are very high, and it derives not its origin from so mean a thing as earth. There are other fires, arising from a small love of God, which any event will extinguish; but not this fire; even though a whole sea of temptations should break in, yet it will not make this fire leave off burning; rather will the fire become master of them. If it be water that comes down from heaven, much less will this extinguish the fire; it even revives it more than the other; they are not contraries, but have the same origin. Do not fear, lest one element should destroy the other: one rather helps the other to produce its effect; for the water of true tears, such are those which come from earnest prayer, is given by the King of heaven, and helps to kindle and rather to make the fire continue; and the fire also helps to cool the water. O my God! how pleasant and how wonderful, that fire should cool and even congeal all earthly affections, when it is united with this living water from heaven: and this heaven is the source whence come those tears mentioned above; and these are freely given to us, not obtained by our own industry. Thus I may indeed assure you, that this water will leave no love for the things of this world, so that the soul should be detained by them, unless it be to kindle this fire, if it can, since it is natural for it not to be content with a little space, but if it could, to inflame the whole world.

The second property of water is, to cleanse dirty things. If we had no water to wash with, what would become of the world? You know how well this "living water," this celestial water, this pure water cleanses – when it is not troubled, and when it contains not any mud. And if we drink of it only once, I am certain it leaves the soul pure, and cleansed from all her faults. For, as I have said, God permits no soul to drink of this water, (since it does not depend on our will, this divine union being something very supernatural), except to purify her and leave her clean, and free from the mire and misery, wherein she was involved by her offences; for other consolations that come by the intervening of the understanding, however much they may effect, draw water which runs on the ground; they do not drink it at the fountainhead: hence, as the water always meets with some dirt in its course, this prevents it from being pure and clean. I do not call this prayer (which goes, as I have said, discoursing with the understanding), "living water;" according to my judgment I say, that however zealously we may desire to labour, our soul always contracts some impurity in spite of our will, and this body and vile nature of ours contribute much thereto. I will explain my meaning a little more. We are perhaps meditating on the character of the world, and how all things come to an end, so as to be excited to despise them; then, almost without our perceiving it, we find our thoughts engaged on things which we love; and though we desire to be free from them, we are distracted a little by thinking what this world has been; what it will be; what we did, and what we shall do. And sometimes, by thinking on what will be of help to us, in order to free us from such thoughts, we fall into new dangers. I do not wish that this meditation should be omitted; but we must fear, and not grow careless. Here, 53 our Lord Himself takes this care upon Him, for He does not wish us to trust in ourselves: He values our soul so much, that He will not allow her to engage in things which may be injurious to her, during the time when He wishes to favour her: He immediately places her near Himself, and in an instant shows her more truths and gives her a clearer knowledge of what all things are than we can attain in this life during many years. Our sight is not free; the dust blinds us as we walk along; here our Lord brings us to our journey's end, without our knowing how.

The third property of water is, that it satisfies and quenches the thirst; for it seems to me, that thirst implies the desire of a something which we stand much in need of, and which, if it cannot possibly be obtained, kills us. A strange thing, which, if we want, kills us; and if taken to excess, also destroys life; just as we see many who die through suffocation. O my Lord! who can be so happy as he who finds himself so engulfed in this "living water," as to end his life therein? But cannot this be effected? Yes! indeed, for the love and desire of God may grow to such a height, that nature cannot endure it: and some persons there have been, who have died thus. I know one54 on whom this "living water" was poured so abundantly, that had not God come to her assistance, her raptures would almost have taken her senses away; I say, "would almost have taken her senses away," because therein the soul does not work. It seems even that the soul, suffocated by not being able to endure the world, revives in God; and His Majesty now enables her to enjoy that, which if she remained in herself she could not, without losing her life. But here we must remember, that since there cannot be anything imperfect in our Supreme God, all that He gives is for our good; and therefore, however abundant this water may be, there is no excess; for no superfluity can be found in anything belonging to God; since if He bestows much, He disposes the soul (as I said), and makes her capable of drinking much, just as a glass-maker, who makes his glasses in whatever way he sees necessary for containing a certain quantity. Merely desiring this water is never without some defect, as such a desire comes from ourselves: if it should have anything good, it is through our Lord's assistance therein.

But so indiscreet are we, that because it is a sweet and delightful pain, we think we can never be satisfied with it: we desire it without measure, and as much as we can, we increase this desire, and so it sometimes kills us. Blessed is such a death! And yet perhaps by living, such a person may help many others to die with the desire of such a death. And this I believe the devil does, because he knows the loss he will receive, if such an one lives; and so he tempts us here to indiscreet penances, which destroy our healthy and so he gains much.

I say then that whoever has this violent thirst, should be very careful, for let him be assured he will meet with this temptation; and though he may not die of thirst, he will lose his healthy and show it by exterior signs, even against his will, which by all means are to be avoided. Sometimes our diligence will avail but little, since we cannot conceal all that we desire. But let us be careful, when these great impetuosities come for increasing this desire, not to add to it; but with sweetness cut off the thread by some other consideration, 55 for it may be that at times our nature will effect as much as love, for there are some persons who very vehemently desire anything, even though it should be bad. These, I think, are not so mortified as they ought to be, for mortification is useful in everything. It seems foolish to prevent so good an action, but it is not so; for I do not say this desire should be destroyed, but only checked; and this, perhaps, may be done by another desire, just as meritorious. I will use an example, to make myself understood.

Some one (let us suppose) has a strong desire of seeing himself immediately with God, and of being freed from this prison of the body, as St. Paul had. Now a pain for such an object, and which in itself is very delightful, will require no small mortification to moderate it; and this cannot be done entirely. But when one sees that it overcomes him in such a way, as almost to take away the judgment, as I saw one not long since, who though impetuous by nature, was still so accustomed to break his own will, that I thought he had quite lost it; yet, by what was seen in other things, I saw this person for a time almost mad with the great pain and violence he used to disguise this passion; then in such a strong case, though it were the Spirit of God, I consider it humility to fear; for we must not think we have so much true love, which places us in such great difficulties. I say then, I shall not think it wrong for a person to change her desire, if she can (though perhaps she cannot at all times); for she thinks that by living, she may serve God more; and by serving God more, may merit to be able to enjoy Him the more; yet let her fear for having hitherto served Him so little. These are consolations fit for so great an affliction, and thus she may lessen her pain and gain much, since in order to serve our Lord, she is willing to suffer here, and live with her cross. It is like consoling one who is in great affliction, or excessive torment, by bidding him have patience and resign himself into the hands of God, and let Him accomplish His will in me, since this resignation of ourselves is in all things the most secure course.

But what if the devil should, in some way, contribute to so vehement a desire? This is possible; as I think Cassian relates concerning a hermit who led a very austere life, and who was persuaded by the devil to cast himself into a well, in order to behold God the sooner. I am confident this man did not live with true humility, nor even a good life, for our Lord is faithful, and His Majesty would never have suffered him to be blinded in so manifest a case; but it is clear, that if the desire had been from God, it would not have hurt him, for it brings with it light, and discretion, and moderation (this is evident); but the sworn enemy of ours, whichever way he goes, seeks mischief: since then he is not idle, let us not be negligent. This is important for many things, as for shortening the time of prayer, however delightful it may be, when the corporal strength begins to fail, or it hurts our head: in everything discretion is necessary. For what purpose do you think, my daughters, have I endeavoured to explain the end, and show the reward before the battle, by telling you the advantages we may derive from drinking of this celestial fountain, and this living water? I have done so, in order that you may not complain of the pains and opposition which are to be found in the way, and that you may go on with courage, and not be weary; for (as I have said) it may be, that after you have arrived at the well, all you may want will be to stoop down and drink at this fountain; and still you may leave all things and lose this advantage, imagining that you have not strength to reach it, and that you are not fit for it. Consider, how our Lord invites all; He being truth itself, there is no reason to doubt. Were not this banquet open to all, our Lord would not call us all; and though He did, He would not say, "I will give you to drink." He might say, "Come to me, all you that labour, and are burdened, and I will refresh you;" or, "If any man thirst, let him come to me and drink." But as He speaks to all without this condition, I consider it certain that all those who do not loiter by the way shall not want this living water. May our Lord, who has promised it, give us in His mercy grace to seek it, as it should be sought.

CHAPTER XX.

SHE SHOWS HOW WE NEVER WANT CONSOLATION IN PRAYER, AND SHE ADVISES THE SISTERS TO LET THEIR DISCOURSES ALWAYS BE ON THIS SUBJECT. IT seems that in the preceding chapter I contradict what I had said before; for in comforting those who do not arrive so far as perfect contemplation, I told them there were different ways whereby to approach to God, as He had many mansions for us in heaven.

The same thing I now repeat again, for as His Majesty knows our weakness, He has so provided for us in His goodness; yet He did not say that some should come by this way, 56 and others by another. But His mercy was so great, that He has forbidden no one at all to strive and come to drink at this fountain of life. May He be blessed for ever, for with how great reason might He have forbidden me. Now, since He did not command me to desist, when I began, but even caused me to be plunged into the depths thereof, I dare certainly say, He forbids no one, but rather calls us publicly and aloud; though being so very good, He does not force us, but gives in many ways drink to those who will follow Him, that so no one may go away disconsolate, or die through thirst. From this rich spring come rivers; some great, some small ones, and sometimes little pools for children; this is sufficient for them, since they would be frightened, if they beheld a great body of water; these are persons who are yet only in their rudiments.

Do not fear then, sisters, you will die of thirst. In this way the water of consolation will never be wanting – in such a way, I mean, as cannot be endured; and since this is the truth, take my advice, and do not loiter on the way, but fight like resolute souls till you die in asserting your right; you are here for no other purpose but to fight. And if you always continue thus firmly resolved rather to die than desist from advancing to the end of the journey, though God should suffer you to endure some thirst in this life; yet in the other, which is eternal, He will make you drink thereof abundantly, and that without fear of ever wanting it. May God grant we may not be wanting to Him. Amen.

Now, in order to enter upon this way which I have mentioned before, so as not to turn aside in the beginning, let us speak a little as to the manner how this journey is to be commenced; this is of the greatest consequence. I say everything depends upon it. I do not mean that whoever has not the resolution which I shall mention hereafter, should neglect to begin, because our Lord will go on perfecting him; and when he makes but one step forwards, it has so great a virtue with it, that he must not fear losing it, or despair of his being very well rewarded. It is, as we may say, like one who has a rosary, to which indulgences are annexed, so that if it be used once, he gains something, and the more the oftener: but if he never make use of it, and only keep it in a chest, it would be better if it had no indulgences attached. Hence, though afterwards one should not go along the same way, the little progress he has made therein will give him light to proceed well in other ways; and the further he goes, the more light he has. In a word, let him be assured that the fact of his having begun will not prejudice him in anything, though he should afterwards forsake it, because good can never do harm. Therefore, daughters, with regard to all persons with whom you may converse, if you are in any way friendly with them, endeavour to remove from such the fear of their commencing so excellent a thing. And I beseech you, for the love of God, that you always direct your conversation for the good of those with whom you converse, since your prayers should be for the welfare of souls: and this you should always beg of our Lord. It would look bad, sisters, not to endeavour to accomplish this object by all means in our power. If you wish to be kind relations, this is true friendship; or to be good friends, you can show it in no other way but this. Let truth enter into your hearts by meditation, and you will plainly perceive what love we are bound to have for our neighbour.

This is not now the time, sisters, for children's play, 57 (for these worldly friendships seem to be nothing else, though they may be good); nor let there be heard amongst you any such words as these, "Do you love me?" or, "Do you not love me?" Such language must not be addressed either to friends or to any one else, except for some important object, or for the good of some soul; for it may happen, that in order to get your relation, or brother, or such like person, to hear a truth and receive it, it will be necessary to dispose them by using such words, and such proofs of love, which are always pleasing to sensuality: it may be that they will be more affected "with one kind word," as they term it; and thereby they may dispose themselves better than by many words spoken about God, that so afterwards they may relish these the better. Hence, while you act with a design to benefit others, I do not forbid you to use those words; but if you do not use them for this object, they can produce no good, but may do harm without your perceiving it. They already know that you are "Religious," and that your employment is about prayer; therefore, never say to yourselves, "I do not wish them to consider me good," for the public benefit depends upon what they see in you; and it is the cause of great evil, that persons who lie under such obligations of speaking only on God (as nuns do), should in such a case approve of any dissimulation in their discourse, except it were for a greater good.

This is your employment and language; whoever wishes to converse with you, let him learn it; if not, be careful lest you learn his, for it will prove a hell to you. If they consider you to be clowns it matters little; if hypocrites, still less. Thereby you will gain this object, – viz. that none will visit you but such as understand this language; for it is unlikely that one who does not understand Arabic, 58 should delight often to talk with him who knows no other language. And thus they will not weary or molest you, since it would be no small trouble to begin to speak a new language, and to spend all your time in learning it. You cannot understand so well as I do – who have experience in this matter – the great mischief it does a soul, which in learning one thing forgets another. It is also a perpetual trouble, which you must avoid by all means in your power, because that which is of great assistance to us, in the way we are beginning to speak about, is peace and tranquillity in the soul. If those who converse with you wish to learn your language (since it is not for you to teach it), you may tell them of the riches that may be gained by learning it; and be not weary of this duty, but perform it with piety, and love, and prayer, thereby to do them some good, that so perceiving the great gain, they may seek a master to instruct them; for that would be a great favour which our Lord would bestow, to excite any soul to seek after so great a good. But in beginning to speak of this way, how many things present themselves even to one who has travelled along the road so badly as I have! God grant, sisters, that I may explain this duty to you, better than I have observed it. Amen.

CHAPTER XXI.

HOW IMPORTANT IT IS TO BEGIN WITH A FIRM RESOLUTION TO MAKE USE OF PRAYER, AND NOT TO HEED THE DIFFICULTIES THE DEVIL MAY REPRESENT. WONDER not, daughters, at the multitude of things which must be considered for commencing this divine journey, 59 which is the royal road to heaven. A great treasure is gained by travelling along this road: in our opinion, that is not much which costs much; but the time will come when you will understand what a mere nothing everything is, for so great a price. Now, to return to those who wish to travel along it, and not stop till they arrive at the source of this water of life, to drink of it and be filled; I say that it is very important – it is everything to have a strong and firm resolution, not to stop till we arrive at the water, come what may, or whatever may be the consequence, or whatever it may cost us. No matter who complains, whether I reach there or die on the way, or have not courage to endure the troubles which I may meet with, or though the world should sink under us; for we are often told, "That there are dangers; that such an one was ruined thereby, and another was deceived; and such an one fell who prayed often," &c. Others say, "These things injure virtue; this is not fit for women, for they may fall into delusions; it is better they should spin; they have no need of such subtilties: a Pater and Ave are sufficient for them." This I also say, sisters, and how sufficient are they! It is a very excellent practice, always to ground your prayer upon the prayers uttered by such a mouth as that of our Lord. They have reason in this; for were not our weakness so very great, and our devotion so tepid, we should have no need of any other collection of prayers, or any other books.

Since then, as I have said, I speak to souls who cannot recollect themselves upon other mysteries which seem to them too artificial; and some minds are so subtile that nothing pleases them, I have now thought it proper to lay down here certain principles, means, and objects relating to prayer, though I do not intend to dwell on high subjects. Thus your books cannot be taken away from you, for if you be studious and humble, you need nothing more. I have always been more affected and more recollected by the words of the Gospels, than by books very correctly written. And especially, if the author were not well approved of, I should take no pleasure in reading the books.

Coming, then, to this Master of Wisdom, He may, perhaps, give me some consideration that may please you. I say not, I will give an explanation of this divine prayer. I dare not presume to do so, for there are many explanations already written. Yet if there were not, it would be improper for me [to attempt the task.60] I will, however, give you some considerations upon the "Pater Noster," our Lord's Prayer; for, on account of the multiplicity of books, it seems that we sometimes lose all devotion for that prayer; and yet it is important we should not forget it. It is quite clear, that when a master teaches anything, he conceives a love for his pupil, that so what he teaches may delight him; it is also of help in learning what is taught. And thus in like manner will our Heavenly Father act towards us; and take no notice of the fears men may raise, and the dangers they may represent to you. It is a curious thing that I should wish to travel in a road, where there are so many robbers, and be without any dangers, and at the same time gain so great a treasure. The world then acts kindly, in allowing you to enjoy such a treasure in peace. But when any trifle connected with their interest is at stake, they will interrupt their sleep for nights together, and on that account they will not let you rest, either in body or mind. When, therefore, you are about to receive, or to obtain by force, these treasures (according to what our Lord says, "The violent alone shall bear it away") – keeping along the royal road, and this is a safe way, along which our King walked, as well as all the saints and elect. I say, when you do this, people represent many dangers to you, and excite in you many fears. As to those who wander out of the way, according to their pleasure, to obtain this treasure, what perils do they not expose themselves to? O my daughters! they endure many more without comparison; and they do not perceive them till they fall headlong into real danger, where there is no one to lend them a hand, and they entirely lose the water, without drinking little or much, either at a puddle or from the stream. Do you see, then, how impossible it is for them to travel along a way where there are so many to contend with, without receiving a drop of the water? It is certain, that at the very best they will die of thirst; for whether we will or no, my daughters, we all travel towards this fountain, though by different ways. Believe me, then, and let no one deceive you by showing you a way different from that of prayer. I do not say now it should be mental or vocal, and that all persons should use either the one or the other: as regards yourselves, I say that you stand in need both of the one and the other. This is the employment of "Religious:" whoever shall tell you there is danger in this, consider him a dangerous person, and avoid him; but do not forget this advice, for perhaps you may stand in need of it. It will, indeed, be dangerous for you not to possess humility, and the other virtues; but God never permits the way of prayer to be a way of danger; for the devil seems to have invented the art of exciting these fears, and hereby he has shown himself crafty in making some fall, who were addicted to prayer. See the wonderful blindness of men, who do not consider the many thousands in the world (as they say), who have fallen into heresy, and other great evils, by not using prayer, or knowing what it was; and if among all these, the devil, in order to accomplish his design the better, has made very few of those to fall who practised prayer, this has excited in some a great fear respecting such practice of virtue. Let those beware who take to this refuge for protection, since they fly from the good in order to escape the bad. Never did I see such an evil invention: it seems to be from the devil.

O my Lord! return and defend yourself: see how men interpret your words to a different meaning; suffer not such weaknesses as these to be in your servants. There is yet one great advantage, sisters, that you will always find some persons to assist you, because this property the true servant of God has, to whom His Majesty has given light to know the true way, that so by these very fears, his desire of not loitering on the road may be increased. He sees clearly where the devil intends to strike, and thus avoiding the blow, he breaks his enemy's head; and this vexes him more than all the pleasure afforded him by others delights him. When, in the time of trouble, the devil has sown his cockle, whereby he seems to lead all men after him, under the pretence of a good zeal half-blinded, God raises some one up to open their eyes; and He bids them observe how the devil has cast a mist before them, that they might not see their way. O! the greatness of God, that sometimes only one man, or two, who seek the truth, prevail more than many others together; He again by little and little discovers to them the true way, and gives them courage. If they say, there is danger, he endeavours to inform them how good prayer is, if not by words, at least by his works. If they say, it is not good to communicate often, he then rather receives the oftener. Hence, if there be one or two who follow what is best without fear, by their means our Lord regains what was lost by little and little.

Banish, then, sisters, these fears: in such cases never pay any attention to the opinion of the people; consider, that these are not times, when we should believe all persons, but only those whom you see walk conformable to the Life of Christ. Endeavour to keep a pure conscience, to have a contempt for all the things of this world, and firmly to believe whatever our holy Mother the Church teaches, and you may then be assured that you have taken a safe course. Cast away these fears, as I have said, wherein you have nothing to fear. If any one should terrify you, show him in humility the way [you are walking along;61] tell him you have a rule, which commands you to pray without ceasing (and so indeed it does), and that you must observe this rule. If they say, "It means only vocal prayer," ask them whether the understanding and the heart are to attend to what you say? If they answer, "They are," (and these men can make no other reply), then you see they acknowledge thereby, that you are compelled to use mental prayer – yea, and contemplation too, if God should bestow it on you therein. May He be blessed for ever. Amen.

CHAPTER XXII.

SHE EXPLAINS WHAT MENTAL PRAYER IS.

KNOW, daughters, that with regard to our prayer being mental or not, the difference does not consist in keeping the mouth shut; for if while uttering a prayer vocally, I do attentively consider and perceive that I am speaking with God, being more intent on this thought than on the words which I pronounce, then I use both mental prayer and vocal prayer together. But if they tell you, you may be speaking with God when you recite the Pater Noster, and yet be thinking of the world, here I am silent. For if you would conduct yourselves as you ought to do, in speaking to so great a Lord, it is proper you should consider to whom you speak, and who you are, if you wish to speak with due respect. For, how can you address a king, and style him "your Majesty," or know the ceremonies which are used in speaking to a grandee, unless you are well acquainted with his dignity, and understand what yours is? He must receive honour according to his rank, and as custom gives it; and with this you should be well acquainted, otherwise you will be sent away as clowns, and gain nothing.

Now what is this? O my Lord! What is this? O my Sovereign! How can it be endured? Thou, my

God, art an Eternal King, for the Kingdom which Thou hast is not a borrowed one.62

I feel especial delight almost every time I hear it said in the Creed – "that your Kingdom hath no end." I praise You, O Lord, and bless You for ever. Never allow any one, O Lord! who speaks of you, to do so only with his lips. What is this. Christians? Do you say, you need not mental prayer? Do you understand yourselves? I certainly think you do not, and therefore you would have us all mistaken with you: and neither do you know what mental prayer is, nor how vocal prayer is to be used, nor what contemplation is; for, did you understand it, you would not condemn on one hand, what you praise on the other.

When I think of it, I must always join mental with vocal prayer, and therefore be not frightened, daughters, for I know whither these matters tend, since I have endured some trouble on this account; hence I wish no one to disturb you, because to walk along this way in fear is very injurious. It is very important to know that you walk along very securely; for if you tell a traveller he is straying from the right way, and has lost the road, he turns from one side to the other; and he is wearied with all the trouble he has taken in seeking the right way; thus he wastes his time, and he only reaches his destination the later. Who can say it is wrong, if any one, beginning to recite the Hours or the Rosary, should first consider with whom he is about to speak, and who he is himself that speaks, in order that he may see how he is to conduct himself? Now, I tell you, sisters, that if you properly discharge the great obligation incumbent on you, for understanding these two points well, before you begin your vocal prayer, you would spend a good portion of time in mental prayer. We should not speak to a prince in the same unprepared manner as we should to a peasant, or poor persons like ourselves; there all is taken in good part, as if we were speaking one to another. It is proper, that though the King be gracious and humble, we should not be rude or unmannerly: and though He knows that I am so rude as not to understand how to speak to Him, yet He refuses not to hear me, nor does He deny me access to Him, nor do His guards repulse me, since the angels who attend Him know well the mind of their Sovereign, who is the more pleased with this rusticity of an humble shepherd, seeing that if he knew better he would speak better than if he used the language, however elegant, but not accompanied with humility, of the most able scholars.63 It is at least requisite, in order to testify our gratitude for the unpleasantness he endures, by permitting such a person as I am to be so near Him, that we should endeavour to understand His purity, and who He is. It is true, we soon discover Him by approaching to Him, as we do the great ones of this world; and with regard to these, when once we are informed who were their parents, what is their annual income, what their title, we need no more to know our duty; for in this world, no account is paid in general to the merit of the persons, but their riches only are the cause of their being honoured.

O! wretched world; my daughters, praise God exceedingly for having enabled you to abandon so base a place, where persons are not esteemed by what they are inwardly possessed of, but by what their farmers and vassals are worth; and hence, when these things fail, then the world refuses to honour the individuals. What a pleasant consideration, to make you merry, when you all meet at recreation! for it is a good source of amusement to consider, how blindly worldlings spend their days. O! my Emperor, Supreme Power, Supreme Goodness, Wisdom itself, without beginning, without end, without bounds to perfections, which are infinite and incomprehensible, a bottomless ocean of wonders, a Beauty including in itself all beauties. Strength itself.64 O my God! would that I had here, at once, all the eloquence of men, and wisdom also properly to understand (as far as can be understood in this world, which in reality is nothing) how to make known on this occasion some of those many things which we might consider for understanding, in some small degree, how great is this our Lord, and our Sovereign Good!

Continue, then, to consider and understand with whom you are going to speak, and with whom you are speaking. In a thousand such lives as ours are, we should never be able fully to comprehend how this Lord deserves to be treated, before whom the angels tremble: who commands all things, can do all things, whose will is the deed. It is proper then, my daughters, that we should endeavour to delight ourselves in these excellencies which our Spouse possesses, and that we understand to whom we are married; and also what kind of life we are to lead. O my God! since here in this life, when a person is married, she first knows with whom she is to live, and who her husband is, and what he has; shall not we, who are already contracted, think on our Spouse before the nuptials, when He is to conduct us to His house? Since then those who are espoused in the world are allowed to have such thoughts, why should we be forbidden from endeavouring to know who this person is, and who is his Father, and what kind of a country that is to which he is to conduct us, and what those good things are which he promises to bestow upon us, what his good qualities are, how I may best please him, and in what I can delight him, and to study how to make my will bend to His? Now, if a lady who is likely to make a good match is advised (omitting other points) to consider well these things, though her husband may be a very insignificant man, are they, O my Spouse! to esteem You less in everything, while others are made so much of? If men would not approve of such conduct towards others, let them leave your spouses to you, to spend their whole lives with you. It is true, when the husband is so jealous that he does not wish his spouse to converse with any other person, it would be very odd if she did not endeavour to comply with his request; it is but reasonable she should do so, since in him she has all that her heart can desire. To understand and practise these truths, my daughters, is mental prayer. If you wish to understand this, and also to pray vocally, you may do it. But do not speak with God, and be thinking of other things, for then you do not understand what "Mental prayer" is. I believe I have explained it sufficiently. God grant we may learn to practise it. Amen.

CHAPTER XXIII.

SHE SHOWS HOW NECESSARY IT IS FOR ONE WHO HAS ENTERED UPON THE WAY OF PRAYER, NOT TO TURN BACK, ETC.

I WISH you then to remember, that much depends on beginning with a strong resolution; and this for many reasons, that would occupy too much time were I to enlarge upon them. I will tell you, sisters, only two or three. The first is, that as God has given us so much, and continues to bestow favours upon us, it is proper that what we resolve to give Him (viz. this "little care" of ours, by which we think of Him, and this not without interest, but with very great gains) should be given with all our heart, and not as one who lends a thing to recall it again. This, in my opinion, is not giving; for he to whom something is lent, always seems displeased when it is taken away again, especially if he stand in need of it, and thought it was already his own. But if they be friends, and if he who lent the thing is indebted to the other for many favours bestowed, without any return, he may justly think it meanness and want of affection, not to consent to leave something with him, as a testimony of his gratitude. What spouse is there, who on receiving from her husband many valuable jewels, gives him not at least a ring – not for the value of it, since all things are now his, but for a proof that she will be his till death? Does this our Lord then deserve less, when we mock Him by giving, and taking away afterwards, the trifle we bestow on Him? If we spend so much time with others, who will not thank us for it, let us give to our Spouse that short space of time which we have resolved to give Him; let us likewise give it to Him, with our thoughts free and disengaged from other things, and with a firm resolution of never recalling it again, whatever crosses may happen to us – whatever contradictions – whatever aridities: but rather, let us think that time as not our own, and remember it may with justice be required of us, when we do not entirely give it to Him. I say "entirely," that you may not imagine it would be resuming it again, were you to spend a day, or a few days, upon some necessary business, or on account of some indisposition. Let your intention be firm, for our God is not punctilious;65 He looks not at small things: thus He will be sure to accept of you – since this is giving Him something. The other way is acceptable to one who is not liberal, but so mean that he has no heart to give: it is a wonder he lends. In a word, do something: for this our Lord takes as payment. He does as we desire; in taking our accounts, He is not strict, but generous: how great soever the debt may be, He considers it nothing to forgive it, in order to gain us. He is so vigilant, that you need not fear He will leave unrewarded even the lifting up of your eyes to think of Him.

A second reason is, because the devil has not so much power to tempt us; he is extremely afraid of resolute souls, for he knows by experience that these do him great mischief; and whatever he invents to hurt them turns to their benefit and that of others, and so he comes off with loss. Still, we must not be careless or trust in this, because we deal with perfidious traitors, who, though they dare not so boldly attack persons who are prepared for them (they themselves being extremely cowardly); yet if they see any negligence, may do great harm. But if they see one fickle, and not strengthened in virtue, and earnestly resolved to persevere, they will not leave him day or night, but will suggest fears and inconveniences without end. This I know very well by experience, and therefore am I able to speak thus on the subject; and I add, that few understand the great importance of it.

A third reason is, that a resolute soul fights with greater courage, knowing that, come what may, he must not turn back. It is just like one engaged in battle, who, knowing that if he be conquered, he must expect no quarter; and if he fall not in the battle, he must die afterwards, fights with greater resolution, and intends to sell his life dearly (as they say), and does not fear the blows so much, because he remembers how important victory is, that his life depends upon it. It is also necessary to begin with a hope, that if we do not allow ourselves to be overcome, we shall succeed in our design; this at least is certain, that however little the gain may be, we shall come off very rich. Fear not that our Lord will suffer you to die of thirst, for He it is who invites us to drink at His fountain. This I have already mentioned, and I wish to repeat it often, because it tends greatly to frighten those who do not as yet know by experience the goodness of God, though by faith they know it. But it is a great blessing to have experienced the friendship and caresses which He bestows on those who walk along this way, and how He defrays, as it were, all their expenses. And as for those who have not experienced this, I do not wonder at their desiring some security, that they will receive interest for what they give. Now you know there is a hundred for one, even in this life, and that our Lord has said, "Ask, and you shall receive." If you do not believe His Majesty, who assures us of this in several parts of the Gospel, then, sisters, it is no use my trying to persuade you of it. Yet if any doubt what I say, be assured that little is lost in trying it: for this way has this advantage, that more is given than is asked, or can be desired. I know this is certain; and I can bring forward as witnesses those amongst you, who, through God's goodness, have experienced it.

CHAPTER XXIV.

SHE SHOWS HOW VOCAL PRAYER IS TO BE USED WITH PERFECTION, AND HOW MENTAL PRAYER IS CONNECTED WITH IT.

LET us now speak to those souls, which (as I have said) cannot recollect themselves, nor fix their understandings on mental prayer, or use any meditation. I do not wish to mention here these two names, for I know there are many persons who seem frightened at the mere name of mental prayer, or contemplation: and such an one may come to this house, since (as I have said) all do not go along the same way. The advice which I now wish to give you (and I might say teach you, for it is lawful, being a mother in the office I hold as Prioress), is to teach you how to pray vocally, since it is proper you should understand what you say, and because it may happen, that those who cannot meditate on God, may likewise be tired with long prayers, I do not wish to interfere with those, but only to speak of that which (as we are Christians) we are all obliged to repeat, viz., the "Our Father, and the Hail Mary;" because people should not say of us, that we speak and understand not, unless we think it enough to go by custom, and imagine it is quite sufficient merely to pronounce the words. Whether it is sufficient or no, I do not now inquire: let the learned decide. That which I wish you to do, daughters, is not to content yourselves with this alone; for when I say "I believe," it is proper, methinks, that I should understand and know what I believe; and when I say "Our Father," love requires I should understand who this Our Father is; and who is the master that taught us this prayer. If you reply by saying, "You know this already, and that you need not be reminded of it," you have no reason in what you say: for there is a great difference between one master and another; and not to remember even those in this world who instruct us, is great ingratitude; especially if they be saints and spiritual directors, it is impossible for us to forget them, if we be good scholars. When we say this prayer then, God forbid we should ever be unmindful of such a master as He is, who taught us this prayer, and with such a love and desire too, that we might profit thereby; however, as we are very weak, we are not always mindful of Him.

As to the first point, you already know that His Majesty teaches, prayer should be made in solitude, for so He Himself always prayed; not, however, for His own wants, but for our instruction. Now, I have mentioned before, that we cannot speak with God and with the world at the same time; and surely it is nothing else, when a person prays vocally on one side, and on the other listens to some discourse, or is thinking on whatever comes into his mind, without checking these distractions. Sometimes, indeed, however much one may strive, he cannot help such thoughts, either on account of some evil humours (especially if the person be melancholy), or through weakness of mind; or else because God permits certain tempestuous seasons to come on His servants, for their greater benefit: then, though they are afflicted, and endeavour to be free from their troubles, they cannot; nor do they mind what they say, though they strive ever so much; neither does the understanding fix upon anything, but seems to be in a frenzy, so disordered does it seem; but by the pain it gives him who has this affliction, he will perceive it is not his fault. And let him not afflict himself (which is still worse), or tire himself in trying to reduce to reason one who at the time is not capable of being reduced, viz., the understanding; but let him pray as well as he can, or not pray at all. Rather he should endeavour to give his soul (as being infirm) some rest, and attend to some other act of virtue. This is intended for persons who take care of themselves, and understand well that they are not to speak to God and the world both at once.

That which we are able to do, is to endeavour to be alone; and God grant that may be sufficient for our understanding with whom we are, and what answer our Lord gives to our petitions. Think you, He is silent? Though we hear Him not. He speaks sufficiently to the heart, when we from our heart pray to Him; and it is proper that we consider it is to every one of us our Lord directs this prayer, and that He teaches it to us. Now, the master is never so far from his pupil, that he should have any necessity to call aloud to him, but he is very nigh. This I wish you to understand, that to say the "Our Father" well, you must not go away, but remain near the Master who teaches it to you.

You will perhaps say, "that this is meditation, and that you neither can, nor do you wish to pray vocally;" and because there are impatient persons who love their own ease; and not being used to this, they find difficulty at first in recollecting their thoughts, and to avoid a little labour, they say they cannot do more, nor do they know how to pray, except vocally. You have reason in saying, that what I teach you is mental prayer: but I assure you I know not how it can be separated if we wish to perform vocal prayer well, and if we understand with whom we are speaking. We are even obliged to endeavour to pray attentively, and God grant that by using these remedies, we may say the Lord's Prayer well, and not finish by thinking on some foolish thing. I have myself sometimes experienced this; and the best remedy I find is to endeavour to keep my thoughts fixed on Him to whom I address the words. Have patience, therefore, and endeavour to accustom yourselves to so necessary a duty.

CHAPTER XXV.

HOW MUCH A SOUL GAINS THAT PRAYS VOCALLY WITH PERFECTION; AND HOW IT HAPPENS THAT THEREBY GOD RAISES HER TO CONTEMPLATION, AND TO SUPERNATURAL OBJECTS.

IN order that you may not imagine little advantage is gained by praying vocally with perfection, I tell you it is very possible, that while you are repeating the "Our Father," or saying some other vocal prayer, our Lord may raise you to perfect contemplation; for by these ways, His Majesty discovers that He hears him who speaks to Him; and His greatness speaks to him also, suspending his understanding and binding up his thoughts, and as the saying is, taking the words out of his mouth; and hence, though he would wish, he cannot speak except with much difficulty. He knows that this Divine Master stands teaching him without the noise of words, and suspends his faculties, because, should they operate, they would then rather hinder than help him. They enjoy without understanding how they enjoy: the soul is burning with love, yet she does not understand how she loves. She perceives that she enjoys what she loves, yet she knows not how she enjoys it. She understands sufficiently that it is not an enjoyment which the understanding obtains by desiring it; the will embraces it without knowing how: but by being able to understand something, it sees that this is a good which cannot be merited by all the united labours of men, which they may endure in this life, for the purchase of it. It is a gift of the Lord and of heaven, who gives like Himself [alone can give."66]

This, daughters, is perfect contemplation. Now, you should understand the difference between this and mental prayer, which is, as I have said, considering and minding what we say, and with whom we speak, and who we are that presume to speak to so great a Lord. Thinking on this and the like truths, such as, how little we have served Him, and how much we are bound to serve Him, is mental prayer. Think not that it is some other unknown tongue, nor be terrified at the name. The recital of the "Our Father" and the "Hail Mary," or whatever other prayer you like, is vocal prayer. Now, consider what bad music this will make, without the former, since without it even the words will not always run in order. In these two kinds of prayer, mental and vocal, we may do something by the Divine assistance; but in contemplation, of which I have just now spoken, we can do nothing at all. It is His Majesty who does everything, for it is His work, and it surpasses our natural strength. But as the nature of contemplation has been very fully explained in the best manner I was able, in the relation of my Life, which, as I have mentioned, I wrote in order that my confessor, who commanded me to write it, might examine it, I will say nothing more on the subject here, but merely touch upon it. If those amongst you who shall have been so happy as to be conducted by our Lord to this degree of contemplation should happen to meet with this relation, it contains some points and advice, which our Lord wished I should properly and truly deliver, in order that they might console you greatly, and also tend to your profit; and this, the relation of my Life is, I think, capable of doing; and others think the same, for they keep it by them through their esteem for it. But it is a shame for men to bid you to esteem anything of mine, and our Lord knows with what confusion I write a great deal of what I say. May He be blessed who thus bears with me. Those who have supernatural prayer, let them procure it67 (as I have said), after my death: those who have it not, need not do so, but let them endeavour to practise what I have said in this chapter, gaining by all possible ways, and using every diligence, that our Lord may give it to them; and let them beg it from Him, and assist one another themselves. Let them leave it to our Lord, for He it is who must bestow it. And He will not deny you it, if you loiter not on the way, and strive courageously to arrive at the end thereof.

CHAPTER XXVI.

ON THE MANNER HOW WE ARE TO RECOLLECT OUR THOUGHTS.

LET us now return to our vocal prayer, that it may be performed in such a way, that without our perceiving it, God may give us the whole together. Now (as I have said), in order to pray as we ought, you already know that the examination of conscience, saying the Confiteor, and making the sign of the cross, are to be done first. Next, daughters, since you are alone (when thus employed), endeavour to obtain some company. And what better can you have than the very Master who has taught the prayer you are going to say? Represent the same Lord with you, and observe with what love and humility He stands teaching you. And believe me, as much as you can, you cannot remain long without such a friend. If you accustom yourselves to have Him near you, and He sees that you do it with affection, and that you still endeavour to please Him, you cannot drive Him from you, as the saying is. He will never be wanting to you. He will help you in all your troubles: you will find Him with you in all places. Do you think it a small favour to have such a friend at your side? O sisters! those amongst you who cannot discourse much with the understanding, nor keep your thoughts fixed without being distracted, accustom yourselves to it: remember, I know you may do it, for I have lived many years under this cross, of not being able to fix the imagination upon one thing. This is a very great affliction. Yet I know our Lord does not abandon us in such a way, that if we humbly approach and beg it of Him, He will not accompany us. And if we cannot obtain this favour in one year, let it be in many, and let us not grudge spending time on one thing. Who hinders us from so spending it? I say that one may accustom herself to this, and be at her work, and so get near to this true Master. I do not now require you to meditate on Him, or to form many ideas, or make high and curious considerations with your understandings. I require of you no more than to look upon Him. And who hinders you from turning the eyes of your soul for one instant (if you can do no more) towards this Lord? Since you can look upon the most ugly objects, can you not look upon something the most beautiful that can be imagined? If He do not appear beautiful in your eyes, I give you leave not to look upon Him: and yet, daughters, your Spouse never takes His eyes off from you. He has endured a thousand abominations committed against Him, and yet they were not enough to make him forbear looking upon you. Is it much then for you, to take off your eyes from these exterior objects, and sometimes to cast a look upon Him? Behold, as the Spouse saith. He stands waiting for nothing else, but that we look upon Him. As you wish for Him, you will find Him. He takes such notice of our casting our eyes upon Him, that no diligence will be wanting on His part to induce us. People say, that if a wife wish to live quietly with her husband, she must do as he does: if he be sad, she must appear sad too: if he be merry, she must appear so likewise (though she may not be in reality). See, sisters, from what a subjection you are freed. Thus, in truth, without any fiction, does our Lord act with us; for He makes Himself the subject, and would have you be the mistress, 68 and He acts according as you wish. If you be cheerful, contemplate Him as risen, for merely imagining how He went forth from the sepulchre will rejoice your soul; but with what brightness, with what beauty, with what majesty! How victorious, how joyful, like one who has so gloriously returned from the battle, where he has gained so great a kingdom, all of which He wishes should be yours! Now, is it much that you should once turn your eyes to look upon Him, who bestows so much upon you? If you be sad or afflicted, consider Him on the road going to the garden; and what sorrow is so great as that which He endured in His Soul, since through patience itself, He speaks of this sorrow, and complains of it? Consider Him again bound to the pillar, full of pains, all his flesh torn to pieces through His great love for you: persecuted by some, spit upon by others, denied by His friends and forsaken by them, without any one to plead for Him; stiff with cold, and placed in such solitude, that it would be easy to console yourselves with Him.

You may consider Him likewise laden with His Cross, so that His enemies would not let Him take breath. He will behold you with those eyes, so beauteous and compassionate, big with tears, and He will forget His own sorrow to comfort you, provided only that you go and solace yourselves with Him, and turn your eyes to look upon Him.

O Lord of the world! my true Spouse! art Thou so far necessitated, my Lord and my God, that Thou wilt admit such wretched company as mine? You should say, sisters, if your hearts have been so softened from seeing your Saviour in the state I have described, that you not only desire to look on Him, but you are delighted in speaking to Him, not in a set form of prayer, but with supplications issuing from the grief of your hearts, what will be your joy when you see Him in heaven? I perceive, O my God! by your looks, that you are pleased with me. Now, how O Lord! is it possible, that the angels should leave Thee alone? That even Thy Father should not comfort Thee? If it be, O Lord! that Thou wilt suffer all this for me, what is it that I suffer now? What do I complain of? I am now so ashamed, since I have seen Thee in such a state, that I wish to suffer, O Lord! all the afflictions which may happen to me, and to take them as a source of great comfort, that so I may imitate Thee in something. Let us go together, O Lord! Wherever You go, I will go too: whatever You pass along, I will pass likewise. Bear your part, daughters, in this Cross: be not troubled, lest the Jews trample upon you, because your Lord will not walk in such pain; heed not what they say of you, because you are deaf to their accusations, stumbling and falling with your Spouse; go not away from the Cross, nor leave it. Consider attentively the weariness with which He travels, and by how many degrees His passion exceeds your sufferings, however great you may fancy them to be, and however much you may feel them, you will always be comforted thereby; for you will see they are but children's play, when compared with our Lord's suffering.

You will perhaps say, sisters, "How can this be done now? Had you seen Him with your corporal eyes, at the time when His Majesty lived on the earth, then you would very willingly have done it, and always looked upon Him." Believe it not; for he who will not now use a little violence to recollect his mind, so as to behold His Lord within himself (and this he may do without danger, and with using very little diligence), much less will he place himself at the foot of the Cross with Magdalen, who saw death before her eyes. And what must our glorious Lady and this blessed Saint have suffered? What threats – what ill words – what shocks – what affronts? With what courtiers had they to deal? Those of hell, who were the ministers of the devil. Doubtless, what they suffered must indeed have been terrible; but the great sorrows of another make them not feel for their own. Imagine not therefore, sisters, you would be fit for such great afflictions, if you are now so unfit for such small matters; by exercising yourselves in these, you may be able to endure other greater afflictions.

In order to help you herein, you may carry about with you an image or representation of this Lord, not merely to wear it in your bosom and never look at it; but to speak often to Him, for He will teach you what to say to Him. Since you find words to speak to others, why should you want them to speak with God? Do not believe this: I at least will not believe you, if you accustom yourself thereto; for if you do not, you will be sure to want them, for not conversing with a person causes a kind of strangeness, and an ignorance how we should speak; it almost seems as if we did not know her, even though a relation; for kindred and friendship are soon lost, for want of conversing together.

It is likewise an excellent thing to take a good book in your own language, in order to recollect the thoughts, that so you may pray well vocally, and by little and little accustom the soul thereto, by caresses and artifices, that so she may not be frightened. Remember, that the soul many years ago went away from her Spouse, and that to induce her to be willing to return to His house, great skill is required to know how to treat her, so depraved are we sinners. We have so accustomed our souls and thoughts to follow their own pleasure, or (to speak more properly) their own pain, that the wretched soul knows not her condition: hence, to make her return and take delight in living at His house requires great skill; for unless she be forced to do this, and that by little and little, she will never effect anything. Again I assure you, that if you carefully accustom yourselves to what I have said, you will thereby gain such great profit that I cannot express, even if I wished. Keep yourselves near then to this good Master, and firmly resolve to learn what He shall teach you; and His Majesty will so order things, that you will not fail to become excellent scholars: nor will He forsake you, if you do not forsake Him. Consider the words69 which that Divine mouth utters, for by the very first you will immediately understand the love He has for you: and it is no small happiness and consolation for a scholar to know that his Master loves him.

CHAPTER XXVII.

SHE DWELLS ON THE GREAT LOVE OUR LORD SHOWS US, AND THE HONOUR HE GIVES US IN THE FIRST WORDS OF THE "OUR FATHER."

"OUR Father who art in Heaven."70 O my God! how justly do you seem to be the Father of such a Son, and how well does your Son appear to be the Son of such a Father! May You be blessed for ever. Was it not enough to bestow so great a favour, at the end of the prayer? At the beginning, Thou fillest our hands and dost bestow so high a favour upon us, that it would be well if the understanding were so filled and the will so taken up therewith, as to be unable to speak one word more to Thee. O! how well, daughters, would perfect contemplation come in here! O! with what great reason should the soul here enter into herself, the better to be able to ascend above herself, that so this Holy Son may make her understand, what a glorious place that must be where He says His Father is, viz., in Heaven! Let us leave this earth, my daughters, since it is proper such a favour as this should not be so undervalued, as that we should still remain on the earth after we understand how great this favour is.

O Son of God! and my Lord! how is it that Thou givest so much in the first word? How is it, that not only dost Thou humble Thyself exceedingly, so as to unite Thyself with us in our petitions, and make Thyself a Brother of what is so vile and miserable, but Thou givest us, in the name of Thy Father, all that can be given, since Thou wishest Him to take us for His sons? Thy word cannot fail: Thou obligest Him to keep it, which is no small burden; since in being a Father He bears with us, however grievous our offences may be, if we return to Him as the prodigal son did. He has to pardon and to comfort us in our afflictions; He has to support us, as such a Father should do, who must of course be far better than all earthly fathers, since there can be nothing in Him but every perfection; and after all this, it is Your wish to make us partners and co-heirs with Thee! Consider, my Lord! that though by reason of the love You have for us, and through Your humility, nothing can hinder You from doing so; (for, O Lord! You were upon earth and were clothed with it; and since You assumed our nature, You seem to have some reason in regarding our benefit) – still, consider Your Father is in heaven: you say so, and therefore it is fit you should have respect for His honour, and since you are exposed to dishonour on our account, leave your Father free; do not oblige Him to so much for one so wicked as I am, and who will so ungratefully repay Him. O! good Jesus! how clearly hast Thou shown that Thou art one with Him, and that Thy will is His, and His thine. What acknowledgment is so clear! How wonderful is the love Thou hast for us. Thou didst endeavour all Thou couldst to conceal from the devil that Thou art the Son of God; and through the ardent desire Thou hast for our good, nothing could hinder Thee from showing us this excessive favour. Who could do it but Thou, O Lord? At least, I see clearly, O my Jesus! that Thou, like a darling Son, didst speak for Thyself and for us, and that Thou art powerful to perform in heaven what Thou sayest on earth. Blessed for ever be

Thou, O my Lord! who art so desirous of giving, that nothing can be too precious for Thee.

Now, daughters, do you think this is a good Master, who, in order to entice us to learn what He teaches us, begins by bestowing on us so great a favour? Do you think it will now be fit, that though we pronounce this word vocally, we should forbear to apprehend it with our understanding, lest our heart, by seeing such love, should break in pieces? And what son is there in the world that does not endeavour to know who his father is, when he hath a good one, who possesses such majesty and power? If He were not such, I should not wonder at our being unwilling to know ourselves to be His sons; for the world is now in such a state, that if a father has a lower dignity than his son, the latter does not think himself honoured in owning him for his father. This is not the case here; for God forbid that ever there should be any mention of such things in this house; it would then become a hell. But let her who is the most noble by birth seldom or ever mention her father's name; for all must be equal here.

O! sacred College of Christ, wherein St. Peter, who was only a fisherman, had more authority than St. Bartholomew, who was a king's son.71 His Majesty knew what would happen in the world about precedency, viz., who was the more noble?72 This is nothing more than to dispute, whether the earth be good for bricks or for mortar. O my God! what an insignificant matter! May His Majesty deliver you, sisters, from such contests as these, though it be but in jest: I trust in His Majesty that He will. When something of this nature shall happen to any one, let a remedy be applied immediately, and let her fear to become a Judas among the apostles; let a penance be given to her, till she thoroughly understand that she deserves not to be even the most vile earth.

Our good Jesus has given you a most excellent Father; let no other Father be owned or mentioned here, and endeavour, my daughters, to be such that you may deserve to be regaled with Him; cast yourselves into His arms, you know already He will not cast you away, if you be good daughters. Now, who will not take care not to lose such a Father? Daughters, what an opportunity is there here, for your consolation! But not to dwell longer on this point, I will leave you to your own thoughts; for, however distracted your mind may be, between such a Father and such a Son the Holy Spirit must of necessity be; and may He inflame your will, and bind it with the most ardent love, since the great desire you have is not sufficient.

CHAPTER XXVIII.

ON THE WORDS, "WHO ART IN HEAVEN." THE SAINT ALSO EXPLAINS WHAT THE PRAYER OF RECOLLECTION MEANS.
CONSIDER what your Master says next: "Who art in Heaven." Do you think it is of little importance for you to know what heaven is, and where your Most Holy Father is to be sought? I tell you that it is very important for wandering intellects, not only to believe this, but to endeavour to understand it by experience, because it is one of those things which strongly bind the understanding and recollect the soul. You already know that God is in all places; now it is clear, that where the king is, there is the court; in a word, that where God is, there Heaven is: you may also believe without doubting, that where His Majesty is, all His glory is.

Consider what St. Augustine says, that he sought God in many places, and came at last to find

Him in himself. Do you think it is of little importance for a distracted soul to understand this truth, and to know that she need not go to heaven to speak with her Eternal Father, or to regale herself with Him? Nor need she speak aloud, for however low she may speak, He is so near, that He will hear us; neither does she require wings to fly and seek Him, but she can compose herself in solitude and behold Him within herself: and let her not separate from so good a Guest, but with great humility speak to Him as a Father, entreat Him as a Father, relate her troubles to Him, and beg a remedy for them, knowing that she is not worthy to be His daughter.

Be on your guard, daughters, against a certain false modesty, to which some persons are addicted, and think it is humility: yet it is not humility, if the King is pleased to show you a favour, not to accept of it; but it is humility to accept it, and acknowledge how much it exceeds your merits, and so you may rejoice in it. A fine humility indeed! – that I should entertain in my house the Emperor of heaven and earth, who comes therein to show me kindness and recreate Himself with me, while I out of humility will neither answer Him, nor stay with Him, nor accept what He gives me, but leave Him there alone; and though He may bid and entreat me to ask Him for something, I through humility must remain poor, and even allow Him to go away, because He sees I have not determined on anything!

Pay no attention to such humility, daughters, but treat with Him as with a father, as with a brother, as with a lord, as with a spouse, sometimes in one way, sometimes in another; for He will teach you what you should do to please Him. Be not too easy, but challenge His word, since He is your Spouse, that He would treat you as such. Consider that you are much concerned in understanding this truth, viz., that God dwells within you, and that there we should dwell with Him.

This kind of prayer, though it be vocal, recollects the understanding much sooner, and is a prayer that brings with it many benefits. It is called the prayer of recollection, because in it the soul recollects73 all the faculties, and enters within herself with her God; and there her divine master comes much sooner to instruct her, and bestow on her the "Prayer of Quiet," than in any other way; for, placed there with Him, she may meditate with herself on the passion, and represent to herself the Son, and offer Him to the Father; and not weary the understanding by going to seek Him on Mount Calvary, or in the Garden, or at the Pillar. Those that can thus shut themselves up in this little heaven of our soul, where He abides who created heaven and earth; and they who can also accustom themselves not to behold, or stay where these exterior senses distract them, let them believe that they walk in an excellent way, and that they shall not fail of being able to drink water from the fountain, and thus they will advance far in a little time. It is like one who makes a voyage by sea, who by having a little favourable weather gets within a few days of his journey's end; whereas those who go by land are much longer.

Those are already out at sea (as the expression is) who, as they have not quite lost sight of land, do nevertheless what they can, by recollecting their senses, to get quite clear of it.

In like manner we very clearly discover whether the recollection be true, for it produces a certain operation (which I cannot explain, but whoever has it will understand it), so that it seems the soul rises up from her play, for such she sees the things of this world are. She seizes the opportunity, and like one who retires to some strong castle, to be out of the fear of the enemy, she withdraws the senses from these exterior objects, and leaves them in such a manner, that the eyes (though unaware) close up so as not to behold them, in order to open wider the eyes of the soul. Accordingly, whoever walks in this way always keeps his eyes shut in prayer; and it is an admirable custom for many reasons, because it is forcing ourselves not to behold things here below. This shutting of the eyes takes place only at the beginning of such recollection, for afterwards it is useless: then more strength is required to open them. The soul seems to strengthen and fortify herself at the expense of the body, and to leave it all alone and enfeebled, and thence she draws a supply of provisions74 against it.

And though at first, this retreat should not be understood because not very great (for in this recollection, there is sometimes more and sometimes less); yet, if it grow into a custom (although in the beginning it may cause trouble, for the body disputes its right, not perceiving that it ruins itself by not acknowledging itself to be vanquished) – if, I repeat, it should be practised for some days, and we use this force to ourselves, the benefit therefrom will appear evident; and we shall perceive that, in the beginning of prayer, the bees immediately repair to their hive, and enter to make honey. And this is without any trouble on our part, because our Lord is pleased, that for the time in which they formerly took some pains, the soul and the will should deserve to be possessed of such a command, that by merely an intimation to them, and nothing more, the senses might immediately obey and retire into her. And though afterwards they go forth again, it is a great matter to have already submitted, because they go forth as captives and subjects, and do not the mischief which they could effect formerly; and when the will recalls them, they come with more readiness, till after having often re-entered, our Lord is pleased that they shall rest entirely in perfect contemplation.

Let what I have said be well considered; for though it may seem obscure, yet whoever will practise it shall understand it. Since then these go by sea, and since it is so important for us not to go on so slowly, let us speak a little as to the manner how we may accustom ourselves to so good a way of proceeding. These are much more secure from occasions, and the fire of Divine Love takes hold of them sooner, because they are so near it, that upon the least breath of the understanding, all will be in a flame, if only the smallest spark should fall upon them; and as there is no obstacle from the exterior, the soul remains alone with her God, and so she is quite prepared to be set on fire.

Let us remember, then, that within us there is a palace of immense magnificence: the whole building is of gold and precious stones: in a word, it is every way as it ought to be for such a Lord. Forget not, also, that you are partly the cause that this edifice is such as it is; for truly there is no building of such great beauty as a pure soul, filled with virtues; and the greater these virtues are, the brighter do these stones sparkle; and that in this palace the great King lodges, who has been pleased to become your Guest; and that He sits there on a throne of immense value, which is your heart. This may, at first, seem ridiculous (I mean to make use of such a figure to make you understand what I say): still it may be of great help, to you especially; for since we women want learning, all this is indeed very necessary to make us understand, that there is within us something else more precious beyond comparison than that which we see outwardly. Let us not imagine we have nothing in our interior. God grant that women only be the persons guilty of this negligence; for if we remember that we have within us such a guest, I think it is impossible we should be so fond of the things of this world, because we should see how base they are, in comparison with those treasures which we possess within us. What more does a brute beast do, which, on beholding something pleasing to the sight, satisfies its hunger by seizing upon it? Now, should there not be some difference between them and us?

Some persons will, perhaps, laugh at me, and say, "All this is very evident," and they may have reason for saying so; but for some time it was obscure to me. I knew well that I had a soul; but I understood not the dignity of this soul, nor knew who lodged within it, because my eyes being blinded by the vanities of this life, I was prevented from seeing Him. Methinks, had I then known, as I do at present, that in this little palace of my soul so great a King is lodged, I would not have left him alone so often, but sometimes at least I should have stayed with Him, and have been more careful to prepare a clean lodging for Him.

But what calls for so much admiration as that He who, by His immensity, could fill a thousand worlds, should be enclosed in so small a place! Thus was He pleased to be confined in the womb of His Most Sacred Mother. He being Lord, brings us liberty with Him; and in loving us much, reduces Himself to our nature. When a soul begins to know Him, He does not discover Himself fully at once, lest she might be troubled to see herself so little, and yet containing within herself so great a being. By degrees He enlarges such a soul, according to what He knows is necessary for that which He infuses into her. Therefore, I say that He brings liberty with him, since He has power to enlarge this palace. The point lies in our giving it to Him as His own, with a full and perfect resolution, that so He may either place there, or take away, whatever He pleases, as it is His own. This is His pleasure, and His Majesty has reason: let us not refuse it to Him. Since He is not to force our will, He takes only what we give Him. But He does not give Himself entirely to us, till we give ourselves up entirely to Him (this is certain, and because it is of such importance, I so often remind you of it); nor does He operate in the soul so much as He does when without any obstacle she is wholly His: nor do I understand how He could operate there, for He is a lover of order.

Now, if we fill the palace with rabble, and with trifles, 75 how can it receive our Lord, with all His court? He does a great deal in remaining, even for a short time, amidst so much confusion. Do you think, daughters, that He comes alone? Do you not hear what His Son says, "Who art in Heaven?" You may be sure such a King is not left alone by his courtiers; but they attend Him, praying to Him for us, and for our welfare, because they are full of charity. Imagine not that it is the same in this world, where if a king or prelate should visit any one for some particular object, or because he loves the person, envious feelings immediately arise in others, and the poor man is calumniated, without having done the others any injury: hence the honour costs him dear.

CHAPTER XXIX.

SHE MENTIONS WHAT MEANS ARE TO BE USED FOR OBTAINING THE PRAYER OF RECOLLECTION.

FOR the love of God, daughters, be not at all anxious for these favours: let each one endeavour to do her duty, and if the superior do not approve of it, she may be sure our Lord will accept and reward it. But have we come here to seek a reward in this life? Let our thoughts be fixed upon that which endures for ever, and let us despise all things here below, since even they do not continue during the period of one's life; for to-day you may be going on well, but to-morrow, if the superior should see more virtue in you, he may like you better; if not, it is of little consequence. Do not give way to such thoughts, which sometimes arise from little things, and may disturb you much. Stifle them by considering that your "kingdom" is not in this world, and how quickly all things come to an end.

But even this consideration is a poor remedy, and not a very perfect one. It is better that your cross should continue, that you should fall into disgrace, and be despised: desire this may be so, for the sake of that Lord who is with you. Cast your eyes on yourselves, and behold yourselves interiorly, as I have said already: there you will find your Master, who will not be wanting to you, and the less exterior consolation you have, so much the more will He caress you. He is very compassionate, and never fails to help the afflicted and disconsolate, if they trust in Him alone. So saith David, "Mercy shall encompass him that hopeth in the Lord." Either you believe these words, or you do not: if you do, why do you torment yourselves? O my Lord! did we truly know Thee, we should not be anxious for anything, for Thou givest plenty to those who wish to trust in Thee. Believe me, friends, if we understand this truth, it will be of great assistance towards enabling us to discover that all the favours of this world are a lie, even should they hinder the soul but a little from retiring into herself. Would that you could understand this truth. I cannot make you understand it; for though I am obliged, more than any one else, to understand it, yet I cannot understand it as I ought to do.

To return now to what I was saying. I should be glad to know how to explain to you, in what manner the soul finds herself in the company of the King of kings, and the Saint of saints, without any impediment to the solitude which she and her Spouse enjoy, when this soul desires to enter within herself into this Paradise with her God, and locks the door after her against all things of the world. I say, "when the soul desires;" for know that is not a matter altogether supernatural, but that it depends upon our will; and we can do it by the help of God's grace, since without this nothing can be done, nor can we of ourselves have one good thought. Here the powers of the soul are not silent, but only shut up within themselves. We can acquire this degree in many ways, as we find written in certain books, viz., by disengaging ourselves from everything, in order thereby to approach interiorly to God; and even amidst business, by retiring into ourselves, though it were only for a moment. It is very useful to remember, that we have "company" within us. What I only aim at is, that we see Him, and remain with Him to whom we are speaking, without our turning our backs upon Him; for, methinks, we do this, when we remain discoursing with God, and thinking on a thousand vanities at the same time. All the evil comes from our not properly understanding that He is near us; but we imagine He is far off, and how far, if we go to heaven to seek Him! Does not Thy countenance then, O Lord, deserve to be looked upon, being so near to us? We think men do not hear us, if, when we are speaking to them, we notice they do not see us; and must we shut our eyes that we may not see You beholding us? How can we know whether You have heard what we say to You? This is only what I would wish to explain; that we should accustom ourselves with facility to quiet the understanding, that so it may know what it says, and to whom it speaks; and for this purpose, it is necessary that we withdraw these exterior senses within ourselves, and there find them something to do; for it is true, that we possess heaven within us, since the Lord thereof resides there. In a word, it is necessary that we should accustom ourselves to taste the sweetness of His presence, without our requiring any words to speak to Him, for His Majesty will clearly show us

He is there.

Thus we shall be able to pray vocally with great quiet, and we shall free ourselves from much trouble; for during the short time that we force ourselves to stay near this Lord, He will understand us (as the saying is) "by signs," so that if we were often to repeat the "Lord's Prayer," He will make us understand, that when we say it only once, He has heard us. He exceedingly loves to deliver us from evil, though we should say but one "Our Father" in an hour, provided we understand that we are with Him, and that we know what we ask, and how willing He is to give, and how glad He is to be with us; He does not wish that we should tire ourselves by speaking too much with Him. May our Lord teach this truth to those among you, who know it not; for myself, I confess I never knew what it was to pray with satisfaction till our Lord taught me this way; and I have always found such great advantage from this practice of recollection and entering within myself, that this is the reason why I have said so much on the subject.

I now conclude. Whoever wishes to arrive at this degree of perfection (and, as I have said, it is in our power to do so), let her not grow weary in accustoming herself to do what I have been saying; and this is, by little and little to obtain the mastery over one's-self, not losing ourselves for nothing, but recalling our senses within us; and this is not a loss for the soul, but a great gain. If she speak, she should endeavour to remind herself that she is about to speak with one within her; if she listen, she should remember. that she is about to hear One who speaks most intimately to her. In a word, let her understand that, if she wish, she need never separate herself from such good company; and let her grieve, when she has, for any long time, left this her Father there alone, of whom she stands so continually in need.

If she can do this often in the course of the day, let her; if not, let her do it at least sometimes; when she has accustomed herself to it, she will gain great profit thereby sooner or later. After our Lord shall have granted this favour to her, she would not exchange it for any earthly treasure: nothing is learnt then without some little trouble. For the love of God, sisters, consider that care well employed, which you all bestow on this matter; and I know that if you practise it for a year, or perhaps only for half that time, you will reach this degree by the Divine assistance. You see then how inconsiderable this labour is, in comparison with the advantage of establishing this solid foundation, in order that if God wishes to raise you to higher things, He may find you disposed, by seeing you so near Him. Amen.

CHAPTER XXX.

ON THOSE WORDS OF THE OUR FATHER, "HALLOWED BE THY NAME," THE SAINT APPLIES THEM TO THE PRAYER OF QUIET.

LET us now consider how our Good Master goes on (with His prayer), and begins to pray to His Holy Father for us. And what does He ask him? It is proper that we should understand this. Who is there, however stupid he may be, that when he is about to ask something of a great person, considers not beforehand how he should speak to him, that so he may please, and not displease him. And does he not also consider what it is necessary he should ask for, and for what purpose he wants what is to be given to him, especially if he should ask for any important favour, as our good Jesus teaches us to ask? This is a point very worthy of being attended to. Could you not, O my Lord! have in one word included all things, and have said: "Give us, Father, that which is expedient for us," since to one who understands all things so well, nothing more seems requisite? O Eternal Wisdom! between You and Your Father this would be sufficient, and so You prayed in the garden: You manifested Your will and showed Your fear: but You resigned Yourself to your Father's will. And You know, O my Lord, that we are not so resigned as You were to Your Father, and that it was necessary to ask for particular blessings, that so we might rest upon the consideration, whether what we ask be good for us: if not, we should not ask it. Our nature is such, that unless we receive what we desire, we would not (on account of our free-will) accept what God shall give us, because though it may be better for us in the end, yet we never think we shall be rich unless we see ready money in our hands. O Lord! what is the cause why our faith is so benumbed and so dormant, both as regards the one and the other? Hence, we neither understand how certain a punishment we shall have, nor how certain a reward. It is therefore proper, daughters, that you should understand what it is you ask for in the "Our Father;" take heed, that if the Eternal Father grant your request, you cast it not back in His face; and that you always think very seriously of what you ask, and whether it be good for you; if it be not, do not ask for it; but desire that His Majesty would enlighten you on this point; for we are blind and squeamish, so that we cannot eat those meats which would give us life, but only those which bring death with them, a death so dangerous, because eternal.

Our Good Jesus tells us to say these words, wherein we petition that such a Kingdom should come to us: "Hallowed be thy name: thy Kingdom come." Now, daughters, consider the great wisdom of our Master. Here I consider, and it is fit we should understand, what we ask for in praying for this "Kingdom." As His Majesty sees we should be unable to sanctify, praise, magnify, or glorify this holy name of the Eternal Father, on account of our very poor ability, if His Majesty had not given us the means, by giving us here His Kingdom; so our good Jesus has been pleased to join both together.76

In order, then, daughters, that we may understand what we ask for, and how necessary it is that we become importunate in our requests, and do all we can to please Him who is to grant our petitions, I will tell you here what I understand: if you do not like it, you may meditate on other considerations; and this our Master will permit, that so we may in all things submit ourselves to the judgment of the Church, as I always do; and even this I will not give you to read, until it has been examined by persons who understand the subject.

The chief happiness which seems to me to be in the Kingdom of Heaven (among many other sources of joy), is this, that there no account is made of any earthly thing; but there is a repose, a glory in the Blessed, a rejoicing that all rejoice, a perpetual peace, a great satisfaction in themselves; and this comes to them, because they see all the inhabitants sanctify and praise God, and bless His name, and that none offend Him. All love Him, and the soul herself minds nothing else but to love Him, and she cannot forbear loving Him because she knows Him. And so we should love Him in this world, did we know Him, though not in such perfection and with such steadfastness:77 but we should love Him in a manner different from what we do now, did we once know Him.

It seems as if I were going to say, we must be angels, in order to present this petition, and to pray well vocally; this our divine Master wishes us to do, since He commands us to make so sublime a request; and doubtless He bids us not ask for things which are impossible. And why should it be impossible for a soul, placed in this land of exile, to arrive at this point, by God's assistance, though not in such perfection as those others do, who are free from this prison of the body, for we are yet at sea, and on a journey? But there are seasons when our Lord places those who are weary of travelling in a state wherein the powers are tranquil, and the soul is quiet; wherein, as it were by signs, He makes them clearly understand how sweet that is which our Lord gives to those whom He brings to His Kingdom; and on those to whom this is given He bestows certain pledges, that by means of them they may conceive great hope of being enabled to enjoy eternally, what they are only allowed to sip here in this world.

If I thought you would not say I was speaking of contemplation, it would in this petition be very proper to say something of the beginning of pure contemplation, which those who are accustomed to it call the Prayer of Quiet. But (as I have said) I am speaking of vocal prayer; and here it may seem that one does not agree with the other. This I will not endure: I know they do agree; excuse me in saying so, for I know many persons who pray vocally, and have been advanced by God, without their knowing how, to a high degree of contemplation. Therefore it is that I urge this so much, daughters, in order that you may perform your vocal prayers well.

I know a person who could never reach further than vocal prayer, and yet by practising this, she possessed everything: if she did not pray vocally, her understanding was so distracted that she could not endure it; but would that all of us practised mental prayer so well. In certain "Pater Nosters," which she recited on the several mysteries of the Passion, and in some few other prayers also, she continued to pray vocally for two or three hours. She once came to me exceedingly afflicted, "because she knew not how to practise mental prayer, neither could she contemplate, but only pray vocally." I asked her what she said, and perceived that though she kept to the "Pater Noster," she enjoyed pure contemplation, and God raised her even to the Prayer of Union. And this clearly appeared in her actions, for she led a very good life, so that I praised our Lord, and even desired to have her vocal prayer. If what I say be true (as it is), you who dislike contemplatives must not suppose you have not contemplation, if you say your vocal prayers as they should be said, and keep a pure conscience.

CHAPTER XXXI.

SHE CONTINUES THE SAME SUBJECT AND EXPLAINS THE PRAYER OF QUIET, ETC.
I WISH, daughters, notwithstanding, to explain this Prayer of Quiet to you, according as I have heard it practised, or our Lord has pleased to let me understand it, perhaps in order that I might explain it to you; and it seems to me that our Lord begins to make known that He has heard our prayers, and that He already begins to give us His kingdom here, in order that we may truly praise and sanctify His name, and endeavour that all men may do the same. This is something supernatural, which we cannot acquire by all our diligence, because it is setting the soul in peace; or rather, to speak more correctly, our Lord leads her into peace by His presence, just as He did holy Simeon, for all the faculties are calmed. The soul understands in a manner different from understanding by the exterior senses, that she is now placed near her God, and that in a very short time she will become one with Him by union. This does not happen, because she sees Him with the eyes of the body, or of the soul; for as holy Simeon saw this glorious little Infant only

under the appearance of poverty, and wrapped in swaddling clothes, and with attendants to follow Him, He might rather have supposed He was the Son of some mean person, than the Son of the Heavenly Father. But the child made himself known to him; and so in the same way the soul understands He is there, though not with the like clearness, for she herself knows not how she understands, but that she sees herself in the kingdom (at least, near the King who is to give it to her), and the soul seems impressed with such reverence, that then she dare not ask anything.

It is as it were an interior and exterior fainting away, 78 so that the exterior man (I mean the body, that you may understand me better) does not wish to stir at all; but like a person who has almost arrived at his journey's end, he rests, in order to be the better able to travel again, for here one's strength is redoubled for the purpose. A very great delight is experienced in the body, and a great satisfaction in the soul. She is so delighted at merely seeing herself near the Fountain, that she is already satisfied even without drinking: she seems to have nothing more to desire. The faculties are so quiet, that they will not stir, and everything seems to be an obstacle to her love. And yet the faculties are not lost, for they can think near whom they stand, since two of them are free. Here the will is a captive, and if she feel any pain in this state, it is to see that she is to return to her former liberty. The understanding does not wish to understand more than one thing, nor the memory to employ itself about anything more. Here they perceive this 79 alone is necessary, and that all things else disturb them. They would not have the body move, because they think they should lose that peace, and therefore they dare not stir. Speaking is painful to them: they will sometimes spend an hour in saying only one "Our Father." They are so near, that they perceive they are understood by signs; they are in the palace close by their King, and they see that He already begins here below to bestow upon them His kingdom. Here flow tears without any feelings of grief, and sometimes even they are attended with great delight. They seem not to be in the world, and they wish neither to see nor to hear of it, but only to hear of their God. Nothing troubles them, and it seems nothing can do so. In a word, while this continues, they are so inebriated and absorpt with the delight and satisfaction contained therein, that they remember not there is anything more to desire; and they exclaim with St. Peter, "Lord, let us make here three tabernacles."

In this Prayer of Quiet, God sometimes bestows another favour, very hard to be understood, unless one has great experience; and if he have such experience, those who have it will immediately understand it; and it will afford them great consolation to know what it is, and I believe God often bestows this favour together with the other. When this favour is great, and continues for a long time, it seems to me that unless the will were attached to something, it could not continue so long in that peace; for it happens that we go on a day or two with this satisfaction, and do not understand ourselves: I speak of those who have it. They see, indeed, they are not entirely taken up with what they do; but that they want the chief thing, which is the will; and this seems to me to be united with God, and to leave the other faculties free, that they may attend to things relating to his service; and for this object they have then more ability; but as regards worldly concerns, they are stupid, and sometimes as it were fools. This is a great favour, on whomsoever our Lord bestows it, for the active and contemplative life are united. Our Lord is then served by all, for the will is busy at her work, without knowing how she works, and continues in her contemplation; the other two powers serve to do the office of Martha; so that she and Mary walk together. I know a person whom our Lord often raised to this state; and because she knew not what it was, she asked a great contemplative, who told her, "It was very possible,"80 for the like had happened to him. I think, therefore, that since the soul is so well satisfied in this Prayer of Union, the will must, during most of the time, be united to Him who alone is able to satisfy it.

Now, here it seems to me, it would be well to give some advice for those amongst you, sisters, whom God, in His goodness, has raised to this state, for I know there are some such amongst you. The first is, that when they see themselves in that joy, and know not how it has come upon them (at least they see they could not obtain it of themselves), this temptation presents itself, that they think they can make it continue, and so they do not wish even to breathe. A foolish error is this; for as we cannot make the day break, so neither can we prevent the night from coming on. It is now no act of ours, for it is supernatural, and we are quite unable to acquire it. The surest means of retaining this favour is to understand clearly that we can neither diminish nor add thereto, but only receive it as being most unworthy of it, and give thanks for it. This we should do, not with many words, but like the publican, not daring to lift up our eyes. It is good to seek for more solitude, in order thereby to make room for our Lord, and let His Majesty work as in something of His own, and to utter, from time to time, some sweet word, like one blows a candle, when he sees it has gone out, in order to light it again; but if the candle be burning, our blowing serves only to extinguish it. This blowing should, in my opinion, be gentle, that it may not trouble the will, by forming many words with the understanding. Pay great attention, my friends, to the advice I will now give you; for you will often find yourselves unable to make use of those other two powers. It may happen, that the soul enjoys very great quiet, and in the mean time the understanding is so distracted, that what happens seems not to be in its house; and so then it seems that it is as a guest in another person's house, and it goes seeking for other lodgings to live in, since that does not please it, for it little knows what it is to continue still in one state.81 Perhaps this has only been my case, and others may not have been so. I think that sometimes I desire to die, because I am unable to remedy this variety of thoughts: other times they seem to be settled in their house, and they accompany the will, so that when all the three powers agree, it is a kind of heaven; just like two married persons who love each other, for what one desires the other does too: but if the husband be bad, it is soon discovered how troubled the wife is thereat.

When the will, therefore, perceives herself in this quiet, let her not heed the understanding, or thought, or imagination (for I know not which of them it is), any more than she would heed a fool; for if she seek to carry any one of these with her, she must of necessity be occupied, and somewhat disquieted; hence, in this degree of prayer, all will be labour and no gain; but we shall lose that which our Lord gives us without any labour of ours. Pay great attention to this comparison, which our Lord suggested to me when in prayer: it suits me exactly, and I think explains my subject. The soul is like a child that sucks, lying at his mother's breast; and she to please him, without moving his lips, forces the milk into his mouth. Even so is it here; for without any labour of the understanding, the will continues loving, and our Lord is pleased that, without her thinking on it beforehand, she should understand that she is conversing with him, that she only swallows the milk which His Majesty puts in her mouth, and enjoys its sweetness, and that she knows it is our Lord who bestows this favour upon her, and that she exults in the enjoyment of it. But let her not be desirous of knowing how she enjoys it, and what that is which she enjoys; let her then have no care for herself, for He who stands near her will not fail to see what is best for her; since if she should contend with the understanding, to give it a share by taking it along with her, she cannot do everything, and must therefore let the milk fall out of her mouth, and so lose that divine nourishment.

This prayer is thus distinguished from that wherein the soul is altogether united with God, for then the soul does not receive this nourishment by swallowing it down; but she finds it within herself, without perceiving how our Lord puts it there. Here it seems He wishes the soul to take a little pains, though this is done with so much ease, that it is scarcely felt. That which torments her here is the understanding, or imagination. This is not the case, however, when there is a union of all the three powers, because He that created them suspends them: and with the delight He then gives them. He employs them all without their knowing how, or being able to understand it. Hence, as I have said, when the soul finds in herself this prayer, which is a quiet and great contentedness of the will, without knowing how to judge distinctly what it is, though she sees clearly it differs exceedingly from all pleasures here below, since dominion even over the whole world, with all the delights thereof, would not be sufficient to make a soul feel in herself the satisfaction which the will has in its interior; for other pleasures of this life are, methinks, relished only by the bark or exterior of the will (as we may call it); when the soul, I repeat, finds herself in so high a degree of prayer, which, as I have said, is now very clearly supernatural, if the understanding, or, to speak more correctly, the thought should run after the greatest fooleries in the world, let her laugh at it and leave it as a fool, and remain in her quiet; for it will go and come, because the will being here a powerful mistress, she will recover it without your afflicting yourselves.82 Yet if she seek by force of arms to bring it to her, she loses the strength which she has against it, and which she obtains by eating and taking that divine nourishment; and neither one nor the other will gain anything, but both will be losers. There is a saying, "that he who strives to grasp at much, loses all at once:" just so, methinks, is it in this case. Experience will make this clear, and whoever has it not, no wonder if he consider what I have been saying to be very obscure: but I have already said, that with a little experience he will understand it, and may thereby benefit himself; and you will praise God that He was pleased to direct me to express so much here. Let us draw the conclusion then, that when the soul has arrived at this degree of prayer, it now seems that the eternal Father has granted her request, viz., to give her in this life His kingdom.

O blessed petition! wherein, without our understanding it, we ask for so great a good! O blessed way of praying! I wish you, therefore, sisters, to consider how we should recite this heavenly prayer of the "Our Father," and all our other vocal prayers. For as our Lord has done us this favour, we should forget all the things of this world, because when the Lord of our soul enters. He drives away the love of all creatures. I say not that all those who have it, 83 must necessarily be separated from the world; but I would have them understand, at least, what is wanting to them; and let them humble themselves, and endeavour to be more and more disengaged from every thought, because otherwise they will stop here.

A soul to which God gives such pledges may be assured He intends her for some important service, and unless it be her own faulty she will advance exceedingly. But if He perceive, that when He erects this "kingdom of heaven" in her house, she returns to the earth, He will not only not acquaint her with the secrets that are in His kingdom, but He will confer this favour on her very seldom, and only for a short time. Now, I may be mistaken in what I say, yet I see and know that this usually happens; and for my part, I consider this to be the reason why there are not many who are more spiritual; for as they do not correspond in their actions with so great a favour, and do not re-dispose themselves for receiving it, but rather take out of our Lord's hands the will which he already considered His own, and apply it to vile things; so He goes seeking for some who love Him, in order to give them more, though He does not altogether take away that which He gave the others, when they live with a good conscience. But there are some, and I have been one of them, to whom our Lord gives tender feelings and holy inspirations, and light to know the nature of all things here below; and at last, He bestows this "Kingdom" upon them, and places them in this Prayer of Quiet; and yet they make themselves deaf, because they love so much to be speaking, and to repeat many vocal prayers in great haste (like one who wants to get through his task), having formerly bound themselves to say them every day, when, as I have said, our Lord delivers His kingdom into their hands, but they do not accept it, imagining they do better in saying these prayers; and so they forget the great favour our Lord offers them. Do not you, sisters, act in this manner: but watch carefully, when our Lord shall bestow this favour upon you; consider that you lose a great treasure, and that you do much more by leisurely saying one word of the "Our Father," than by often repeating it hastily, without understanding it. He to whom you pray is very nigh: He will not fail to hear you; and believe me, hereby we may truly praise and sanctify His name, for now you glorify our Lord as if you belonged to His house, and you praise Him with more ardent affections and desires; and it seems you cannot help knowing Him much better, when you have tasted "how sweet He is." Thus I exhort you to be careful, since it is very important for you to be so.

CHAPTER XXXII.

SHE EXPLAINS THE WORDS, "THY WILL BE DONE ON EARTH, AS IT IS IN HEAVEN," ETC.

OUR good Master having now asked for us, and having also taught us to ask for a favour of such value, which includes all the things which we can desire in this world; and having bestowed so great a favour upon us, as to make us His brethren, let us consider what He wishes us to give to His Father, and what He offers to Him for us, and what He desires of us; since it is proper that we should serve Him by something answerable to such great favours. O good Jesus! who givest so little (little on our part), whereas thou askest much from us, although if we consider the thing in itself, it is nothing in comparison to what we owe so great a King. But it is certain, my Lord, that since Thou hast given us thy kingdom, Thou dost not deprive us of everything; and we give all that we can, if we give it as we say in the next words, "Thy will be done on earth, as it is in heaven,"

You did well, our good Master! in making the above petition, that we may be able to accomplish what you offer to us. Were it not so, O Lord! this seems to me impossible to do: but because your Father performs what you desire Him, about giving us here His kingdom, I know we shall also find you faithful, in giving Him that which you offer for us. For when earth shall become heaven, it will be possible to accomplish your will in me; but without this, and in a soil so barren as mine is, I know not, Lord, how it can be possible. It is a great favour which you offer. And when I think of this, I smile at those persons who dare not beg crosses of our Lord, because they think He must needs send them immediately. I speak not of those who wish not to have them out of humility, because they consider themselves unable to bear them; though for my part I consider, that He who gives them such a great love of Him, as to desire so sharp a means of expressing it, will give them strength to bear these crosses also. I would ask those who do not pray for crosses, through fear of their being sent to them immediately, what they say when they beseech our Lord to accomplish His will in them? It is indeed to say that which all say, but not to do it. This, sisters, would not be well. Consider that our good Jesus seems here to be our Emperor, and to be willing to mediate between us and His Father, and this to His no small cost. Now, it would not be proper, that what He offers for us, we in reality should fail to perform: let us rather not say the words.

I will now show it another way. Consider, daughters, this promise must be fulfilled, whether we will or no: take my advice then, and believe me, and make a virtue of necessity. O! my Lord, what a great consolation is this to me, that Thou wouldst not leave to so bad a will as mine the accomplishing or not accomplishing of Thy will. Were the accomplishment of Thy will in heaven and on earth in my hands, what a condition should I be in! I therefore now freely give you mine (although at a time when it is not free from much self-interest), for I have tried, and this by long experience, what gain is obtained by resigning my will to Yours. O! my friends, what a great benefit is acquired here! O! what a great loss, when we do not perform what we promise God in the "Our Father," respecting what we offer Him.

Before I tell you what is gained thereby, I will show you what you offer, lest you afterwards should consider yourselves deceived, and say you did not understand it. Let us not be like certain religious women, who do nothing but promise; and when they do not keep their promise, they give this excuse, and say, "We did not understand what we promised." It may now be the case here; for, to say we will resign our will to that of another, seems very easy, till by trying it we discover it is a most difficult thing to be done, if it be done as it ought to be; it is easy to utter, but hard to execute; and if they thought one was not more important than another, they understood it not. Make those understand it, who shall make their profession in this house, by a long trial of them: let them not suppose they are to bring words only: they must bring works also. Yet superiors do not always guide us with rigour, because they see we are weak; and sometimes they rule the weak and the strong in the same manner. But here it is not so, for our Lord knows what every one can bear; and when he sees one that has strength, He does not desist till He has accomplished His will in him.

I wish, then, to inform and remind you what this His will is; do not fear that it is to give you riches, pleasures, and honours, or any worldly advantages; our Lord has greater love for you, and He highly values what you give Him, and desires to reward you amply, since even when you are alive, He gives you His Kingdom. Do you wish to see, then, how He acts towards those who say this to Him in sincerity? Ask His glorious Son, who said this when He prayed in the garden; as He uttered it with resolution and an entire will, see if He accomplished in Him, by giving Him such an abundance of troubles, pains, injuries, and persecutions, till at last He ended His life by the death of the cross. Here then you see, daughters, what He gives to Him whom He loved most; and hereby we may know what His will is. Thus these are His gifts in this world. He acts conformably to the love He has for us. To those whom He loves more, He gives these gifts the more; to those less, whom He loves less; and so in proportion to the courage He sees in every one, and to the love He has for His Majesty. He sees that he who loves Him much, can suffer much for Him. To him that loves little, He gives little. For my part I think, that the rule of being able to bear great or little, is that of love. Hence, sisters, if you possess this, endeavour that the words which you address to so great a Lord, be not words of compliment: but force yourselves likewise to suffer what His Majesty shall be pleased to send you. For if you give up your will in any other way, it is like a person who shows you a jewel, and offers it, yea begs of you to take it; and when you stretch out your hand to receive it, he holds it fast and will not give it. These are not jests which we are allowed to put upon one who has endured so many for us; for if there were nothing else, it is no reason why we should mock Him so often; since it is not seldom that we say this to Him in the "Our Father." Let us now, once for all, give Him the jewel freely, which we have so often pretended to give. It is true He gives it to us first, in order that we may give it to Him again.

Secular persons will do much, if they have earnest resolution to fulfil it: and you, daughters, will do a great deal also, by saying and by doing in word and work, as indeed it seems we Religious do. And yet sometimes we not only offer to give Him the jewel, but we put it into His hands, and take it again. We suddenly become so generous, and afterwards so parsimonious,84 that it had been better in some respect we had been more cautious in giving. Now because all that I have advised you to do in this book, is directed to the object of inducing to give yourselves up entirely to your Creator, of resigning our wills to His, and disengaging ourselves from Him (of which you already understand the great importance), I will speak no more about it. But I will mention the reason why our good Master places here those words mentioned above, for He is one who knows how much we shall gain by doing this service to His Eternal Father, since by accomplishing these words, we dispose ourselves, in a very short time, to see ourselves arrived at our journey's end, and drinking of the "living water" of the already mentioned; for without resigning our own will entirely to our Lord, to regulate everything regarding us according to it, He will never allow us to drink of this water.

This is perfect contemplation, which you desired me to write about; wherein, as I have shown, we do nothing on our part: we neither labour, nor negotiate at all, nor is more requisite, for all else disturbs and hinders us, except saying: "Thy will be done." May your will, O Lord! be fulfilled in me, in whatever way You shall please: if You wish it to be fulfilled by afflictions, only grant me strength, and let them come: if by persecutions, sickness, disgrace, and poverty – lo! here I am: I will not turn away my face, O my Father! Nor is it fit I should turn my back.85 Since Your Son offered, in the name of all this my will also, there is no reason I should fail on my part. But do me the favour to give me Your Kingdom, that I may be able to accomplish Your will, since He asked it of You for me; dispose of me as one entirely Yours, according to Your will

O my sisters! how powerful is this gift! If it be presented with the resolution it should be, it even induces the Almighty to become one with our baseness: it transforms us into Himself, and unites the Creator with the creature. Consider, whether or no you are well rewarded, and whether you have a good Master, who knowing by what means His Father's affection is to be gained, instructs us how and by what manner we are to serve Him. Now the more resolute the soul is, and the more she shows by her actions that these are not words of mere compliment, the closer does our Lord unite us with Himself, and exalt us above all things here below, and even above ourselves, in order to dispose us for receiving great favours. For even in this life, He is never tired with rewarding our services, so much does He value them; so that we know not what more to ask, and His Majesty is never weary with giving; for not content with having made such a soul one with

Himself, by uniting her with Himself, He begins to regale Himself with her and discover secrets to her, and He is pleased that she should understand what she has gained, and should know something of that which is to be given to her afterwards. He makes her lose the exterior senses, in order that no other object may occupy her attention: (this is a rapture). He also begins to converse with her so very familiarly that He not only restores her will to her, but with it gives her His own; for as our Lord converses so familiarly with her, He is pleased that they "command by turns," 86 as the expression is, and fulfil what the soul requests of Him (as she performs what He requires of her): and this is done so much better, because He is powerful, and can do whatever He wills, and He never ceases to will. In the mean time, the poor soul cannot do what she desires, though she would wish; nor indeed can she do anything, except strength be given to her. And this is her greatest riches, to be the more indebted, the more she serves Him; and oftentimes is she afflicted to see herself exposed to so many inconveniences, obstacles, and bonds, as the prison of this body brings with it, because she would be glad to pay off some part of what she owes. But she is very foolish to afflict herself so much; for though she may do all that lies in her power, what can we pay, who, as I have said, have nothing to give but what we receive? We can however know ourselves; and this we do by His assistance, viz., perfectly to resign ourselves to His will. All else is a hinderance to a soul which our Lord has advanced so far; it does harm, and not good.

Observe, that I speak of a soul which our Lord has been pleased to join to Himself by union and perfect contemplation, for humility alone is that which does everything; and this is not acquired by the understanding, but by a clear truth, which comprehends in a moment what the imagination by labouring cannot reach in a long time, that we are "a very nothing," and that God is everything. One caution I give you, not to think of reaching this degree by your own strength or diligence, for it is vain: even if you had devotion, you will remain cold, but only say with humility and simplicity, which obtain everything – "Thy will be done."

CHAPTER XXXIII.

OF THE WORDS, "GIVE US THIS DAY OUR DAILY BREAD."

SINCE, as I have said, our good Jesus understands how difficult a thing this was which He offered us, and knowing our weakness, how we often make ourselves believe that we do not understand what the will of God is, as we are so weak, and He is so merciful, He saw a remedy for this was necessary; and therefore He asked for us of His Eternal Father this heavenly bread. He saw it was in no way necessary for us, to omit giving what was given, because in this consists all our gain. But to accomplish the object without this favour, He perceived was very difficult. For tell one who fares deliciously, and is rich, that it is God's will he should live moderately, that so others who are even dying with hunger, may at least have bread to eat, He will urge a thousand reasons for not understanding the divine will, except for his own purpose. Tell a detractor that it is God's will he should love his neighbour as he loves himself, he cannot fulfil it with patience, nor can reason make him understand it. In a word, tell a Religious who is accustomed to liberty and excess, that he should consider he is bound to give good example, and that he should remember he ought to fulfil this petition, when he says it, not with words merely, but that he has sworn and promised to fulfil it, and that it is God's will he should perform his vows, and that he must consider how directly he goes against them, should he give scandal; and that he has taken a vow of poverty, which he is bound to observe without seeking to be free from it, for such is the will of our Lord: even such considerations cannot induce some of these men to desire to do His will. What would become of us then, had not our Lord performed the principal part by the remedy which he has applied? There had been surely but very few who would have fulfilled these words, which He spoke for us to His Father, "Thy will be done." Our good Jesus, therefore, seeing our necessities, sought out an admirable means, whereby He showed us the extremity of the love He bore us; and in His own, and in the name of His brethren, He made this petition, "Give us this day our daily bread."

Let us, sisters, for the love of God, understand what our good Master prays for, since it is very important that we should not pass over this petition hastily, and consider that to be very little which you have given, since you are to receive so much. It seems to me at present (bowing to another better judgment) – that our good Jesus, seeing what He had given for us, and how the giving of it concerned us, and the great difficulty there would be, as I have said, because we are by nature so inclined to what is base, so exceedingly destitute of love and courage, that the sight of His ardent love was necessary to awaken us, and that not once but every day, was here obliged to resolve to remain with us. But as it is a matter of such great importance, He wished it to come from the hand of His Eternal Father, because though they are both one, and though He knew that what He did on earth, God would ratify in heaven, and esteem as good, since His will and that of His Father were one; yet such was the humility of our loving Saviour, that (as man) He wished to ask leave as it were for it, though He already knew he was beloved by His Father, and that He delighted in Him. He knew very well that He asked for more in this petition than in the rest, because He knew the death they would make Him suffer, and the disgrace and affronts He would have to endure.

Now, my Lord, what father can be found, who having given us a Son (and such a Son!) who was so ill used, would consent still to remain among us, in order to suffer new injuries? Certainly none, O Lord! but your Son would have done so. You know well to whom you pray. O God! what excessive love in the Son! and what immense love is that of the Father! Yet, I am not much surprised at our good Jesus, for having already said, "Thy will be done!" He was to fulfil it, being what He is. I know He is not like us. Remembering, therefore, that He accomplished it by loving us as Himself, He accordingly endeavoured to seek the means of fulfilling this command with greater perfection, though it was to be at His cost. But how did you consent, Eternal Father? How could you see your Son daily in such wicked hands, having permitted it to be done once, and how could you consent thereto? Since then you see how they have used Him, how could your goodness see Him endure daily such injuries? And how many affronts are now offered to Him in the Most Holy Sacrament? In how many of his enemies' hands must His Father behold Him, and how numerous are the insults of these heretics! O eternal Lord! how can you admit such a petition! How can you consent to it? Look not at His love, who for the perfect accomplishment of your will, and for our benefit, will even allow Himself every day to be cut in pieces. It is your part, O my Lord! to consider this, since your Son does not hesitate at anything. Why must all our good come at His cost? Why does He conceal everything, and seem not to know how to speak for himself, but only for us? Must there be no one, then, to plead for this most loving Lamb?

I have observed how in this petition only He redoubles the words, for He speaks firsts and then prays, "Give us this day our daily bread," as much as to say, that since He gave it to us, He would not take it from us again till the end of the world; but let it serve for our help and service every day. Let this consideration, my daughters, melt your hearts, into loving your spouse, since no slave willingly professes himself to be so, and yet our good Jesus thinks Himself honoured by it. O Eternal Father! how exceedingly meritorious is this humility! With what treasures can we purchase your Son! We know how to sell Him, for that was done for thirty pieces of silver; but to buy Him, no price is sufficient. He is made here one of us, by that portion of our nature which He possesses. And as He is Lord of His own will, He reminds His Father, that since it is His, He can give it to us, and therefore He says, "Our bread." He makes no difference between Himself and us, but makes us one with Himself; that so, by His Majesty daily joining our prayer with His own, ours may obtain from God what we request.

CHAPTER XXXIV.

THE SAME SUBJECT IS CONTINUED, AND APPLIED TO THE RECEPTION OF THE MOST BLESSED SACRAMENT.

SINCE these words "every day" seem to mean for ever, I have been considering why our Lord, after He had said "daily," should add, "Give us this day."87 I will show you my foolishness, for it will appear to be such, by my venturing to speak on this subject. The word "daily," means (it seems so me), that we enjoy Him here on earth, and shall do so in heaven also, if we make good use of His company here in this world, since He has remained with us for no other reason, but to aid, encourage, and sustain us in doing His will, which, as we have said, must be accomplished in us. The saying "this day," seems to me to imply one day, viz., while the world lasts, and no more; and indeed it is but one day, as it were, for those wretches who are condemned to hell, who do not enjoy it in the other life. But it is not our Lord's fault, if they allow themselves to be conquered, for He will not fail to animate them to the end of the battle: they will then have nothing whereby to excuse themselves, or to accuse the Eternal Father, because He took it away from them at the best time. Hence, His Son begs of Him, that since it is for no more than one day, He would let Him spend it with His friends, notwithstanding the indignities some persons offer to Him; for since His Majesty has given Him to us, and sent Him into this world through His own goodness and will, He now willingly desires not to desert us, but to stay here with us, for the greater glory of His friends, and the grief of His enemies; so that He now asks nothing more than only for "to-day" because as He has once given us this most sacred bread, we are certain that He has given it to us for ever. As I have mentioned, His Majesty gave us this nourishment, and manna of the humanity, 88 that so we may find it when we please, and not die of famine, except through our own fault; for in every way which the soul can desire to feed, she will find in the Most Holy Sacrament sweetness and consolation. There is no poverty, trouble, or persecution, which is not easy to bear, if we once begin to taste and relish His sufferings.

Ask the Father, therefore, daughters, together with this Lord, to let you this day have your spouse, that you may never see yourselves in this world without Him; and this will be sufficient to moderate so great a pleasure, that He remains thus disguised under these accidents of bread and wine; and this is torment enough for one that has nothing else to love, nor any other comfort; beseech Him not to desert you, but to grant you a disposition to receive him worthily. Be not solicitous for any other bread, for you have truly resigned yourselves to the will of God; I mean at those times of prayer, when you are treating about more important matters; for there are other times in which you may work and earn your food, though not with solicitude. At no time busy your mind about this: but let the body labour (for you ought to get your living), and let the soul rest: leave this care to your spouse, as I have exhorted you in another place more at length: He will always take it on himself. Never fear, lest He will forget you, if you fail not in what you have promised about resigning yourselves to the will of God. And truly, my daughters, for myself I tell you, that should I now, through malice, fail in wanting resignation (as I have often done before), I would not entreat Him to give me bread, or anything else to eat: let me die of hunger. For why should I desire to live, if every day I am exposing myself more and more to eternal death? Hence, if you sincerely give yourselves up to God, as you say here, He will take care of you. Just as when a person enters upon a service, he is anxious to please his master in every thing, and the master is bound to find the servant in food while he remains in his house and serves him, except he become so poor that he has nothing, either for himself or for the servant. But here this is not the case, since our Master ever is and ever will be powerful and rich. Now, is it fit, a servant should every day be asking for victuals, when he knows His master takes care, and must take care to provide him with food? He might with reason tell him to be careful in serving him and pleasing him, for by fixing his thoughts on what he should not, he does nothing right. Hence, sisters, however anxious others may be in asking for this bread, let us beseech the Eternal Father, that we may deserve to ask of Him our eternal bread. And as the eyes of the body cannot take delight in beholding Him, because He is so veiled, let us hope He will discover Himself to those of the soul, and make Himself known to be another kind of pleasant and delicious food, and that He may thus preserve our life.

Do you think that this most holy food is not nourishment for these bodies, and an excellent remedy even against corporal maladies? I know it is, for I am acquainted with one subject to grievous diseases, who being often in great pain, was hereby freed from it, as by the touch of one's hand, and afterwards continued in perfect health. This was very usual, in diseases too which were well known, and which in my opinion could not be counterfeited. And because the wonders which this most holy bread effects on those who worthily receive it are well known, I do not relate many which I could mention, with regard to the person I speak of, and I know they are not false. Our Lord had given her so lively a faith, that when she heard some persons say they wished they had lived at the time when Christ our Lord (our Sovereign Good) conversed in this world, she smiled to herself, and thought that since men enjoyed Him in the most Holy Sacrament as really as if He were alive, what need they care for any more? I know with regard to this person, though she was not one of the most perfect, that for many years when she communicated, she endeavoured to revive her faith, as much as if she had seen with her corporal eyes our Lord coming into her soul. And this she did (believing that our Lord entered into her poor cottage), in order that she might disengage herself, as much as possible, from all exterior things, and enter in with Him. She endeavoured to recollect her senses, that they might all understand so great a good; I mean, might not hinder the soul from understanding it. She imagined herself to be at His feet, and with blessed Magdalen she wept as much as if she had seen Him with her corporal eyes in the house of the Pharisee; and though she might have felt no devotion, yet faith told her that there she was well; and there she stood discoursing with Him. For unless we wish to make ourselves stupid and blind our understanding, there is no doubt that this is not a representation of the imagination, as when we consider our Lord upon the cross, or in some other stages of his passion: there we represent these things as past. This is now present, and is an absolute truth: hence, we need not seek Him out in some remote place; but as we know, that while the natural heat has not consumed the accidents of bread, our good Jesus stays with us, we do not lose so good an opportunity, but join ourselves with Him.

Now, if when He lived in this world, He healed the sick by the mere touch of His garments, what doubt is there but that He will perform miracles, since He is so intimately within us, if we have a lively faith; and that He will grant us what we ask of Him, while He is in our house? His Majesty is not accustomed to be a bad pay-master, if we give Him good entertainment. If you are troubled at not seeing Him with your corporal eyes, consider it is not expedient for us; for it is quite one thing to see Him glorified, and another to see Him as He was, when He lived and conversed on earth. No one would be able to bear it, such is our weak nature; there would be no world, nor would any one be able to stay in it, because by seeing this eternal truth, it would evidently appear that all those things which we value here, are a lie and a cheat. And seeing so great a majesty, how should such a sinner as I am, who have so highly offended Him, dare to be so near Him? He is accessible under those accidents of bread; for if the King be disguised, it seems we are not troubled to converse with Him, without so many ceremonies and reverences; it even appears that He is obliged to suffer this, because He has not made Himself known. Who dare approach Him with such tepidity, such unworthiness, and with so many imperfections?

As we do not know what we ask, how much better has His wisdom ordered it! To those whom He sees likely to profit thereby, He discovers Himself; though they see Him not with their corporal eyes, He has many ways of disclosing Himself to such a soul, by great internal sentiments, and that in different ways.

Stay willingly with Him: lose not so fair an opportunity of negotiating, for after you have communicated is the time. Consider that this is a great benefit to a soul, and wherein our good Jesus delights much – see that you keep Him company. Make great account, daughters, of your not leaving Him. If obedience enjoin you some other duty, endeavour that your soul may be still with our Lord: He who is your Master will not fail to teach you, though you understand it not; but if you immediately fix your thoughts on something else; and if you mind Him not, nor esteem Him who is within you, then complain of no one but yourselves.

This, then, is the proper time for our Master to teach us, and for us to hear and kiss His feet, because He has been pleased to instruct us; and let us beseech Him not to depart from us. If you make this request on beholding a picture of Christ, it seems to me to be folly, to leave at such a time the Person Himself, in order to see His likeness. Is it not the same, as if possessing the picture of one whom we love dearly, and on the individual coming to visit us, we should neglect to speak to him, but converse entirely with his picture? But do you wish to know at what time this is no less useful than holy, and when I take a very great pleasure in it? When the person himself is absent, and wishes us to understand that he is so by many avidities, then it is a great pleasure to see his picture, whom we love with such great reason: on whatever side I turn my eyes, I should wish to see it. On what more delightful object can we fix our sight, than on one who loves us to such a degree – on One who comprises all good things in Himself? Unhappy heretics, who by their own fault have lost this as well as other consolations.89

But after you have received your Lord, endeavour to shut the eyes of the body and open those of the soul, since you possess His very Person within you; for I tell you again (and I wish to tell you often), that if you adhere to this practice every time you communicate, and endeavour to keep such a conscience that you may be admitted frequently to the enjoyment of this good, He will not come so disguised, but as I have said He will make Himself known by many ways, according to the desire we have of seeing Him; and you should earnestly desire, that He may wholly reveal Himself to you. But if we make no account of Him, and after we have received Him, go away from Him to seek after other base objects, what can He do? Must He drag us by force to seek Him, because He loves to be known by us? No, for men did not treat Him well, when He openly exposed Himself to the gaze of all, and told them plainly who He was: there were very few who believed in Him. It is therefore a great mercy which He shows us all, that His Majesty will allow us to understand it is He who is present in the Most Holy Sacrament. But He does not like to be seen openly, nor to communicate His favours and bestow His graces, except on those who He knows earnestly desire Him, because such as these are His true friends. For let me tell you, whoever is not so, and approaches not to receive Him as such, never let him importune our Lord to manifest Himself to him. He does not think the hour goes soon enough, wherein he has fulfilled what the Church commands, when presently he goes out of his house, and endeavours to drive our Lord away also. Hence, such a person seems, by other affairs, and occupations, and tumults of the world, to make all the haste he can, that our Lord may not take possession of his house.

CHAPTER XXXV.

SHE CONCLUDES THIS SUBJECT WITH AN EXCLAMATION TO THE ETERNAL FATHER.
I HAVE thus here entered into details (though I have spoken on the subject in the Prayer of Recollection,) showing how very important it is thus to enter alone into ourselves with God. And when you do not communicate, daughters, and yet hear mass, you may communicate spiritually, which is a very beneficial practice: you may do the same about retiring afterwards into yourselves, for thus the love of our Lord is deeply imprinted on our heart. When we dispose ourselves to receive, He never fails to give, in many ways unknown to us. Just as when we are coming to a fire, which though very great, yet if you stand at a distance from it and hide your hands, you can hardly get warmth from it, though it gives more heat than is felt where there is no fire at all. But it is another thing for us to desire to come near this fire; since if the soul be well disposed, (I mean, if she be desirous of expelling the cold), and if she continue therein for some time, she keeps the heat she gets for many hours, and a small spark flying out from it sets her all on fire. Indeed, it is so important for us to dispose ourselves for this favour, that you should never wonder, daughters, at my repeating it so often.

But remember, sisters, that if you should not succeed well at the beginning, you must not be troubled thereat: for the devil, perhaps, may bring on you some trouble of mind and anguish, because he knows the great harm he receives thereby. He will make you believe there is more devotion in other things than in this: but believe me, do not leave off this method, for thereby our Lord will try how much you love Him. Remember, there are few souls who accompany and follow Him in troubles: let us suffer something for Him, since His Majesty will reward us. And remember, likewise, there will be some who not only love not to stay with Him, but with rudeness drive Him from them. We must, therefore, suffer something, that He may discover we have a desire to see Him and to be with Him. And since He endures, and will still endure, all things, for the sake of finding only one soul to receive and retain Him in herself with affection, let this soul be yours: because were there none such, with reason would the Eternal Father be unwilling to abide with us. But He is so great a friend to His friends, and so good a Master to His servants, that as He knows the will of His dear Son, He will not hinder so noble a work, wherein His love is so perfectly seen.

Since, then, Holy Father who art in Heaven, Thou willest this, and dost accept it (and it is evident you would not refuse a favour so beneficial to us), there must, as I said at first, be some one who will speak for Your Son.

Let us, daughters, be those persons, though it is a bold attempt, considering what we are: yet, relying on our Lord's command that we should ask, and adhering to this obedience in the name of our Good Jesus, let us beseech His Majesty, that seeing He has left nothing undone, by bestowing on sinners so great a benefit as this, He may in His Goodness be pleased to apply some remedy, that He may not be so unworthily treated here; and that since His Holy Son has proposed so good a means, viz., that we may often offer Him up in sacrifice, so precious a gift may be of service in stopping the further progress of such immense evils and irreverences as are practised in places where this Most Holy Sacrament has been, viz., among the Lutherans, who demolish churches, kill so many priests, and abolish the Sacraments. What an affliction is this, my Lord and my God! I beseech You, O Eternal Father! allow this evil to continue no longer: stop this fire, O Lord! for if You will, You can.

Consider that Your Son is still in the world; through respect for Him, let such foul, filthy, and abominable doings cease; and for the sake of His beauty and purity also let them cease, for He does not deserve to lodge in a house where such things are. Do it not for our sakes, O Lord! for we do not deserve it; do it for Your Son's sake, since to beseech You that He should not abide with us, this we dare not ask. He has, however, obtained from You the favour that for "to-day," that is, as long as the world shall last, You would leave Him here: for otherwise, all things would come to an end; and what would become of us? If anything can appease You, it is our possessing here90 such a pledge.

Since, then, my Lord, some remedy must be found, let Your Majesty apply it. O my God! who could importune You so much, and serve you so much, as to be able to request so great a favour, in recompense for His services, since You send none away unrewarded! But I have not done so, O Lord! but rather I am one, who perhaps have so exasperated You, that through my sins such great evils have happened.91 What then ought I to do, my Creator! but to present You with this most Sacred Bread? And though You gave it to us, yet I must give it back again, and beseech You, by the merits of Your Son, to do me this favour, since He has merited it by so many ways. Now, O Lord! now do calm this sea.92 Let not this Ship of the Church be always tossed about in such a tempest:93 save us, O Lord, or we perish!

CHAPTER XXXVI.

SHE EXPLAINS THE WORDS, "FORGIVE US OUR TRESPASSES," ETC.

OUR good Master seeing, then, that with this celestial food all things become easy to us (unless it happen otherwise by our own fault), and that we may very easily perform what we have promised the Father in order that His will may be done in us, now beseeches Him that He would forgive us our "trespasses," since we forgive others; and so proceeding in His prayer, He uses these words, "And forgive us our trespasses, as we forgive them that trespass against us." Observe, sisters. He does not say, "As we shall forgive," that we may understand whoever asks for so great a gift as the preceding94 is, and whoever has already resigned his will to God's will, must have done this duty already; and, therefore, He says, "As we forgive them." Hence, whoever truly says these words to our Lord, "Thy will be done," ought to have done it all, at least, in his resolution. You see here how the saints rejoiced at injuries and persecutions, because in forgiving them they had something to present to God, when they prayed to Him. But what shall such a poor wretch as I do, who have so little to forgive, and so much to be forgiven me? O my Lord! if there be any to keep me company, and who never yet understood this point, – if there be any such, in your name I beseech them to remember this, and to make no account of certain trifles which they call injuries; for, like children, we seem to build houses of straw, by taking notice of these punctilios of honour.

Would, sisters, that we understood what a thing honour is, and in what the loss of it consists! I speak not of you now (since it would be a great shame, not yet to have understood this), but of myself, when I look back upon the time in which I valued honour so much, not knowing what it was, and following the example of the multitude. O! at how many things was I displeased, of which I am now ashamed! And yet I was not one of those that paid much regard to these things, but I stood not on the main point of honour, because I did care for the honour which brings some advantage with it: this is the honour which benefits the soul. O! how true are the words, "Honour and profit cannot stand together." I know not whether He spoke the words exactly in this way; yet it is quite true to say, that the soul's profit and honour can never agree together. It is astonishing to see in what opposite ways the world goes on. Blessed be God, who has brought us out of it. May His Majesty grant that it may be always as far (as it now is) from this house. God deliver us from monasteries where points of honour are observed, in such there will never be much honour given to God.

But take notice, sisters, that the devil does not forget us: he likewise contrives honours for monasteries, and settles his laws for their rising and falling in dignities, like those of the world; and they place their honour in certain trifling matters, at which I am astonished. The learned must go according to their learning: this I do not understand, viz., that he who has got so far as to read divinity, must not condescend to read philosophy, for this is a point of honour, which honour consists in ascending, and not in descending; and even in his own judgment, if it were enjoined him under obedience, he would consider it an affront, and find some to defend him, and say, "It is an injury," and immediately the devil discovers reasons, that even in the law of God there seems to be some ground for it. Even among nuns, she that has been prioress must be thought unfit for any other inferior office; the senior must be considered, and this we never forget: and sometimes it seems that we deserve merit, because the order enjoins it. This is a matter only fit to be laughed at, or rather deplored: I know the order does not forbid our having humility. It commands this, for preserving good order; but I am not to be so strict in this respect, in things concerning my own reputation, so as to take as much care of this point of order, as of other things relating to it, which, perhaps, I observe very imperfectly. Let not all our perfection consist in observing this: others will mind it for me, if I be careless. And in such a case, since we are inclined to ascend higher (even though we should thereby lose our ascent to heaven), it seems we must not think of descending.

O my Lord! are you not our pattern and example? Certainly you are. Now, wherein did your honour consist, O honoured Master? Did you not in reality lose it, by being humbled even to death? No! Lord, but you gained it for us all. O! for the love of God, sisters, consider how much we shall lose our way, if we follow this road, since from the beginning it is the wrong one; and God grant no soul may perish for observing these miserable points of honour, without considering in what honour consists, lest afterwards we come to imagine that we have done a great deal if we forgive some little trifle of this kind, which was neither an affront nor injury, nor anything; and like one who has done some extraordinary action, we come and beg of God to forgive us, since we have forgiven others. Make us understand, O my God! that we know not ourselves, and that we come with empty hands; and do you, in your mercy, pardon us.

But how highly must God here value our loving one another, since our good Jesus might have proposed other things to His Father, and have said, "Forgive us, O Lord, because we do great penances, or because we pray and fast much, and have left all things for you, and because we love you exceedingly, because we would lose our lives for you." Many other things of the like nature I could mention; and yet our Lord only said, "As we forgive them;" because, perhaps, He knew we were such great lovers of this miserable honour; and because it is a duty so difficult to be performed by us. He therefore mentioned it, and offered it in our behalf.

Now, observe carefully, my sisters, that He says, "As we forgive," speaking of something as already done. And mark this well, that when some of these things happen to a soul, and she does not rise from the prayer of Perfect Contemplation (of which I have spoken already), firmly resolved to forgive, and when occasion offers, does not actually forgive an injury, however great it may be, though these injuries are only trifles, she need not trust much in such prayers; for these trifles do not affect that soul, which God unites to Himself in such sublime prayer, nor does she pay any more regard to being esteemed than despised. I have not spoken correctly; for honour afflicts her more than dishonour, and great delight and repose, than troubles. Since God has given her His kingdom here, she now desires it not in this world; and she understands that, in order to reign more powerfully, this is the true course to pursue. She has also seen by experience the benefit that she gains, and how much a soul advances by suffering from God: for seldom does His Majesty confer so great a favour, except upon such as have cheerfully endured many troubles for His sake; and as I have said elsewhere in this book, great are the afflictions of the "Contemplative," for our Lord selects those who have had experience therein.

Know then, sisters, that those who already sufficiently understand what all things are, should not stay long upon any transitory object. If some grievous cross or injury should trouble them upon the first assault, yet they scarcely feel it thoroughly, when reason on the other hand comes to their assistance, and seems to erect a standard for them, and leaves this trouble defeated, as it were, by the joy which the soul takes in seeing how God has presented her with an opportunity, whereby she gains before His Majesty in one day more graces and lasting favours, than she could possibly gain in ten years by labour voluntarily undertaken by her. This is very common, as far as I can understand, for I have spoken with many contemplatives, who value afflictions as others esteem gold and jewels, for they have learnt that these enrich them the most. These persons are very far from esteeming themselves on any account; they delight in having their sins known, and in mentioning them, when they see others esteem them. They act in like manner with regard to their noble birth, for they know that in the kingdom which never ends they shall gain nothing thereby; should they delight in being of noble descent, it would only be when it might conduce more to the honour of God and His service; if it should not tend thereto, they are troubled for being taken far more than they are, and without any pain, or rather with some delight, they undeceive others herein. The reason must be, because he on whom God bestows the favour of obtaining this humility and great love of God becomes so forgetful of himself, and despises himself so much in whatever tends to his praise, that he cannot even believe that others think differently of him, nor does he consider it an injury.

These effects which I have mentioned above, belong to persons who have arrived at a higher state of perfection, and to whom our Lord very commonly grants the favour of uniting them to Himself by perfect contemplation. As regards the first point, viz., resolving to bear injuries, however painful they may be, I say that he to whom God grants the favour of arriving at union obtains this grace in a very short time; and if he should not obtain it, nor find he has acquired much strength after this prayer, let him believe that this was not a favour from God, but some illusion of the devil, in order that we might esteem ourselves to be the more excellent. It may be, that when our Lord at first confers these favours, the soul has not this strength immediately; but if our Lord continue to bestow them, die will obtain this strength in a short time; and though she may not have it in other virtues, yet she has strength to forgive injuries.

I cannot believe, that a soul which has arrived so near to Mercy itself, where she knows what she is, and how many sins God has forgiven her, should not instantly and willingly forgive others, and be pacified and wish well to every one who has injured her, because she remembers the kindness and favours our Lord has shown her, whereby she has seen proof of exceeding great love, and she is glad to have an opportunity offered to show some gratitude to her Lord.

I say again, I know many persons on whom God has bestowed the favour of exalting them to a supernatural state, bestowing on them this prayer, or the contemplation mentioned above; and though I have noticed many defects and imperfections in them, yet not one have I noticed, when they were in possession of this favour; nor shall I ever notice any, I believe, if these favours come from God, as I have said. Let him observe who receives great favours, how these effects go on increasing in him: and if he find none, let him fear much, and not believe that these favours come from God, since He always enriches the soul to which He comes. This is certain, that though the favour and consolation soon pass away, yet in time they are discovered by the benefits left in the soul. And as our Good Jesus knows this very well, He confidently tells His Father that we forgive those who injure us.

CHAPTER XXXVII.

ON THE EXCELLENCE OF THE "LORD'S PRAYER," AND HOW WE MAY IN MANY WAYS RECEIVE CONSOLATION FROM IT.

IT ought to excite us to praise God exceedingly when we consider the great excellence of this heavenly prayer, composed as it was so well by such a good Master, so that, daughters, every one of us may apply it to our wants. I am astonished to see how every kind of contemplation and perfection is comprised in such few words; for if we study only this book, we seem to stand in need of no other. Herein our Lord has already taught us every kind of prayer and high contemplation, from that of mental prayer, to the Prayer of Quiet and Union; hence, were I able to express myself well, I could compose a large book on prayer built on such a solid foundation. And here our Lord already begins to let us understand the effects He leaves us, when they are His favours, as you have seen.

I have sometimes thought, why His Majesty did not manifest Himself more in things so high and obscure, that so we might all understand them; and it seemed to me, that because this prayer was intended for all persons, that every one might ask according to his intention and receive comfort (thinking he understands the sense well), our Lord left it thus indefinite, that so contemplatives who seek not after earthly favours, and persons already much devoted to God, may ask heavenly favours, which through God's goodness are attainable here on earth.95 Those also who yet live in the world (and it is fit they should live according to their respective states) may ask likewise for their daily bread, since they must maintain their families, and this is very just and pious; and so with regard to other things suitable to their necessities. But let them observe, that the two points in this prayer, viz., the resigning our own will, and forgiving injuries, are necessary for all persons. It is true, indeed, there is more and less in it, as I have already mentioned. The perfect will resign their will, because they are perfect, and forgive with the perfection above mentioned: we also, sisters, will do what we can; since our Lord accepts all. And it seems a kind of agreement made on our behalf with His Eternal Father, as if He should say, "O my God! do this, and my brethren will do that."96

We may be quite sure that He does not fail on His part; that He is a very good Paymaster, and rewards without measure. We may say this prayer once in such a manner, that our Lord, not discovering any duplicity remaining in us, but that we intend to act as we speak, will make us rich. He loves exceedingly, that we should treat with Him in sincerity, plainness, and clearness, and not speak one thing and mean another. He always gives more than we ask. As, therefore, our Good Master knows that both those who tend to perfection in thus praying, shall rise to so high a degree by reason of the favours which the Eternal Father is to bestow upon them; and understanding that those are already perfect, or that they walk in the way of perfection (who fear nothing, nor ought to fear, as they have the world under their feet) from the effects which He works in their souls, these may entertain very high hopes that His Majesty resides there; and that being inebriated with these delights, they would not willingly remember there is another world, or that they have any adversaries. O Eternal Wisdom, O excellent Instructor! O! what a great blessing, daughters, is a good, prudent, and cautious Master, one who prevents dangers! This is all the spiritual happiness that a spiritual person can desire in this world, for it gives us great security.

I cannot express in words how important this is. As our Lord, then, sees it was necessary to awaken them, and remind them that they have enemies, and how much more dangerous it is still for them to become careless, and that they stand in need of far greater assistance from the Eternal Father (because they would fall from a higher place); and also that they may not go on "deceived," without their ever perceiving it. He presents these petitions, so necessary for all men while we live in this land of exile, viz., "And lead us not into temptation, but deliver us from evil."

CHAPTER XXXVIII.

ON THE WORDS, "LEAD US NOT INTO TEMPTATION, BUT DELIVER US FROM EVIL."

WE must here understand and meditate upon great things, since we ask for such. Now observe, sisters, that I consider it very certain that those who arrive at such perfection do not herein beg of our Lord to free them from afflictions, from temptations, and combats, for this is a very certain sign that it is the Spirit of God, and that there is no illusion in the contemplation and favours which His Majesty bestows on them, since, as I said a little before, they rather desire them, and even ask for them and love them. They are like soldiers, who are the most pleased, when there is the most fighting, because they hope to obtain more booty.97 If there be none, they serve for their pay, but they see they cannot benefit themselves much thereby.

Believe me, sisters, that the soldiers of Christ, I mean those who have arrived at contemplation, long to meet with occasions of fighting. Public enemies they never dread much, because they know them already, and sufficiently understand that by the strength which God gives them they have no power, but are always defeated, and they themselves gain very great profit and never turn their backs. Those indeed whom they fear, and it is proper they should always fear them, and beseech God to be delivered from them, are certain treacherous enemies – the devils, who transform themselves into angels of light: they come in disguise, and will not let themselves be known till they have done much harm in the soul, sucking out our very blood and destroying our virtues, so that we fall into a temptation, and never perceive it. Let us, daughters, often pray in the "Our Father," and beseech God to deliver us from these enemies, and not permit us to fall into temptation, lest they delude us: let us pray that the poison may be discovered, and that they hide not the light from us. And indeed, with what great reason does our Good Master teach us to ask this blessing, and He Himself asks it for us! Consider, daughters, that they do evil in many ways; think not this consists in making us believe that the favours and caresses which they can counterfeit in us come from God. This seems to me to be the least part of the mischief which they can do us: on the contrary, it may happen that thereby they make some travel faster, because being allured by that pleasure, they spend more time in prayer: and as they are ignorant that it comes from the devil, and seeing themselves unworthy of these caresses, they will never desist from giving thanks to God, and therefore they consider themselves the more obliged to serve Him: they will also strive to dispose themselves, that God may confer more favours upon them, thinking they all come from His hand.

Always endeavour, sisters, to acquire humility; and consider that you are not worthy of these favours, and therefore do not seek them. I am confident, that by this means the devil will lose many souls, while he thinks to bring about their ruin, and our Lord works our good from the evil the devil intends doing. His Majesty beholds our intention, which is, to please and serve Him by remaining with Him in prayer, and our Lord is faithful. It is good to proceed with caution, that so no breach may be made in humility by any vain-glory; and beseech our Lord to deliver you from this; and be not afraid, daughters, that His Majesty will suffer you to be caressed much by any but by Himself. But that by which the devil may do great mischief, without our discovering it, is in making us believe we have virtues which we do not possess; this deceit is a very pestilence, for in caresses and favours we seem only to receive something, and we remain so much the more obliged to serve our Lord: but here it seems that we give something, and that our Lord is bound to pay us, and thus by little and little great evil is produced. On the one hand, our humility is awakened, and on the other we neglect to acquire that virtue which we think we already possess. And thus we imagine we go on securely, without perceiving it, and we fall into a ditch from which we cannot get out; and though it may not be evidently a mortal sin, which always leads us to hell, it so disables us,98 that we cannot travel along the road of which I began to speak, for I have not forgotten it.

I tell you that this is a very dangerous temptation. I know by experience a great deal about it, and so I can explain it to you, though not so well as I could wish. And what is the remedy, sisters, for this? The best, in my opinion, is that which our Master teaches us, viz., prayer, beseeching our Eternal Father not to suffer us to fall into temptation. I will also tell you another remedy. If we think our Lord has already given us any virtue, we are to understand it is a blessing we have received, and that He may take it from us again, as indeed it happens many times, and not without great providence on the part of God. Have you never perceived this, sisters, in yourselves? I have, and sometimes I think I am very disengaged from earthly things; and indeed, when it comes to the trial, I am so. At other times I find myself so attached, and this to things perhaps, at which I should have laughed the day before, that I hardly know myself. Another time I seem to have great courage; and as regards anything which would tend to promote God's honour, I would not turn my back upon it, and upon trial I find I have it in some things; the next day it happens that I find I have not so much courage as would be sufficient to kill an ant for God's sake, should I meet with any opposition. Sometimes methinks, I do not care at all for whatever people may say about me, or however much they may detract me; and I have sometimes found it so by experience, and it has rather pleased me. There are days again, when a single word afflicts me, and I would willingly leave this world, since here, it seems, everything disgusts me. And in this respect I am not alone; I have observed this in many persons better than myself, and I know it happens so.

If this then be the case, who can say of himself that he has virtues, or that he is rich, when at the very time that he stands in need of virtue, he finds himself destitute of it? We must not say so, sisters; but let us always think ourselves poor, and not run into debt, when we have no means of paying, for our treasures must come from another quarter, and we know not when our Lord may leave us in the prison of our own misery, without giving us any assistance. And if others or we should think ourselves good, because He shows us favours and grants us honours, which I said are only lent us, both they and we too shall find ourselves deceived. The truth is, that by our serving with humility, our Lord at last helps us in our necessities; but if this virtue be not really in our soul, our Lord will leave you to yourselves in everything. This is an exceeding great favour on His part, in order that you may greatly esteem this virtue, and understand that we have nothing, except what we receive.

Observe, also, another remark which I will make. The devil makes us believe we have some virtue (suppose the virtue of patience), because we resolve to suffer, and we make frequent acts of suffering much for God's sake, and we think we really should so suffer; and on this account we are greatly pleased, and the devil helps us to believe this. I advise you not to make any account of these virtues, nor let us think we know them except by name, or that God has bestowed them upon us, till we discover some proof of this. It may happen that one word will be spoken which displeases you, and then your patience may fall to the ground. When you suffer often, then praise God, for He begins to teach you this virtue; and strive to suffer, because it is a proof He wishes you to repay it to Him, since He gives it to you: but consider it only as something deposited, as I have already told you.

Another temptation the devil makes use of is, to make you believe that you are truly poor; and he has some good reason, because in words you have taken a, vow of poverty, as every Religious does, or because you desire in your heart to be such, as persons do who practise prayer. Poverty then being thus bound, or if she thinks she is poor, she thus speaks to herself, "I desire nothing: this I have because I cannot be without it; in a word, I must live to serve God, and He wishes us to support these bodies." A thousand other things I might mention which the devil, disguised as an angel of light, persuades her to believe, because all this is good; and so he makes her believe that she is poor already, and that she has this virtue, and that everything is done which can be done.

Let us now come to the proof, for this cannot be known in any other way than by continually reflecting on our actions; and if we take any care, the temptation will immediately discover itself. One person, for instance, has an estate which is superfluous. I speak of what is necessary, and not that he should keep three servants, when he can do with one: he is sued for some money, or a poor farmer neglects to pay him his rent, and this troubles and afflicts him as much as if he were not able to live without it. He will reply, perhaps, that his trouble arises lest he might lose his estate through his own neglect; and thus there is always some excuse. Now, I do not here mean to say he should neglect his business, but rather he should mind it; so that if it prosper, well and good; and if not, it is well also. For one who is truly poor, esteems these things so little, that though he attends to them for certain reasons, yet they never disturb him, because he never imagines he shall be in want; and even if he should be in want, this does not trouble him much. He considers it as a thing accessory, and not the principal;99 having higher thoughts, he is occupied on the other hand only by force. A religious man or woman who is poor, (or, at least, ought to be so), possesses nothing, because sometimes they have it not; but if a person bestows anything upon him, it would be a wonder, it would be wonderful, if he were to consider it superfluous; he always loves to have something preserved; and if he can have a habit made of fine stuff, he asks not for a coarse one: he will have some small article, which he can pawn or sell, though it may consist of books, because if sickness comes, he will require better nourishment than usual. Wretched sinner that I am! Is this what you have promised, to forget yourselves, and leave the matter to God, come what may? If you go on providing for the future, you may with less distraction enjoy a fixed revenue. Though this may be done without sin, yet it is proper that we understand these imperfections, in order that we may see how much we want towards possessing this virtue, and that we may ask it of God, and obtain it; for if we imagine we possess it, we grow careless, and (what is worse) are deluded.

The same happens to us with regard to humility, for we think we do not desire honour, nor care for anything: but when an occasion presents itself relating to some trifle, it will immediately appear by what you feel and do, that you are not humble, for if anything should happen which tends more to your honour, you do not reject it; nor do those poor, of whom we spoke, reject what is more beneficial to them, and God grant they may not seek it too. But they have the words so often in their mouths, viz., that they desire nothing (and they really think so), that even the habit of saying this makes them more ready to believe it. It is very important for this purpose always to watch over ourselves, in order to discover this temptation, and also to be watchful in other matters, as well in the things I have already mentioned. For when our Lord gives only one of these virtues, it seems to draw all the rest after it; this is a truth well known. But I wish to remind you again, that though you may think you possess the virtue, yet you must fear being deceived, for the truly humble man is always doubtful of his own virtues; and those which he sees in his neighbour very frequently appear to him to be the most certain and valuable.

CHAPTER XXXIX.

THE SAINT GIVES ADVICE TO ENABLE US TO RESIST CERTAIN TEMPTATIONS OF THE DEVIL, ETC.

BE on your guard, daughters, against certain false humilities, which, with great uneasiness to ourselves, are suggested by the devil, respecting the greatness of our sins; for hereby he is accustomed to disturb souls in many ways, in order to dissuade them from the holy communion, and from using prayer offered up for particular intentions, (for the devil persuades them they are unworthy); and when they approach to receive the most blessed sacrament, the time in which they may receive some favours from God is mostly spent in discussing whether they have been well prepared or not. The enemy prevails so far as to make a soul believe that, because she is such a great sinner, God has forsaken her to such a degree, that she almost doubts of his mercy. Whatever she says seems dangerous, and her actions fruitless, however good they may in reality be. She is quite discouraged, because she has no power to do any good, for that which appears good to her in others, looks bad in herself.

Pay very great attention, daughters, to this point, which I shall now tell you; for at one time it may be humility and virtue to consider ourselves to be bad, and at another time it may be a very great temptation; and because I have experienced this, I know it to be true. However great our humility may be, it does not disturb or disorder the soul, but brings peace, delight, and calmness. Should any one, seeing herself to be wicked, clearly understand that she deserves to be in hell, and can scarcely dare ask for mercy, if this be true humility, this grief has a certain sweetness and satisfaction attendant upon it, so that we would not wish to see ourselves without it: it does not disturb nor straiten the soul, but rather enlarges her, and disposes her for serving God the more fervently. But the other kind of grief troubles and disorders everything, and quite throws the soul into confusion, and is very painful. I believe the devil tries to make us think we have humility, and at the same time (if he can) to make us distrust God. When you find yourselves in this state, avoid, as much as you can, thinking on your own misery, and meditate on the mercy of God, and how much He loves you, and how much He suffered for you. If it be a temptation, you will not be able to do even this; for it will not suffer such thoughts to rest, or fix themselves on anything, unless to torment you the more: it will be much, if you can discover it to be a temptation. The same may be said of indiscreet penances, for thereby the devil tries to make us believe we are more mortified than others, and that we do something. If you conceal yourselves from your confessor or superior; or if they command you something, and you do not obey, this is evidently a temptation: endeavour to obey, though it may cost you more trouble, since herein our greater perfection consists.

The devil uses another dangerous temptation likewise, which is a certain security, by which we imagine that on no account shall we return to our former faults, and the delight of the world, for we already know it, and understand how soon all things will end, and that the things of God give us more solid pleasure. If this temptation come at the beginning, it is very bad, because by this security we become careless, and throw ourselves again into the occasions of sin, and thus we fall. God grant the relapse may not be far worse; for when the devil sees there is a soul which can injure him, and do good to others, he does all he can that she may not rise again. Hence, the more caresses and pledges of His love which our Lord gives you, yet never be so secure as not to fear you may fall again, and keep yourselves also from dangerous occasions.

Be very careful to communicate these favours and consolations to one who can give you light, and do not conceal anything: use such care, that in the beginning and end of your prayer, however sublime your contemplation may be, you may always conclude with the knowledge of yourselves; since if it be from God, even though you be not desirous of it, yet you will do it very often, because it brings humility along with it, and leaves us with more light, in order that we may understand what a nothing we are. I will not enter into more details, because you may meet with many books which will give you the same advice: what I have said, I have said from experience, and have sometimes been in such troubles, and all that can be said cannot afford a perfect security.

What then, O eternal Father! are we to do, but to repair to You, and beseech You, that these our enemies lead us not into temptation? Let public assaults come, for by Your aid we shall better defend ourselves; but these treacheries who can understand? O my God, we need continually beg a remedy of You: suggest to us, O Lord, something whereby we may understand ourselves, and assure ourselves; You know already that many do not go this way; and if they must travel amidst so many fears, much fewer will go. A strange case this is! It seems as if the devil would not tempt those who do not go by the way of prayer, and that all should be more terrified and astonished at one whom, when arrived nearer to perfection, he deceives, than at a hundred thousand whom they see in error and in public sin: one need not examine whether they be good or bad, since this can be seen a thousand leagues off. But indeed they have reason, because there are so very few whom the devil deceives, among those who say the "Our Father," in the manner already mentioned, that like some new and unusual thing, it excites astonishment. It is very usual with men to pass lightly over that which they commonly see, and wonder greatly at that which comes very seldom, or almost never: the devils themselves cause them to wonder, because it suits their purpose well, since they lose many souls by one who has arrived at perfection. I say the miscarriage of such is so astonishing, that I do not marvel at their wondering, because unless it be their own great fault, these go much safer than those who take another way; just as they do who stand on a scaffold to see a bull-fight, rather than those who expose themselves to its horns. This comparison I heard, and it seems to me a very proper one. Be not afraid, sisters, to travel along these ways, of which there are many in prayer, for some will be freed from temptation sooner, by being near our Lord. The way is safe. But you will be sooner free from temptation by being near our Lord, than by being far off. Beg this favour from Him, as you so often do every day in the "Our Father."

CHAPTER XL.

SHE MENTIONS TWO REMEDIES, WHEREBY WE MAY SAFELY PASS AMIDST OUR NUMEROUS TEMPTATIONS, VIZ., THE LOVE AND FEAR OF GOD.

O OUR good Master! give us then some remedy, in order that we may escape the snares of our enemy in so dangerous a war. That which we are able to use, daughters, and which His Majesty has given us, is love and fear; for love will make us quicken our pace, and fear will make us be cautious where we set our feet, in order that we may not fall on the road, where there are so many things to make us stumble, along which we must travel while we live: thus warned, I can safely assure you we shall not be deceived.

You may ask me, by what means you shall discover that you possess these eminent virtues? You have reason for so asking, for a certain and clear proof thereof cannot be given, because were we sure that we possessed love, we should be also sure of our being in a state of grace. But observe, sisters, there are some proofs which it seems even the very blind see; they are not secret, and though you may not wish to hear them, they send forth cries that make a great noise, for there are few who have these in perfection, and therefore they are the more manifest. The love and fear of God are like two strong castles, from which war is made against the world and the devil. Those who really love God, love all good – seek all good – encourage all good – commend all good – always join themselves to the good, and acknowledge and defend the good. They love nothing but truth and things worthy to be loved. Do you think it possible for those who sincerely love God, to love vanities, or riches, or worldly things, or pleasures, or honours? They have no quarrels; they bear no envy – all their object is to please only their Beloved: they are dying with the desire that He would love them, and thus they spend their lives in studying how they may please him most. It is impossible that the love of God, if it be indeed love, should be concealed much. Behold it in St. Paul, in blessed Magdalen. In three days St, Paul began to perceive he was sick with love, and Magdalen perceived it from the first day. And how plainly was it perceived! There is sometimes more and sometimes less; and so love makes itself known, according to its strength: if it be little, it discovers itself a little; if great, it manifests itself greatly: but yet, whether it be little or great, if there be the love of God, it is always seen.

But respecting that which we are now speaking of (viz., the deceit and illusions which the devil causes in contemplatives), in them love is strong; their love is ever great, or they could not be contemplatives: and thus love is readily discovered, and in different ways. Being a great fire, it cannot but cast a great light around. If love, then, be wanting in any, let them walk with great caution: let them know they have good reason to fear: let them endeavour to understand what the matter is, and make use of frequent prayer; let them live in great humility, and beseech our Lord not to lead them into temptation; for truly, if we have not this mark, I fear we shall fall into temptation: but by our walking in humility, endeavouring to know the truth, being obedient to our confessor, and treating with him in sincerity and simplicity (as I have said), God will be faithful. Believe me, that if you conceive no malice, nor discover any pride, then the devil is instrumental in giving you life, by that wherewith he thinks to give you death, though he may seek to delude and affright you. But if you feel this love of God, which I have spoken of, and his fear whereof I shall now speak, be cheerful and quiet, for the devil, in order to disturb your soul that it may not enjoy such great blessings, will suggest a thousand false fears, and will also cause others to raise them in you: for as he cannot gain you, he endeavours at least to make you losers in some way, and those to lose likewise who might gain a great deal by believing that such great favours as He bestows on such a wicked creature, come from God; but they consider it impossible for Him to bestow them, because it seems that sometimes we have forgotten His ancient mercies.

Do you think it matters little to the devil to raise these fears? No, for he does two evils hereby: one, by intimidating those who hear it from approaching to prayer, thinking that they also must be deceived; the other, that many would give themselves more easily to God, by seeing (as I have said), Him to be so good, that it is possible for Him to communicate Himself so much now to sinners. This excites in them a great desire for the like favour; and they have reason, for I know some persons who, encouraged by this, have begun prayer, and in a short time have become true contemplatives, our Lord bestowing on them great favours. Hence, sisters, when you see amongst you one on whom our Lord bestows these favours, praise Him greatly for them; yet do not, therefore, consider her safe, but rather help her with more fervent prayers; for no one can be secure while he lives, being engulfed in the dangers of this tempestuous sea.

Thus you will be sure to discover where this love is, for I do not see how it can be hid. When we love creatures here below, this is said to be impossible, and the more persons endeavour to conceal it, the more it discovers itself; and yet it is a thing so base as not to deserve the name of love, being based upon a mere nothing: it even makes me sick to make use of this comparison; and how then can divine love be concealed, which is so strong? It is a love so just, that it always goes on increasing; and as it has so great an object to love, it sees nothing to induce it to cease loving, and it has many motives to love, all grounded on such a good foundation as that of being rewarded with a return of love. Of this there can be no doubt, for it has been so clearly proved by the great sorrows, and labours and afflictions, and shedding of blood, even to the loss of life, that so we might not have the least doubt of His love!

O my God! What a vast difference must there be, between one love and the other, to a soul who has experienced it! May His Divine Majesty make us understand it, before He takes us out of this life; for it will be a great comfort at the hour of our death, to see we are going to be judged by Him whom we have loved above all things: we may rest secure about the subject of our debts; we are not going to a strange land, but to our own native country, since it is His whom we love so exceedingly, and who loves us: and this love (beyond all the rest) has this advantage over other earthly loves, viz., that in loving Him, we are sure that He loves us.

Remember, my daughters, the gain which this love brings with it, and also what a loss it is when we have not love; for then we fall into the hands of the tempter, into hands so cruel, so hateful of all good, and so bent upon all evil. What will become of the poor soul, which immediately falls into such hands, when she has just been freed from the pains and torments attendant on the pangs of death? What a poor repose does she find! How quickly does she descend into hell, cut into a thousand pieces!100 What a multitude of serpents surround her in various ways! What a dreadful place it must be! What a miserable lodging must be there! If any trouble can scarcely be endured here in this world, by a rich person delicately brought up (and such as these must go there), how will that unfortunate soul, think you, endure such torments for ever? Let us not desire delicacies, daughters, for we are well enough in this house. The poor accommodation is, as it were, but for one night: let us praise God, and force ourselves to do penance in this life. But how sweet will death be to one who has done penance for all his sins, and escapes purgatory! Perhaps even from this time he begins to enjoy heavenly glory. He shall find no fear within him, but solid peace. Now if we do not reach this degree, sisters (since it is possible), it will be great cowardice on our part. Let us beg of God, that if we must suffer immediately after death, it may be in a place where we may endure our sufferings willingly, with the hope of being released from them; and where we may not lose His friendship and grace which He gives us in this life, that so we may not fall into temptation without our knowing it.

CHAPTER XLI.

ON THE FEAR OF GOD, AND HOW BY IT WE MAY AVOID VENIAL SINS.
TO what a length have I spoken! And yet not so much as I could wish, for it is sweet to speak on such a love; what then will it be to possess it! O my Lord! do give it to me; let me not leave this world till I desire nothing in it, nor be capable of loving anything but You: neither let me apply this name of love to what is nothing, since all things are false: if the foundation be such, the building will not last. I know not why we wonder when we hear it said, "This man has not behaved well to me; that other does not love me." I laugh to myself, and say, "Why should he love you, or how else should he requite you?" Hereby you may learn what the world is, since it afterwards punishes you by that very love which you have for it: and this is what torments you, viz., the will is very much displeased that you have kept her so deeply immersed in children's play.101

Let us now speak of the fear of God, though I am not troubled at discoursing for a short time on this love of the world: for I know it well, and wish you to know it also, that you may always keep yourselves from it: but because this would be wandering from my subject, I must not enter upon it.

The fear of God is likewise a subject which is well understood by him who has it, and by those that treat of it, though I wish you to understand that in the beginning it is not so perfect, except in some persons, to whom (as I have said) our Lord gives in a short time so much, and whom He raises to such a high degree in prayer, that it is then clearly discovered. But where the favours do not come in such abundance, that the soul (as I said) is enriched, by one approach, with all virtues, then this fear goes on increasing by little and little its strength, and augmenting each day its forces. It is perceived from the very beginning, for the persons immediately forsake their sins, and the occasions thereof, and their evil company, and other proofs are discovered. But when the soul has already arrived at contemplation (of which we principally speak here), the love as well as the fear of God are very easily discovered; they are not concealed even in the exterior. These persons, though narrowly observed, will not be found to walk carelessly; for however closely we may watch them, our Lord so preserves them that they would not wilfully commit a venial sin, however much it might be for their interest to do so: mortal sins they dread as much as fire. These are the illusions, sisters, which I wish you to fear so much; and continually beseech God that the temptation may not prove so strong, so as to offend Him, but that it may be proportioned to the strength which He shall give us to overcome it; if your conscience be pure, it can do you little or no harm. This is the point to our purpose; this is the fear which I desire may never be taken away from us, and which will avail us in all our wants.

O! how very important is it, in order that we may chain up those infernal slaves, that we should not offend God, since at last all must serve Him, however unwilling they may be; they perhaps are forced to do so: we do it willingly. Hence, if our Lord be pleased, they will all be kept within bounds, and they shall be able to do nothing to hurt us, however much they may bait us with temptations, and lay secret snares for us. Treasure up this instruction in your interior, for it is very necessary that you be not negligent, till you find in yourselves so strong a resolution of not offending God, that you would lose a thousand lives rather than commit one mortal sin; and as to venial sins, be extremely careful not to commit them wilfully. But who does not commit many which are involuntary? There is, however, one kind of advertence so deliberate and another so sudden, that committing a venial sin and adverting to it are almost the same thing. But may God deliver us from a wilful sin, however small it may be; for I do not understand how we can have the boldness to act in opposition to so great a Lord, even though it were but in a very small matter: how much more when there is nothing little which offends so immense a Majesty, especially as we see that He stands looking at us:102 hence this seems to me to be a premeditated sin, as if one said: "Lord, though this sin may displease You, yet I will commit it: I now see You behold it, and you dislike it; this I am well aware of: but I prefer to follow my own fancy and passion rather than do Your will." Now, in a case of this nature, is there anything little? To me the fault seems not little, but great, and very great too.

Consider, sisters, for the love of God, that if you wish to obtain this fear of God, it is very important you should understand how grievous it is to offend God; and reflect upon this truth very frequently in your mind, for our eternal life depends upon it. Strive much more to have this virtue deeply rooted in your soul; and till we possess it, we must continually use the greatest care, and withdraw ourselves from all the occasions of sin, and from all company that does not help us to approach nearer to God. Take care, whatever you do, to subdue your will: and endeavour also, that whatever is spoken may tend to edification: fly from that company, where the discourse is not of God. Much is required on our part, in order deeply to imprint this fear in the soul, though if there be love, it103 is soon obtained. But when the soul has discovered in herself this strong resolution of which I have spoken, viz., that she would not commit an offence against God for any consideration, though she may sometimes fall afterwards (for we are frail, and have no reason to trust ourselves, since when we seem to be strong, then we ought to be the least confident in ourselves; for whence should our confidence come? It must be from God), let her not be discouraged, but endeavour immediately to ask pardon. When once we perceive in ourselves what I have mentioned, then it is not necessary to be so pensive and scrupulous, since our Lord will assist us, and our good habit will help us not to offend Him; and we shall go on with a holy liberty, treating with whomsoever it shall be proper, though they may not be good persons; for those who were poison to you, before you had this true fear of God, and were instrumental in destroying the soul, will often give you afterwards an opportunity of loving God and of praising Him for having delivered you from what you were in great danger. And if formerly you were instrumental in increasing their weaknesses, you will now help them to refrain from them, because they are in your presence; for without your seeking this honour, you will find it.

I often praise our Lord; and considering how it happens that, without speaking a word, a servant of God may sometimes stop the discourses which are uttered against God, I conclude it must be in the same manner as when we have a friend, there is always such respect shown him, as to induce us not to do him, in his absence, any injury before one who is known to be acquainted with him; and since this person here is in the state of grace, that same grace must certainly cause respect to be be given him, however poor he may be, and that no rudeness be offered to him in a matter which it is known he feels so much; viz., offending God.104 The truth is, I know not the reason, but this is very common. Hence, you should not afflict yourselves too much; for if the soul once begin to grow timorous, it is a very bad disposition as to all kinds of good, and sometimes she becomes scrupulous; and lo! here it is unserviceable, both for herself and others; and suppose she fall not into scrupulosity, it may be well for herself, but she will not bring many souls to God, when people see so much fear and anxiety. Such is our nature, that it frightens and stifles persons, and (through fear of the like trouble), they relinquish the desire of taking the course which you take, though they clearly perceive it to be more conducive to virtue.

Hence also another evil arises, viz., that in judging of others (who do not go that way, but with greater sanctity, in order to benefit their neighbours, converse with freedom, and without reservedness), they will immediately seem to you imperfect. If they use a holy alacrity, it will seem a laxity of morals; especially in us, who want learning, and who know not how far we may converse with others without sin, it is a very dangerous thing. It is also very bad to be continually tempted (and this is unpalatable, because it is to the prejudice of our neighbour), and to fancy, that except all persons scruple in the same way that you do, they do not go on so well. There is also another evil, viz., that in some matters of which you are to speak, and it is but reasonable you should do so, you will, through a dread of exceeding in something, not dare to speak; or perhaps you will speak well of that, which it were better you should hate and abhor. Endeavour, therefore, sisters, as much as you can, to be affable, without displeasing God; and so conduct yourselves to all persons with whom you may have to speak, that they may love your conversation, and admire your manner of life and discourse, and that they may not be terrified at virtue. This is of great importance for religious women; the more holy they are, the more sociable they should be with the sisters; for though you may be much troubled, because all their discourses are not such as you might desire, yet never be unfriendly with them, and thus you will be loved, and do them much good. We ought to endeavour, as far as we can, to be affable, and to please and content those persons with whom we converse, and especially our sisters.

Endeavour, therefore, my daughters, to understand this truth, that God does not regard such trifles as you imagine; and let not your soul and spirit be too restrained, for they may lose many advantages. Let your intention be right, and the will determined (as I have said) not to offend God: but let not your soul hide herself in a corner; for, instead of acquiring more sanctity, she will contract many imperfections, into which the devil will drive her by other ways; and, as I said, she will not benefit herself or others so much as she might. Here you see how with these two virtues, the love and fear of God, we may travel along this road gently and quietly, though, as the fear must precede, we must not travel carelessly; for while we live we cannot enjoy security, because it would be too dangerous: and this our instructor understood, who at the end of this prayer, utters these words to His Father, "But deliver us from evil," being one who well understood their necessity.

CHAPTER XLII.

ON THE WORDS, "DELIVER US PROM EVIL."

METHINKS our good Jesus has reason to desire His Father to deliver us from evil (that is, from the dangers and troubles of this life), both for our own interest, because, while we live, we are exposed to great danger; and for His own interest, since we already see how weary He was of this life, when at His last supper He said to His apostles, "With desire have I desired to eat this Pasch with you:" since we see how sweet death was to Him. But now, those who are a hundred years old are not weary of life, but always desire to live: but we do not lead so miserable a life, nor endure such sufferings and such poverty as His Majesty did. What was His whole life but a continual death, as He always had before His eyes that cruel death His enemies were one day to make Him suffer? And yet this was the least part of His sorrow, when compared with the innumerable offences which He saw would be committed against His Father, and with the immense multitude of souls that would be lost. If this consideration be to one of us in this world so great a torment, provided we have any love, what must it have been to the boundless and immense love of our Lord! What great reason, then, had He to beg of His Father to deliver Him now from so many afflictions and evils, and to grant Him eternal repose in His Kingdom, since He was the lawful Heir thereof? Hence it was that He added "Amen;" in which, because by this word all prayers usually end, I think our Lord besought His Father that we might be delivered from all evil for ever: and so I beseech our Lord to deliver me from all evil, since by living longer I do not discharge what I owe; but it may be, I plunge myself deeper every day. And what is not to be endured, O Lord! is this, that I cannot know for certain I love you,105 or whether my desires are pleasing to you.

O my Lord and my God, deliver me now from all evil, and be pleased to conduct me there, where all good things are. What do those expect here in this world, to whom you have given some knowledge of what a nothing this world is, and who have a lively faith of that glory which their heavenly Father has reserved for them? To ask for this with an intense desire, and a firm resolution to enjoy God, is a sure sign for "Contemplatives" to know, that the favours which they receive in prayer come from God. Hence, let those who have it value it highly. When I ask it, I do not do so in this manner (I mean, it is not to be understood in this sense); but as I have lived so ill, I am now afraid to live any longer, and am weary of so many crosses.

No wonder that those who receive Divine consolations long to be there, where they receive them not by drops; and that they do not wish to remain in a world, where so many obstacles prevent them from enjoying so great a good; and that they desire to be there, where the Sun of Justice never sets. Everything will look dark and obscure to them, when they have seen earthly joys: and hence, I wonder how they can live. He cannot surely live with any pleasure, who has begun to enjoy God, and who has already received here the promise of His kingdom, wherein he is to live – not after his own will, but according to the will of his King.

O! what a different kind of life must this be, where death is not wished for! How differently inclined is our will here, from God's will! His will wishes us to love the truth, and we love a lie;

it wishes us to love the Eternal, and we love things which pass away; it wishes us to love objects which are noble and sublime, and we love things which are base and earthly; it wishes us to seek what is certain, and we love here what is doubtful. All is vanity, daughters, except to beseech God to deliver us for ever from all evil; and though we may not express this desire with very great perfection, yet let us force ourselves to make our demand. And what does it cost us to ask much, since we ask One who is powerful? It would be a shame to ask a great emperor for a farthing. But in order that we may succeed, let us give up our will to His, since we have already surrendered it to our superiors. May His name be always hallowed in heaven and on earth, and may His will always be done in me. Amen.

See now, sisters, how our Lord has relieved me of the trouble, since He Himself teaches both you and me, the "way"106 which I began to show you; and He has made me understand what great things we ask, when we say this heavenly prayer. May He be blessed for ever, since it is certain I never imagined this prayer comprised such great mysteries. You have already seen how it includes in itself the whole way of perfection, from the very commencement, till God engulfs the soul in Himself, and makes her drink abundantly of the fountain of Living Water, which flows at the end of the road: and it is true, that as I have come out of this fountain (I mean this prayer), I am now unable to go any further. It seems our Lord was pleased to make us, sisters, understand the great consolations which are contained therein, and that this prayer is exceedingly useful for persons who cannot read: did they understand it well they might gain much instruction from it, and much comfort to themselves.

Let us profit then, sisters, by the humility with which our good Master teaches us; let us also beseech Him to pardon me for having presumed to speak on such sublime subjects, since I did so through obedience. His Majesty knows well, that I was not capable of writing on the subject, had He not taught me what I have said. Thank Him for it, you my sisters, since He has certainly assisted me, being moved by the humility wherewith you requested me to write, and desired to be instructed by so miserable a creature. If the Rev. Dr. Bañez, 107 my confessor (to whom I shall deliver the manuscript before you see it), should perceive that it will promote your good, and shall allow you to read it, I shall receive comfort from your consolation. But should the manuscript be unfit for any one's perusal, you will accept my good-will inasmuch as I have endeavoured to comply with your request; and I shall consider myself sufficiently rewarded for the trouble I have taken in writing (not certainly in practising) what I have said. May God be eternally blessed and praised, from whom cometh all the good we speak, and think, and do. Amen, Amen.

LAUS DEO.

CONCEPTIONS OF DIVINE LOVE.

PREFACE.

FATHER GRACIAN informs us that, among the various books which St. Teresa wrote by the express command of her superiors, one was composed by her, consisting of very sublime meditations on Divine Love, on Prayer, and other heroic virtues, in which certain words of the Book of Canticles were explained; hence the title, "Conceptions of Divine Love on some Words of the Book of Canticles,"108 The Saint herself, at the end of the seventh Chapter, gives us the reason why she composed the book. "My design when I began," she says, "was to let you understand, daughters, how you might delight yourselves when you hear any words of the Canticles, and that you might meditate on the great mysteries contained in them, though in your own opinion they may seem obscure," &c.

Unfortunately, only seven Chapters remain of this work, which, judging from the four Chapters I have translated, must in every respect have equalled her other admirable books. When the Saint had finished the work, she showed it to one of her confessors,109 who, thinking it a dangerous thing for a woman especially to write on so difficult a part of the Holy Scripture, commanded her instantly to commit the book to the flames. St. Teresa did so, with her usual heroic obedience and humility. But our Lord was pleased that a certain nun should previously copy the seven first chapters, which we now possess.

However good may have been the motives of the confessor, who commanded the Saint to burn the work; yet I think he was bound first to have perused the whole of the book, before he pronounced judgment upon it. He would then have seen that it was not a Commentary but only an Explanation of certain words in the Canticles, which she had either heard in sermons, or read in her Breviary. Deeply, then, do we deplore the loss of such a book, and sincerely do we regret that the confessor gave such a rash command to the Saint.110

The manuscript of the seven Chapters came into the hands of Father Gracian, who published them at Brussels, in 1612. Another edition appeared at Valentia the following year, and a third was published at Madrid in 1615.

The Saint seems to have composed the book about the year 1517; because in it she refers to the "Castle of the Soul," which was written in the same year. (See Bollandists, p. 454.)

D'Andilly expresses his highest admiration for the fragment we possess. It certainly abounds in most noble and sublime sentiments, which cannot but excite the reader's affections, and enkindle the love of God in his heart.

J. DALTON.

CONCEPTIONS OF DIVINE LOVE.

CHAPTER I.

LET HIM KISS ME WITH THE KISS OF HIS MOUTH, FOR THY BREASTS ARE BETTER THAN WINE." (Chap. i. v. l.)

I HAVE frequently observed, that the soul (according to what she understands here) seems to be discoursing with one person, and asking peace from another, because she says, "Let him kiss me with the kiss of his mouth," and immediately she seems to say to him with whom she is speaking, "Thy breasts are better;" I do not understand how this is, and not understanding it gives me great consolation; for truly the soul is not so much to consider or respect her God in the things which it seems we may comprehend here below by our poor understanding, as in those things which we cannot in any way understand. I therefore earnestly recommend you, when you read any book, or hear a sermon, or meditate on the mysteries of our holy faith, that you do not fatigue yourselves about what you cannot perfectly understand, nor tire your brain with subtile discussions. This is not fit for women, nor often even for men. When our Lord wishes us to understand the subject, He does it without any trouble to us. This I say with regard to men and women, who are called upon to maintain the truth by their learning: and as for those whom our Lord has appointed to explain it to us, it is evident they must labour, and they gain thereby. But we must take what God gives us with simplicity; and what He does not give us, we must not torment ourselves about, but rejoice in considering that our God and our Lord is so great, that one of His words may include a thousand mysteries in it, and thus we do not understand it properly. No matter if it were in Latin, in Hebrew, or in Greek: it is the case even in our own language. How many things are there in the Psalms, which, when explained to us in Spanish, are as obscure as if they were in Latin? Be always, then, on your guard against perplexing your mind or tiring yourselves, since women need no more than what suits their capacity; and in this respect God confers a favour upon us.

When His Majesty is pleased to give it to us without care or trouble, we shall discover the meaning; as to the rest, let us humble ourselves, and (as I have said) be glad to have so great a Lord, whose words cannot sometimes be understood, even when spoken in our own tongue.

You may think that in these Canticles there are some words which might be expressed in another way: I do not wonder at this, considering our dulness, and therefore I have heard some persons say, that they avoid even hearing them. O! how great is our misery! For, as venomous creatures turn all they eat into poison, so it is with us here, in spite of the great favours our Lord bestows upon us, in allowing us to understand the great blessings which the soul enjoys that loves Him, and in His encouraging her, that so she may be able to address His Majesty, and regale herself with Him, whereby we ought to conceive a greater love for God, yet we give meanings to those words, corresponding with the cold affections of divine love which we have attained.

O my Lord! what bad use we make of all the blessings you have conferred upon us. Your Majesty seeks out ways and means to declare the love you have for us; and we, because little experienced in loving you, so undervalue it, that our thoughts, not accustomed to it, tend to those things which always occupy them, and neglect considering the great mysteries contained in those words, which are inspired by the Holy Ghost: these we avoid.

What do we require more to inflame us with His love, than to consider that this mode of speaking[11] is not used without great reason? I remember well I once heard a religious man make a very excellent sermon and the greater part of his discourse was about those caresses of the Spouse with God; but the sermon caused great laughing among the audience; and everything that he said was taken in such bad part (for he spoke on love, being commanded to do so by his Superior, and to preach on certain words of the Canticles), that I was astonished. I see clearly, that (as I have said) it is owing to our having too little practice in the love of God, which makes us think a soul cannot speak with God in such expressions.

But I know some persons, who have, on the contrary, gained such great benefit thereby, and so much consolation and security from their fears, as often to give our Lord particular thanks, for leaving so salutary a remedy for souls who love Him with a fervent love, and who see and understand how God abases Himself; but had they not had experience thereof, they would still be fearful. I know a person who for many years lived in great fear, and nothing could comfort her, till our Lord was pleased she should hear certain words from the Canticles, and by them she understood her soul was going on well. I think (as I said) that the soul, being enamoured of Christ her Spouse, suffers all these delights – swoonings – deaths – joys – and afflictions with Him, after she has left for His sake the pleasures of the world, and has now entirely resigned herself into His hands. And this is not only in words (as it happens in some), but with a love in every way sincere, and perfected by deeds.

O! my daughters, what a good paymaster God is; and you have a Lord and a Spouse from whom nothing escapes, for He sees and understands it; and, therefore, though they may be very trifling matters, do not neglect, for love of Him, to do all you can, because His Majesty will reward you for them, as if they were great, since He only considers the love wherewith you do them.

I conclude, then, with this advice: that you never detain yourselves longer than I told you, for anything you do not understand, either in the Holy Scriptures, or in the mysteries of our faith; neither terrify yourselves at the amorous words, which you may hear passing in them between God and the soul. The love He has had, and still has for us, astonishes and confounds me the more, considering what we are; and knowing and seeing there is no exaggeration of words whereby He might prove His love for us, which He has not exceeded by deeds. When you arrive there, I beseech you to stay a little, and think on what He has discoursed to us and done for us; then we plainly perceive, that the love He bears us was so powerful and strong as to make Him suffer so much: what more words can be required to astonish us again?

But to return to what I was saying, there must needs be great things and deep mysteries in these words of such immense value, since learned men have told me so, upon my requesting them to explain to me what the Holy Ghost meant to say therein; but yet they did not give any meaning which was quite satisfactory. Hence, you may suppose my pride is very excessive in undertaking to explain to you something out of the "Canticles," but this is not my intention (however little may be my humility), nor do I think I shall be able to arrive at their true meaning.

My intention here is, that as I receive consolation in what our Lord allows me to understand, when I hear something mentioned from the "Cantiles," so I desire to tell you that which may perhaps comfort you and me; and if what I shall say do not agree with the meaning, it is at least suitable to my purpose, since as long as we do not depart from what the Church holds, and the Saints believe (and the learned, who understand the matter, will examine what I say before you see it in print), I think our Lord will allow us to do this, as indeed He does when, meditating on His sacred passion, we often think on those labours and torments which doubtless our Lord there suffered, besides what is written by the Evangelists. If this be not done through curiosity (as I mentioned at first), but if we receive whatever His Majesty shall enable us to understand, I consider it certain He is not displeased at our thus consoling and delighting ourselves in His words and works. In the same manner as it would delight a king to see a shepherd, on whom He had bestowed some favour, expressing astonishment on viewing his embroidered robe, and pondering how it was made, and what it was; so we women are not to be so hindered from enjoying the riches of our Lord, and from speaking of them, as to conceal them entirely, thinking that thereby we do well. We should rather first show our writings to learned men; and if they approve them, then communicate them to others. Neither do I think (God knows well) that I succeed in what I write; but I only do as the shepherd does, whom I have mentioned above; I rejoice to communicate my meditations to you, as to my daughters, though I do so with many imperfections.

And so I begin with the assistance of my King, and likewise with the leave of my confessor. God grant, that as it has pleased Him to enable me to effect something in other things which I have said, or rather His Majesty by me (perhaps in order to do you good), so I may succeed in this also. But if not, I shall consider the time well spent which I employ in writing and musing with my own thoughts on a subject so divine, that I do not deserve to hear it spoken of.

Methinks that in this which I mentioned at first, the Spouse speaks with a third person, and that the Holy Ghost gives us to understand there are two natures in Christ, the one divine, and the other human. I do not wish to dwell on this point, because my intention is to speak of that which I hope may do us good, who treat of prayer (though everything serves to encourage and astonish the soul, which loves our Lord with ardent desires). His Majesty knows well, that though I have sometimes heard the explanation of these words, which, at my request, have been explained to me, yet it was not frequently, and I do not now remember anything of the explanation; for I have a bad memory, so that I can say nothing except what our Lord shall teach me, 112 and what I think will suit my purpose. I do not remember having ever heard any explanation of this beginning, "Let him kiss me with the kiss of his mouth."

O my Lord and my God! what words are these for a worm to utter to its Maker! Blessed be thou, O Lord! who by so many ways hast instructed us. But who, my King! dare utter these words, but by your permission? This astonishes one; and some perhaps may be astonished at my saying that none can utter them. They will say, "I am a fool; for the Spouse does not wish to speak so, since the words 'kiss' and 'mouth' have many significations: it is also evident we should not speak such words to God, and therefore it would be good if simple people did not read these things." I acknowledge these words may have many meanings; but the soul that is so inflamed with love as to make her a fool, desires nothing else but to utter these words, that God would not take away His love from her. O Lord! what are we astonished at? Is not the deed more to be admired [than the words?] Do we not unite ourselves with the Most Holy Sacrament? I was likewise thinking whether the Spouse here requested the favour which Christ afterwards bestowed upon us, when

He became our food. I also considered whether she desired that close and intimate union, which was afterwards effected by God becoming man. and that friendship which He contracted with mankind; for it is evident that a kiss is a sign of peace, and of great friendship between two persons. May our Lord help us to understand how many kinds of peace there are.

One thing I wish to say, before I proceed further, and in my opinion it is important, though it might be more seasonable at another time; but I will mention now, lest I might forget it (for I consider it most certain), and it is this, that many persons will come to the Most Holy Sacrament in mortal sin, and would to God I were deceived; and if they should hear a soul, which is consumed through her love of God, utter these words, they would be greatly surprised, and would consider it a great boldness; at least, I am sure they would not express themselves in these or such-like words that are found in the "Canticles." Love utters them; and as these people have it not, they may read the "Canticles" every day, yet will not practise them, or even dare to pronounce them; for truly the very hearing of them excites their fear, because such words carry with them a great majesty. Thou, indeed, O Lord! art very majestic in the Most Holy Sacrament; but as they have not a lively but a dead faith, these persons beholding you so humble under the appearance of bread, and as you say nothing to them, because they do not deserve to hear you, presume so much on this account to receive you.

Hence these words, taken literally, would of themselves excite fear in one, if he that utters them were in his perfect senses. But they do not terrify those whom our Love and our Lord have ravished out of themselves. You will pardon me for saying this, and even more, though it be a boldness. And, O my Lord! if a kiss implies peace and friendship, why do not souls beg of You to ratify it with them? What better thing can we ask of You? That which I request of You, my Lord! is to grant me this peace "with a kiss of Your mouth." This, my daughters, is the highest kind of petition, as I shall afterwards explain to you.

CHAPTER II.

SHE MENTIONS NINE KINDS OF FALSE PEACE, IMPERFECT LOVE, AND DECEITFUL PRAYER.

MAY God deliver you from many kinds of peace which worldlings have; God grant we may never experience them, for they raise a perpetual war. There is one peace, when a worldly man goes on very quietly, plunged in great sins, and yet so secure in his vices, that his conscience does not trouble him in anything. This peace you have already heard, that he and the devil are friends, and that as long as he lives he will not make war upon him, because in order to avoid such a war, and not for the love of God, they would return a little to our Lord and correct themselves. But those who act in this manner will never continue long in His service; and the devil, knowing this, continues to give them pleasure, and they return again to his friendship, till he makes them understand how false their peace was. Of these I have no occasion to speak: let them enjoy their quiet; I trust in God so great an evil will not be found amongst us.

The devil may also begin [to attack us] in little things, by another kind of peace; and thus, my daughters, whilst we live we must always fear ourselves. When a Religious begins to grow relax in some things, which in themselves seem small, and if she continue in this state a long time and find no remorse of conscience, this is a false peace; and thereby the devil makes her very bad. Such is breaking any rule of the constitution, in itself perhaps no sin, and carelessness in performing what our superior commands us, though this may be done without malice; still he in reality holds the place of God, and it is good always to obey him, since it is for this purpose we have come here; and we should continually notice what is his will in any other little matters which happen, and though in themselves they may seem to be no sins, yet they are imperfections, and will infallibly happen, because we are women, I do not deny it: but what I mean to say is, that they are sorry for them, when they commit them, and know they have done wrong: for otherwise (as I was saying) the devil may be glad of it, and by little and little he may go on making a soul insensible. Regarding these small matters, I tell you, daughters, that when the devil shall be able to attain his end, he has gained a great deal.

And because I am afraid to proceed further, therefore take great care, for the love of God, since there must be a war in this life; for, among so many enemies, it is not possible for us to stand with our hands across; but we must be continually on our guard, and observe how we proceed both in our interior and exterior. I also tell you, that though in prayer our Lord may confer favours upon you, yet when you are not engaged in it, there will come a thousand stumbling-blocks and little occasions; as, for instance, breaking this rule through negligence, not observing another, besides internal troubles and temptations. I do not say that this war is always to continue, or that it is very common; nor yet that troubles and temptations must never happen, for sometimes they are rather great favours of God, and thus the soul improves: in this world it is not possible to become angels; for this is not our nature.

The truth is, I am not troubled when I see a soul in very great temptations, because if she have a love and fear of our Lord, she will gain a great deal: this I know. But if I see any persons always going on quiet, and without any kind of war (for I have met with some who, though I did not see them offend our Lord, always kept me in fear), I am never secure of them, and therefore I do often prove and try them all I can (since the devil does not), that so they may see what they are. I have indeed met with few such; but it is possible that, our Lord having raised a soul to a high degree of contemplation, one may acquire this method of proceeding, and possess a certain internal joy. Still, for my part, I consider that they know it not: and having examined the subject, I perceive that sometimes they have their little combats also, but these are more rare.

Yet so it is, that I do not envy these souls, for I have seriously considered the case. I see that they advance much further, who sustain the combat I have mentioned, and have as sublime prayer in matters of perfection as we are able to conceive in this world.

Let us now leave those souls who are so much improved and mortified, after having endured this for many years, that they find themselves, as it were, dead to the world; the rest are commonly accustomed to enjoy peace, yet not in such a way as not to perceive the faults they commit, and be very sorry for them. Hence you see, daughters, that God conducts us in many ways: but I am always fearful for you (as I said), when you have no remorse for a fault which you commit; since even for a venial sin, I think you would be grieved to the heart, as, thanks be to God, I believe you now feel.

One thing observe and remember for my sake. If when a person is alive, you prick her even very slightly with a needle, does she not feel it? Or with a thorn, however small it may be, does it not pain her? Now if the soul be not dead, but have a strong love of God, is it not a great grace for her to feel grieved for any little thing she does, which is not in accordance with our professions and obligations? O! what an honour it is for a soul, to whom God gives this solicitude, to make a bed of roses and flowers for His Divine Majesty! It is quite impossible He should refuse to come and regale Himself with her, even though late. O God! though we have left the world, what are we doing in a monastery? Wherefore came we here? In what can we employ ourselves better than making in our souls lodgings for our Spouse, since we take Him for such, when we make our profession?

Let scrupulous persons understand me, for I do not speak of a fault committed once, or of faults that cannot be known, nor always perceived; but I speak of one who commits them very frequently, without making any account of them, esteeming them as nothing, experiencing no remorse of conscience, nor endeavouring to correct them. I say again, that this is a dangerous peace, and beware of it.

What, then, will become of those who give way to frequent relaxations of their rule? God grant there may be none such. The devil may, however, introduce the evil in many ways, since God permits it on account of our sins. But there is no necessity to speak of it here. I thought it useful to say a little, in order to put you on your guard against it.

Let us now pass on to the peace and friendship which God begins to show us in prayer, on which I shall say what His Majesty may give me to understand. But I thought fit to speak a little to you at first of the peace which the world gives, and our own sensuality affords us. Though what I may explain is in many respects better explained by others who have written on the subject; yet being poor, you may perhaps want money to purchase the books, and you may find no one to bestow an alms upon you; but what I say is kept in the monastery, and you can all see it together.

A person may be deceived many ways, in the peace which the world gives. I will mention some of these ways, that we may bewail our misery exceedingly, who through our own fault do not arrive at an intimate, but are content with a slight friendship with God. O Lord! would that we did not thus content ourselves, but remember the reward is great and without end; and that having already arrived at this great familiarity, God even here below bestows this happiness upon us; and many tarry at the foot of the mountain, who might ascend the top! In other little things which I have written for you, I have often told you this; and now I repeat it again, and beseech you that our thoughts may always be courageous, for hereby it may happen God will give you grace, that your affections may be so likewise. Believe me, this is very important.

There are then some persons who have obtained the friendship of the Lord, for they make a good confession of their sins, and repent of them; but scarcely have two days passed by, before they return to them again. Now, you may be sure, this is not the peace and friendship which the Spouse desires. Daughters, always endeavour not to be going every time to your confessor, to acquaint him with the same fault. It is true we cannot be without them; but at least let them be changed, that they may not take root; for then they will be eradicated with more difficulty, and it may even happen that from them may spring many other roots. If we water every day a plant or shrub that we have set, it will grow so large that we shall afterwards require a spade and mattock to dig it up. And so it seems to me it is the same thing when we daily commit the same fault, however little it may be, if we do not correct it; but if it should be allowed to grow only one or ten days, and then be rooted up immediately, all will be easy. This amendment you must beg of our Lord in prayer, for of ourselves we can do little: we should rather add to our former entreaties, and in that dreadful judgment at the hour of deaths they will help us, and those especially whom the judge chose in this life for His spouses.

O great condescension of God! which excites and induces us to walk on with diligence. Strive to please this Lord our King. But how ill do those persons repay His friendship, who so soon again become His mortal enemies! Great, indeed, is the mercy of God! What friend shall we find so patient? When a breach happens even for once between two friends, it is never forgotten, and never are they such friends again as they were before. But how many times do we violate our friendship with God! How many years does He wait for us in this manner! Blessed be Thou, O my Lord! who waitest for us with such great compassion, that you seem to forget your own greatness, in order not to punish so perfidious a treason as ours! This appears a dangerous state to me; for though the mercy of God be such as we see it is, yet we often observe that many die without confession. May God in his mercy deliver you from so dreadful a fate.

There is another peace and friendship of the world less evil than this, viz., that of persons who are careful not to offend God mortally. But these people keep themselves from mortal sins; yet, I think, from time to time they sin almost mortally, for they take no care to guard against venial sins, though they commit many in the day; and thus they come very near to mortal sin. "Do you scruple at this?" they say; and many speak thus (for I have heard them), "This holy water is sufficient, and so are the remedies which our Mother, the Church, uses." O! how are these words to be deplored! For God's sake, daughters, use great caution here, so as never to become careless about committing a venial sin (however small it may be), under the pretext of such a remedy; for it is very important always to have so clean a conscience, that nothing may hinder you from praying to our Lord, to grant you that perfect friendship which the Spouse desires.

But this is not what I have now mentioned, for that is a very suspicious friendship on many grounds, because it tends to pleasures which disturb the soul, and disposes us to great tepidity; nor do such persons know well whether they commit a venial or a mortal sin. May God deliver you from this; for, because they imagine they are not under the guilt of great sins, as they see others are, they continue in this false peace. It is not, likewise, a sign of perfect humility to judge our neighbours to be worse than ourselves, since it may be that they are much better, because they bewail their sins, and this sometimes with great sorrow, and perhaps with more firm resolutions than we do; and besides, many even go further, so as never to offend God afterwards, either in great or little things. But these others, thinking they do not commit a grievous offence, give greater scope to their delights, and taking care that their vocal prayers should for the most part be properly said, they are not carried to any higher degrees.

There is another kind of peace and friendship which our Lord bestows on some persons, who, though they would not absolutely offend Him in anything, yet do not so carefully avoid the occasions of sin. Now, though these individuals often observe their appointed times for prayer, and our Lord gives them tears and tenderness; still they do not wish to give up the pleasures of this life, but prefer to have an easy and delightful life, for they think that this quiet suits them well for living at their ease.

This life carries with it many changes, and it will be very difficult for such as these to persevere in virtue; for as they do not withdraw themselves from the delights of the world, they will soon become relaxed in the way of our Lord, because there are powerful enemies to turn us aside from it.

This, daughters, is not the friendship our Spouse wishes; nor do you desire it, but always keep yourselves even from the least occasion, however small, if you wish your soul to advance in perfection, and to live with security. I know not why I mention these things, except that you may understand the dangers to which you expose yourselves, by not resolutely quitting the pleasures of the world, in order to avoid many faults and many troubles.

But there are so many ways by which our Lord begins to enter into friendship with souls, that it seems to me it would be endless to mention those I have known, 112 though I am a woman. What then may not confessors tell us, and those persons who more particularly converse with such souls? Some of them quite astonish me, because nothing seems to be wanting to them for being the friends of God. I will give you some account of one individual especially, with whom I conversed not long ago very familiarly.

She was a person who loved to communicate very frequently, and never did she speak ill of any one. She had tenderness, and lived in continual solitude, for she dwelt in a house by herself; she was of such a sweet disposition, that nothing could make her angry, which was a very great perfection; she uttered no unbecoming language; had never been married, neither was she now of an age to marry; and besides, she had suffered great afflictions, with her usual peace and tranquility. When I noticed these good qualities, I thought they were signs of a soul far advanced, and of very high prayer. At first, I esteemed her exceedingly, because I saw she committed no offence against God, and I heard from others also, that she was careful not to commit any. But when I conversed a little more with her, I began to perceive that all went on well with her till her interest or self-love were touched; then her conscience was not so tender, but gross enough: for I discovered that though she suffered all things that were said to her with patience, yet she still adhered to points of honour or esteem, being thus immersed in this misery which held her captive. She was also so much addicted to listening and inquiring after what was said and done in the world, that I wondered how such a person could continue one hour alone: she was likewise very fond of her own ease. All her actions she gilded over, and excused from sin; and, according to the reasons she gave, I thought people would have wronged her in some things, had they judged otherwise: but in other matters (as the case was evident) they could not well understand her proceedings. She quite captivated me, and almost every one considered her to be a saint. But I afterwards saw that, respecting the persecutions which she mentioned as having suffered, she ought not to have represented herself as being free from all blame; and I did not envy her way of living, nor her sanctity. She and two more whom I have seen in my life, who were saints in their own opinion, have terrified me more than all the sinners I ever saw. Beseech our Lord to give us light; and, daughters, praise Him exceedingly who has brought you to these monasteries, where, how much soever the devil labours, he cannot delude you in the same way that he does those who live in their own houses.

There are souls who seem to want nothing for soaring to heaven itself, since, in their own opinion, they attain perfection in everything; but no one can understand them, because in monasteries I have never failed to understand them, since they cannot do there what they like, but only what they are commanded; and though in a secular life they might sincerely desire to understand themselves, because they are desirous of pleasing God; yet they cannot, because in whatever they do they follow their own will; or if sometimes they deny themselves, still they are not much accustomed to such mortification. Some persons, however, are to be excepted, to whom for many years our Lord has given light, to enable them to find one who can understand them, and whom they can obey, and whose great humility carries with it little self-confidence; and though they may be more learned, yet do they resign themselves to another's judgment.

Others there are who have left all for our Lord, having neither house, nor estate, nor any desire for pleasures (for they are penitents), nor for the things of the world, since our Lord has already enlightened them to know how miserable they are; but yet they place a great value on reputation, and do nothing which is not very pleasing to men, as well as to God. What great discretion and prudence! These two qualities but ill agree together; and the misfortune is, that without perceiving their own weakness, they prize their own character with the world, almost more than their friendship with God. These souls are generally affected with the least thing which is spoken about them; though it may be true, it disturbs them: they do not carry their cross, but drag it along the ground, and thus it burdens them, and wearies them, and torments them exceedingly: for if the cross be loved, it is carried with delight; this is certain. This then is not the friendship which the Spouse expects; and therefore, my daughters (since you have taken the vow I mentioned in the beginning). be very careful you dwell not in the world. Everything is only a torment to you; if you have forsaken more than others, forsake the world also, its amusements, its pleasures, and riches; all of which, though false, do yet please some men. What do you fear? Know that you do not well understand the matter, since for obtaining one favour which by a word the world can bestow upon you, you must first load yourselves with a thousand cares and obligations, of which cares there is such abundance (if we desire to please worldlings), that to avoid being tedious, it would be out of place here, and indeed quite impossible to mention them.

There are other souls (and with these I conclude), in whom, if you observe them, you will find certain signs by which it is manifest that they begin to advance; and yet they stop in the midst of their course. Though these neither care for the words of men, nor for their own reputation; yet they are not accustomed to mortification and to the denial of their own will: and hence it seems the world has not departed from their body; and even though they seem prepared to suffer all things, and already to be saints, yet in important matters concerning the honour of our Lord, they look to their own honour, and neglect that of God. They do not perceive this fault, nor imagine that they now fear the world, but only God; still they fear what may happen, and that a good work114 might be the beginning of some great evil, which it seems the devil suggests to them; they prophesy a thousand years beforehand what is to come! These are not the souls to imitate the act of St. Peter, and cast themselves into the sea; or what many other Saints have done, to risk their rest and their very lives for the good of souls. They wish by a quiet way to attract souls to God, but not to expose themselves to danger; nor does faith effect much in them, because they always follow their own resolutions. One thing I have observed, viz., that out of religion, we see but few in the world who trust in God for their support. I know but two persons who have such a confidence. But in religion115 they already know they will want for nothing, though I believe that whoever enters into it sincerely, for God's sake only, will not so much as think of this. But how many are there, daughters, who would not abandon what they have, were it not for the security they have in religion? And because, on other occasions, where I have given you directions, I have spoken at length116 of these pusillanimous souls, and shown what harm they receive thereby, and what immense good they derive by having at least great desires, when noble deeds cannot be done, I shall say here nothing more about them. Since, then, our Lord raises them to so high a state, let them serve Him therein, and shut themselves up in a corner; for though they be religious, if they cannot otherwise benefit their neighbours (especially women); yet by heroic resolutions and ardent desires of helping souls, their prayers will have great power; and either in their lifetime, or after their death, our Lord perhaps will be pleased to make them instrumental in doing good, just as He is doing now with regard to our holy brother Diego, who was a layman, and knew nothing but to serve; yet God revives His memory so many years after his death, in order that He may be an example to us, by which we shall be excited to praise His Majesty.

As, then, my daughters, our Lord has raised you to this state, you want but little towards obtaining that peace and friendship which the Spouse desires. Cease not to implore it with continual tears and fervent desires: do all you can on your part to induce Him to give it to you, though it is evident that this state is not the peace and friendship which the Spouse asks. Still our Lord confers a great favour on those whom He raises to this degree, because it is bestowed only after they have practised prayer, penance, humility, and many other virtues.

May our Lord be blessed for ever, who bestows all these upon us. Amen.

CHAPTER III.

ON TRUE PEACE – WHICH IS THE LOVE OF GOD, AND UNION WITH CHRIST.

"Let him kiss me with the kiss of his mouth." (Canticles, chap, i.)
O HOLY Spouse! we now come to that which you ask, viz., that blessed peace which makes a soul expose herself to a war with all the world, she herself remaining in perfect quiet and security. O! what a great happiness it is to obtain this favour! It is the union of a soul with the will of God, so that there may be no division between Him and her, but one and the same will, not in words and desires only, but supported by deeds; hence, when she knows that she can serve her Spouse better in something, she feels such a great love and desire to please Him, that she listens not to the reasons which the understanding offers to the contrary, nor does she heed the fears it represents to her; but she allows faith to operate. Hence she regards not her own profit or quiet, but understands now that therein consists all her benefit.

You may think, daughters, that what I have said is not exactly correct, since it is so commendable to act with discretion. But you should notice one thing, viz., to know (as far as you can, for it cannot be known for certain) whether our Lord has heard this your petition, "to kiss you with the kiss of His mouth." If you once discover this by the effects proceeding from it, you must not detain yourselves with anything, but forget yourselves in order to please so dear a Spouse.

His Majesty makes Himself, in many ways, perceived by those who enjoy this favour. One sign is, undervaluing all earthly things, and esteeming them as they really are; not desiring any earthly good, because you already know it is vanity; taking no delight except with those who love our Lord – to be weary of this life – to value riches just as they deserve, and so on. This is what He teaches those who have raised them to such a state. A soul who has arrived there has nothing to fear, unless her not having deserved that God should be pleased to make use of her, in giving her troubles and occasions whereby she may do Him some service, though it may cost her much.

Here, then (as I have said), love and faith work, and the soul does not make use of that, of which the understanding informs her. This union coming between the two spouses, has taught her other things which the understanding cannot reach, and which she therefore despises and treads under her feet.

In order that we may understand this better, I will make use of a comparison. In the country of the Moors, there is a slave, who has a father, or some great friend, very poor; and yet, unless he can redeem him, he has no means of being free. To effect this object, his whole estate is not sufficient; he must become a slave himself for this captive. The great love he has for him obliges him to prefer his friend's liberty before his own. But discretion immediately steps in with her many reasons, alleging that he is more bound to himself; and it may be, that he has less courage to bear such a captivity than the other; that possibly he may be forced to deny his faith, and that it is not proper to expose himself to such danger, and so on. But O! powerful love of God! How it thinks there is nothing impossible to one who loves! Happy the soul who has been able to attain this peace of her God, which this Lord gives in spite of all the dangers and afflictions of the world, none of which she fears in serving so dear a Spouse and Lord; nor does she heed the reasons such as the friend does whom we have just mentioned.

You have read, sisters, of a certain Saint named Paulinus, bishop and confessor, who, not for the sake of any son or friend, but because he must certainly have arrived at this happy state, viz. this peace of our Lord, and to please His Majesty, and in something to imitate all that He has done for us, went into the country of the Moors, 117 to be exchanged for a son of a certain widow, who came to him in great affliction; you have read how well he succeeded, and what great profit he gained thereby.

Lately, in our own times, I knew a person who came to visit me, whom our Lord moved with such great charity, that it cost him many tears to obtain leave to go and exchange himself for a slave. He spoke on the subject with me (for he belonged to the Discalced Fathers of Peter of Alcantara); and, after many entreaties, he obtained leave from his general: but when he was four leagues from Algiers (whither he was bound, in order to accomplish his desire), God took him to Himself, and no doubt he received a blessed reward. Now, how many discreet persons were there who told him it was a foolish undertaking? It seems such to those amongst us also, who have not arrived at such a great love of our Lord. And yet what greater extravagance, than for us to end the sleep of this life in such great prudence? God grant we may deserve to enter heaven, but much more to be of the number of those who have advanced so far in loving God.

But I now see that, in order to effect such things, we have need of His powerful assistance; and therefore I advise you, daughters, that with the Spouse, you always beg this sweet peace, because you may thus triumph over all the little fears of the world, and resist them with every kind of quiet and tranquillity. Is it not clear that on whomsoever God shall bestow so great a favour as to unite Himself in such close friendship with his soul, he will thereby become exceedingly enriched with His blessings? For truly these goods cannot come from us, but only by requesting and desiring that our Lord would bestow this favour upon us, and even this, too, by His assistance. As to the rest, what can a poor worm do when sin makes it so cowardly and miserable, that we measure all virtues exactly according to our mean capacity. Now, daughters, what remedy is there for this? To desire with the Spouse, "Let Him kiss me with the kiss of His mouth."

If a poor country girl should marry a king, and have children by him, are not those children of blood royal? Now, if our Lord confer so great a favour on a soul, as to unite Himself so inseparably to her, what desires, what effects, what children of heroic actions, 118 might not come from this union, unless it happen otherwise by her own fault! I am certain, that did we once come to the Most Holy Sacrament with great faith and love, that once would be sufficient to enrich us; how much more if we come frequently! But it seems our coming to Him is only a compliment, and, therefore, we derive such little benefit. O wretched world! that keepest so closely shut the eyes of those who live in thee, as not to discern the treasures with which they might purchase everlasting riches! O Lord of heaven and earth! how is it possible that, though living in this mortal life, one may enjoy you with such particular friendship, and that the Holy Ghost should so plainly express it in these words; and yet that we will not understand what are the caresses wherewith His Majesty regales souls in these Canticles? What courtings, what sweet attractions! Only one word would be sufficient to dissolve us into you. Blessed be you, O Lord! for we shall lose nothing on your part. By how many ways and means do you express love for us! By labours, by so cruel a death, by torments, by suffering every day, and pardoning injuries; and not only thus, but by certain words which wound the soul who loves you, which you scatter in the "Canticles," and which you teach her to say to you! I know not how these could be endured, except you helped him that feels them to endure them, not as they deserve, but in proportion to our weakness.

Now, my Lord, I ask you nothing else in this life but "to kiss me with the kiss of your mouth;" and this in such a way that I should not be able, even though I wished, to withdraw myself from this union and friendship. O Lord of my life! let my will always be so docile that it may never depart from yours; and that there may be nothing to hinder me from saying, "My God and my glory! 'your breasts are better than wine.'"

CHAPTER IV.

ON THE SWEET, PLEASANT, AND DELICIOUS LOVE OF GOD, WHICH ARISES FROM GOD DWELLING IN THE SOUL BY THE PRAYER OF QUIET, SIGNIFIED BY THE WORDS, "THE BREASTS OF GOD."

"Thy breasts are better than wine, smelling sweet of the best ointments." – (Canticles, chap, i.)
O MY daughters, what great mysteries are concealed under these words! God grant we may feel

them, for with difficulty can they be expressed. When His Majesty vouchsafes, in His mercy, to grant the spouse this petition, He begins to contract a friendship with the soul, which only those among you who have experienced it can understand. On this subject I have treated in two books, 119 (which, if our Lord please, you will see after my death), at great length, because I think you required it, and therefore I shall only touch on the matter here. I know not whether I shall explain it in the same words with which our Lord was pleased to enable me to explain in the books I wrote.

There is excited in the interior of the soul so great a sweetness, that it makes her perceive very clearly our Lord is very near to her. This is not that kind of devotion which excites one much to tears; for though these cause a certain tenderness when one weeps either over our Lord's passion, or over our own sins, yet it is not so great as this prayer I speak of, and which I call the "Prayer of Quiet," on account of the repose it produces in all the powers, so that the person seems to possess God just as he wishes most. It is true, that sometimes one finds it otherwise, when the soul is not so engulfed; but with this sweetness the whole interior and exterior man seems to be delighted, as if some very delicious ointment were poured into the inmost part of the soul, just like an exquisite perfume! It is as if we suddenly came into a place where it is exhaling, not only from one, but from many things; and we know not what it is, nor from which of them the scent comes, but they all penetrate us. And so this most delicious love of our God seems to enter into the soul with such great sweetness, as to content and satisfy her, though she cannot understand what it is.

This is the meaning of what the Spouse says here: – "Thy breasts are better than wine." And yet she knows not how, nor whence that good comes, which she would fain not lose. She would not so much as stir, or look aside, that it might not go away. And because, where I have spoken in what I wrote, I mentioned what the soul is to do here for her benefit (and this is only to let you understand something of what I have written), I will say no more here than tell you that, in this friendship our Lord now discovers to the soul, He is pleased to keep so strict an union with her, in order that nothing maybe divided between them both. Here great truths are imparted to her, for this light is such that it dazzles her in such a way, that she cannot know what the light is: it makes her see and understand the vanity of the world; though she does not see the master who teaches her, yet she already understands He is with her. She is then so well instructed, and this with such great effects and strength, in all virtues, that she afterwards knows not herself; nor would she do or say anything but praise our Lord. And when she is in this enjoyment, she is so immersed and absorpt, that she seems not to be herself, but rather to be seized with a kind of divine ebriety, 120 that she knows not what she wishes, nor what she asks. In a word, she knows nothing of herself, yet she is not so much out of herself as not to understand something of what passes.

It is true, that when this most opulent Spouse is pleased to enrich and more sweetly to caress souls, He so converts them into Himself, that like a person swooning through excessive delight and pleasure, the soul seems to herself to be suspended in those Divine arms, and to rest on that Divine side, and those Divine breasts: and she does nothing but enjoy herself, being supported by Divine milk, wherewith her Spouse feeds and strengthens her, that He may be able to regale her, and make her increase every day in merit.

When she wakes out of that sleep and that heavenly ebriety, she remains as it were astonished and stupid, and is seized with a kind of holy foolishness, so that it seems to me she may use these words, "Thy breasts are better than wine." When she was in the beginning of that ebriety, she thought she could ascend no higher; but when she saw herself in a more sublime degree, and wholly plunged in that immense greatness of God, whereby she perceives herself more supported, she affectionately compared it to breasts; and therefore she saith, "Thy breasts are better than wine." For as a child does not understand how he grows, nor knows how he sucks, for (even without his sucking the nipple, or doing anything on his part) often is the nipple put into his mouth; and so it is here; for the soul, of herself, is wholly ignorant whether she does anything; nor does she know how, nor whence, so great a good comes to her.

You must understand this is the greatest good that can be enjoyed in this life, even though all the delights and pleasures of the world were united together. She sees herself nourished and strengthened, without knowing when she merited it: she is also taught great truths without seeing the Master who taught her; she is confirmed in virtues, and caressed by Him who knows how and who is able to do it; she knows not what to compare it to, except to the caresses of a mother, who, tenderly loving her infant, nurses and fondles him.

O my daughters! may our Lord grant you to understand, or rather, to speak more correctly, to taste (for otherwise it cannot be conceived) what the joy of the soul is when she is thus affected. Hither let worldlings come, with their riches and lordships, with their pleasures, honours, and trinkets; for though they could enjoy all these without the troubles that inevitably follow them (which is impossible); yet they could not, in a thousand years, enjoy the pleasure which in one moment a soul possesses, which our Lord has brought to this state. If St. Paul says, that the sufferings of this life are not worthy to be compared with the glory to come, I say they are not worthy nor able to merit one hour of that delight which God gives here to the soul; and in my opinion, no joy or delight can be compared therewith, or can merit from our Lord so sweet a consolation, a union so close, a love which so evidently makes one understand the baseness of worldly things. Very pleasant labours those are here below, to be compared with this delight! For if they are not endured for God's sake, they are worthless; but if they should, His Majesty always proportions them according to our strength, since, being so miserable and cowardly, we are so afraid of them,

O my daughters! let us awake at length, for God's sake, out of this dream of the world, and consider that he reserves not for us in the other life the reward of loving Him, but He begins His payment in this. O my Jesus! who can declare the benefit that comes to us from casting ourselves into the arms of our Lord, and making a covenant with His Majesty, so that "I am for my Beloved, and my Beloved for me." Let us not love ourselves so excessively as "to pull out our own eyes," as the saying is. I repeat again, O my God! and I again beseech You, by the blood of Your Son, to bestow this favour upon me, "of kissing me with the kiss of Your mouth," and of giving me Your breasts, for without You, what am I, O Lord? If not united with You, what am I worth? If I turn away in the least from Your Majesty, where shall I stop? O my Lord, my Mercy, and my Good! what more excellent blessing can I wish for in this life, than to be so united to You, that there may be no division between You and me? In such company, what can appear difficult? When You are so near, what may not be attempted for You? What is there for which I can thank myself, and not rather blame myself exceedingly, for not serving You? With St.

Austin, I therefore beseech You with a fervent resolution; "Give what You command, and command what You please,"121 and I shall never, with Your assistance and grace, break Your commandments.

APPENDIX.

No. I.

1. THE earth which is uncultivated, though very fertile, will produce briers and thorns; and so will it be with a man's understanding.

2. Speak well of Spiritual things, such as religious men, priests, and hermits.

3. Among many persons, always speak little.

4. Conduct yourself modestly in all you do or say.

6. Never contend much, especially in matters of little moment.

6. Speak to every one with a well-regulated cheerfulness.

7. On no occasion show contempt.

8. Never blame any one without judgment, and humility, and self-confusion.

9. Accommodate yourselves to the temper of those you converse with; with the joyful be glad, and with the sorrowful sad: in a word, become all to all, that so you may gain all.

10. Never speak without weighing your words well, and fervently recommending them to our Lord, that so you may speak nothing which may displease Him.

11. Never excuse yourself, but upon very good grounds.

12. Never mention anything about yourself deserving of praise, such as your knowledge, virtues, descent, except you have some hope it may do good; and then mention it with humility, remembering that all these gifts come from the hand of God.

13. Never exaggerate anything; but give your opinion with moderation.

14. In every discourse and conversation, always bring in some spiritual subject, for this may prevent idle words and detraction.

15. Never assert anything without first being certain of it.

16. Never offer to give your opinion on all matters, except it be asked, or charity require it.

17. When any one speaks to you on spiritual subjects, hear him with humility and as a disciple, and take to yourself the good he shall say.

18. Discover all your temptations to your Superior and Confessor, and also your imperfections and difficulties, that he may give you advice and a remedy to overcome them.

19. Do not remain out of your cell, nor go out without a reason; and when you do go out, beg God's grace not to offend Him.

20. Neither eat nor drink, but at the usual time, and then give many thanks to God.

21. Do everything as if you were really in the presence of His Majesty, for by this means a soul gains much.

22. Never hear or speak ill of any one, except yourself: and when you rejoice in this, you are going on well.

23. Every action you do, offer it to God, and pray that it may tend to His honour and glory.

24. When you are merry, use no immoderate laughter, but an humble, modest, affable and edifying mirth.

25. Always imagine yourself to be the servant of all, and consider Christ our Lord in all, and thus you will show them respect and reverence.

26. Be ever ready to obey, as if Christ our Lord, in the person of your Superior, had commanded you.

27. In every action, and in every hour, examine your conscience; and having observed your defects, endeavour to correct them by the divine assistance: by this means, you will soon attain perfection.

28. Take no notice of the defects of others, but only of their virtues: mind your own defects.

29. Always have strong desires of suffering for Christ, in everything on every occasion.

30. Every day make frequent oblations of yourself to God, and do this with great fervour.

31. What you meditate upon in the morning, place before you all the day, and use much diligence in this point, for it will be of great benefit to you.

32. Observe carefully the thoughts with which our Lord may inspire you, and execute the desires which He shall give you in prayer.

33. Always shun singularity as much as possible, for it does great harm to a Community.

34. Often read the Constitution and Rules of your Order, and observe them faithfully.

35. In every creature consider the providence and wisdom of God, and in all things praise Him.

36. Disengage your heart from every object. Seek and you will find God.

37. Never show outwardly more devotion than you have within: but you may lawfully hide any indevotion.

38. Do not discover your devotion, but for some great necessity: "my secret to myself," said St. Francis and St. Bernard.

39. Complain not of your diet, whether good or bad: remember the gall and vinegar of Jesus Christ.

40. Speak to no one at table, nor lift up your eyes to look at another person.

41. Think on the table of heaven and its food, viz., God: and its guests, viz., the angels: raise up your eyes to that table and desire to sit down at it.

42. Before your Superior (in whom you should consider you see Christ himself), never speak except what is necessary, and with great reverence.

43. Never do anything which you would not do before every one.

44. Make no comparisons, for they are odious things,

45. When you are blamed for anything, receive the reproof with interior and exterior humility; and pray to God for your reprover.

46. When one Superior commands you something, do not tell him that another commands the contrary; but imagine they have all pious intentions, and obey each one in what he commands.

47. Be not curious to discover or ask questions about things that do not concern you.

48. Remember to bewail your past life and your present tepidity, and how unprepared you are for going to heaven; that so you may live in fear, which is the cause of great good.

49. Always do what those in the House desire of you, if it be not contrary to obedience; and answer them with humility and sweetness.

50. Desire nothing peculiar concerning diet and apparel, except upon some urgent necessity.

51. Never desist from mortifying and humbling yourself in all things, till death.

52. Ever accustom yourself to make frequent acts of love, for they inflame and soften the soul.

53. Make acts of all other virtues.

54. Offer all things to the Eternal Father, together with the merits of His Son Jesus Christ.

55. Be gentle to all, and to yourself severe.

56. On the Festivals of the Saints meditate on their virtues, and beseech God to endow you with them.

57. Use great care every night in the examination of your conscience.

58. On the day that you Communicate, let your prayer be to consider, that being so miserable a sinner, yet you are allowed to receive God; and at night, consider that you have received Him.

59. When you are Superioress, never blame any one in anger, but only when it is over, and thus your rebuke will do good.

60. Diligently aim at perfection, and conduct all your affairs with devotion.

61. Exercise yourself frequently in the fear of the Lord, for it keeps the soul in compunction and humility.

62. Consider well how soon persons change, and how little reason we have to trust them: adhere, therefore, closely to God, who is unchangeable.

63. Endeavour to treat on the affairs of your soul with a Confessor, who is spiritual and learned.

64. Every time you Communicate, beg some gift of God, through the great mercy wherewith He is pleased to come into your poor soul.

75. Though you may have many Saints for your advocates, yet choose particularly St. Joseph, for he is very powerful with God.

66. In time of sadness and trouble, do not omit the good works of prayer and penance you were accustomed to do; for the devil tries to make you omit them: but rather practise them more than formerly, and you will see how soon our Lord will relieve you.

67. Do not discover your temptations and imperfections to those of the House who are less advanced (for thus you may hurt both yourself and others), but only to the more perfect.

68. Remember that you have only one soul; that you can die but once; that you have but one short life; that there is but one glory, and this is Eternal, and thus you will endure many things.

69. Let your desire be to see God; your fear lest you lose Him; your grief that you do not enjoy Him; your joy at that which may bring you to Him; and thus you will live in great peace.

The following Maxims or Sentences are also supposed to have been composed by the Saint: –
Let nothing disturb you.   Nada te turbe.
Let nothing terrify you.   Nada te espante.
All things pass away. Todo se pasa.
God is unchangeable. Dios no se muda.
Patience gains everything.   La paciencia todo lo alcanza.
He who adheres to God wants nothing.   Quien à Dios tiene nada le falte.
God alone is sufficient.   Solo Dios basta.

No. II.

A LIST OF ST. TERESA'S WORKS.

1. Comes her "Life," written by herself, at the command of her Confessor. The Saint began to write it at Avila, in 1561: she completed it at Toledo the following year. She soon after divided it into Chapters, and added the History of the Foundation of St. Joseph's Convent. For remarks on this wondrous Life, see Preface to the English Translation. (Dolman, 1851.)

2. Next come what are called "Relations" (Relaciones), which seem to be additions to her Life. They consist of the First, Second, and Third Relation, and refer to a variety of spiritual subjects. The first was written in the Monastery of the Incarnation, 1560; and the second was composed the following year. The third is the most sublime and spiritual of the three. This was composed in 1576.

3. Is the "Way of Perfection" (Camino de Perfecion). See Preface to the Translation.

4. Is the "Interior Castle" (Castillo Interior), or "The Mansions" (Las Moradas). The Saint composed this work in obedience to her Confessor, Dr. Velasquez, who afterwards became Archbishop of Compostella. She commenced it at Toledo in the year 1577 and finished it at Avila the same year. It is divided into Seven Mansions. In the first Mansion, souls are described who have already some good desires; who pray mentally or vocally, though not so often nor with such great attention as they ought, being distracted with worldly pleasures or business. These persons are represented as being aware of their present state of misery, and seek help by prayer.

In the Second Mansion are souls who have partly overcome the great difficulties they suffered in the first Mansion, by the Divine assistance, and have left off some of their former sins: but they cannot conquer their will so far as to avoid the occasions of temptations to evil. They endure great afflictions and combats.

In the Third Mansion are souls who abstain from occasions of sin, and also from many venial sins: they are lovers of penance, prayer, and recollection, and sometimes enjoy great pleasure and sweetness, and likewise tenderness and the gift of tears: yet they are troubled with aridities, &c.

In the Fourth Mansion souls are advanced to the first degree of supernatural prayer, in which the will remains united to God, and certain spiritual delights and consolations are infused into the soul, which cannot be attained by human industry.

In the Fifth Mansion souls are still further united with God, by which the faculties of the soul are suspended, so that the imagination is unable to think of anything but God; and the body remains deprived of speech, sense, and motion. The soul also attains the Prayer of Union.

In the Sixth Mansion, the souls enjoy a total suspension of the faculties, joined with several acute, yet most delightful internal pains, which do not continue long, but often return.

In the Seventh Mansion, souls attain the highest and most sublime degree of supernatural prayer: they feel the presence of the Most Blessed Trinity in their interior, and derive the greatest joy from it. Raptures and ecstasies cease, and the senses and other faculties are not suspended.

Though this work is not so practical as the "Way of Perfection," yet it is more sublime, and more closely resembles the life. It was evidently written under the influence of divine inspiration, as the acts of her canonization testify. The purity of the style, and the sublimity of her doctrine are wonderful. What the Saint says in general terms in her "Life," is here reduced to method and order. Yepes, and Ribera, and Palafox, &c., speak in the highest terms of this work; and, indeed, St. Teresa herself prefers it to her "Life." (See Letter 44th, tom. ii.)

6. The "Foundations" (Libro de las Fundaciones) are a continuation of her "Life." They have been translated, and I hope will soon be published. In the preface I have given every particular respecting them. Our Lord Himself commanded the Saint to write them. She commenced the book in the year 1573.

It displays, in a most remarkable manner, all the heroic virtues for which the Saint was so wonderfully distinguished. No novel was ever so interesting, if I may be allowed such a comparison. The Foundation of the Monastery at Granada was added by the Ven. Anna à Jesu, by the command of P. Gratian.

6. "The Method of Visiting the Convents of Discalced Nuns," I have already translated: it is published by Duffy. The prudence, wisdom, judgment, and other virtues, which this short treatise displays, make it highly valuable.

7. "Conceptions of Divine Love on certain words of the Book of Canticles:" (Conceptos del Amor de Dios sobre algunas Palabras de los Cantares de Solamon). These "Conceptions" seem to have been written about the year 1577, or the beginning of 1578. They unfortunately consist of only seven chapters. Father Gratian informs us that the Saint wrote these "Conceptions" by the command of one of her confessors. But another priest (whose name the Saint does not mention),

to whom she soon after went to confession, commanded her to burn the manuscript, without having seen it, thinking, no doubt, that it was dangerous for an illiterate woman to write on so difficult a part of the Sacred Scripture. Saint Teresa immediately obeyed the command, and thus perished a work which, judging from the few chapters that remain, must have been in every way equal to her other books. The seven chapters were preserved by another person, who copied them before the manuscript was burnt. The confessor, no doubt, acted from the best and purest motives, but he ought certainly to have perused the manuscript before he gave the command: he would then have discovered that what the Saint wrote, was not an explanation of the "Book of Canticles," but only sublime meditations on prayer and the love of God.

Father Gratian published these seven chapters at Brussels, in the year 1612. D'Andilly says of them, "That he never remembers to have read anything so beautiful, and which so powerfully tends to raise up the soul to admire the infinite majesty of God, and the wonders of His grace."

8. "Exclamations of the Soul to her God," were first translated by the illustrious Bishop Milner (London, 1790). They were written in 1579, and not in 1569, as several writers mistake. It is also incorrect to style them "Exclamations after Communion." The Spanish title is, "Esclamaciones, o, Meditaciones del Alma à su Dìos." The language is high, clear, and penetrating, and full of divine aspirations.

9. "The Admonitions to her Nuns," I have translated in Appendix No. 1.

10. The Saint wrote some spiritual Hymns, called in Spanish, "Glosa." Under the name of a third person, the Saint thus alludes to her poetic effusions in the sixteenth chapter of her "Life:" – "I know a certain person who, though she was no poetess, made very feeling verses extempore, declaring the sweet pain she suffered; and these were not composed by her understanding," &c. In Appendix No. 4, annexed to the Translation of the Life, I have given the most sublime and remarkable of the poetic pieces, together with a French translation, by De La Monnoye. Woodhead has given an English translation, but it is a very poor one. Indeed, it is almost impossible properly to translate the original.

11. The "Letters" of the Saint are exceedingly valuable and interesting. She carried on a most extensive correspondence with Bishops, Monks, Nuns, Superiors, and friends and relatives, &c., for many years of her life. The number which has been published amounts to 342; and eighty-seven fragments of letters. The Spanish edition extends to four volumes quarto. It was first published in 1658, with the valuable notes of Palafox. The Abbé Migne published in 1840 three new letters of the Saint, which he discovered in the Convent of the Carmelites, at Paris. M. Pelicot was the first who translated the Saint's letters into French. (Anvers, 1707.) Another translation was made by Chappe de Ligny, but it does not include all the letters. Marie Marguerite de Maupeau, published another translation, which, though praised by many for its elegance and fidelity, does not, on the whole, seem to meet with the approbation of the Bollandists. (See vol. vii. p. 458.)

Several of the Saint's letters have unfortunately been lost. It is said that she commanded the Ven. Anna à Jesu to destroy all the letters she had ever received from her. St. John of the Cross also destroyed many of them, when he was persecuted for having taken the part of the Saint.

So powerful were the influence and sanctity of her life, that the reformation of her Order may be said to have been effected solely by her letters; and were these the only writings we possessed of the Saint, they would alone be a lasting monument to her fame. The purity and beauty of the style is perfect.

12. The Saint also drew admirable "Constitutions" for the government of her Reformed Order.

Among most of the Spanish editions and French translations, are found "Meditations on the Lord's Prayer." Several writers attribute them to St. Teresa. But the Bollandists prove that they ought not to be included among the genuine works of the Saint; first, because the style is quite different from St. Teresa's; second, because the tradition of the whole Order is against their being attributed to the Saint; third, because most of her biographers pass them over in silence, which they would not certainly do had they been convinced the "Meditations" were written by the Saint; fourth, why should she think it necessary to explain the Lord's Prayer when she had already done so in the "Way of Perfection?"

Still the "Meditations" are very useful. I translated them because I once thought they were genuine.

"It is by studying the Saint's Works," as Ribera observes, "that her seraphic virtues and sublime genius are discovered, and with what fulness of grace our Lord caressed her." (Lib. v. cap. xxxv.) The Bull of the Saint's canonization thus bears testimony to the excellence of her works: – "Præter hæc omnia divinæ beneficiæ munera, quibus hanc Dilectam suam, quasi pretiosis monilibus decoratam esse voluit Omnipotens, aliis etiam gratiis et donis abundè ipsam locupletavit: adimplevit enim eam spiritu intelligentiæ, ut non solum bonorum operom in Ecclesiâ, Dei exempla relinqueret, sed et illam cœlestis sapientiæ imbribus irrigaret, editis de Mysticâ Tbeologiâ, aliisque etiam multâ pietate refertis libellis, ex quibus Fidelium mentes uberrimos fructos percipiunt, et ad supernæ patriæ desiderium maximè excitantur." (15.) I know of no Saint's works which have received such unqualified praises, as are here bestowed, by the highest authority in the Church, on the writings of St. Teresa.

Luis de Leon thus expresses his high opinion of the Saint's works: – "The Holy Spirit has left us, in the writings of St. Teresa, a most rare and admirable example; for she far outstrips the genius of many authors, in the sublimity of her subjects, and the clearness and depth with which she handles them. As to the purity of her diction, and the elegance of her style, which are so pleasing to her readers, I know no one in our language who can be compared with her. Hence, as often as I read her works, I cannot help admiring them exceedingly; nay in many parts, it seems to me that I hear not a woman speaking, but the Holy Spirit Himself, for I am firmly persuaded that He often directed her pen, and inspired her with thoughts and expressions," &c. (Preface to the Saint's Works.)

Nicolas Antonio (in Bibl. Hisp. art. Teresia) thus expresses his admiration: – "The most difficult subjects, which are far above the powers and genius of the most learned men, this simple and illiterate virgin explains in her works with such clearness and penetration, that one must acknowledge (as indeed the Saint herself does) that she acquired her learning from above." Don

Eugenio de Ochoa has published some of the select works of the Saint, and in his preface to the "Way of Perfection," he uses these words:– "Plena del amor de Dios y mirando con horror todo lo que pudiese ofenderle o' apartarle de él, da à sus palabras un baño, por decirlo asi, de ternura, y á sus imagenes un no sé qué de infantil, de dulce, de sencillo que arrebata el alma, abrasa el corazon, y seduce los sentidos... Como escritora y como muger Santa Teresa fué admiracion del siglo de Felipe II. y el objeto de los elogios de los Prelados y mas aventaja dos escritores de aquel y de los siguientes reinados; y si las alabanzas dc hombres de conscido talento dan mayor brillo á la auréola de gloria que circunda un nombre, pocas serán tan radiosas comola de la Santa, pues le dieron su luz los Luises, los Palafox, los Yuepes, los Ripaldas, los Riberas, el Maestro Avila, los Ibañez, y otros insignes letrados."

The testimonies of other learned men may be seen in the Bollandists (vol. vii. p. 461).

It is remarkable, that the illustrious and profound Leibnitz exceedingly esteemed and praised the works of our Saint. (See his Epist. to Andreo Morelli, anno 1696.)

No. III.

F. Louis de Leon mentions, that some papers came into his hands written by St. Teresa, among which he found the following "Relations," which he thought worthy of being published. They come (in the Antwerp ed. 1649) immediately after the Saint's Life.

"Our Lord one day said to me: Thinkest thou, daughter, that merit consists in enjoying? No: it is only in working, in suffering, and in loving? (Piensas, Hija, que estè el merecer en gozar? No: està sino en obrar, en padecer, y en amar.) Thou hast never heard that St. Paul was admitted to heavenly joys, except once, but that he suffered often; and thou seest my whole life was full of sufferings, and only once hast thou heard of my joy on Mount Thabor. Think not, when thou seest my mother holding me in her arms, that she enjoyed the delight without grievous torments. From the time when Simeon spoke these words: "Thine own soul a sword shall pierce," my Father gave her a clear light to see what I was to suffer. The great Saints who lived in the deserts did great penance, and besides had very great conflicts with the devil and with themselves, and they passed a long time without spiritual consolation. Believe me, daughter, that whom my Father loves best, He afflicts the most, and His love is proportioned to the crosses He sends them. In what can I express my love for you more, than by desiring for you what I chose for myself? Behold these wounds: your sorrow will never equal these."

"When I began to apply myself that day to prayer, I felt such a violent pain in my head, that I thought it would be almost impossible for me to pray. Our Lord then said to me: 'By this, daughter, thou mayst see the reward of my suffering, for since thou wantest health to speak with me, I have spoken to thee and caressed thee.' It is certain that I remained recollected afterwards, for about an hour and a half, during which He spoke to me the words I have just mentioned. I knew not where I was, and I experienced such great joy that I cannot express it. My head also got well, at which I wondered much, though I had an extreme desire to suffer.

"On Palm-Sunday, after I had communicated, I was seized with a great rapture, so that I could not swallow the heart; and as I kept it in my mouth, I thought when I came to myself, that my mouth was full of blood, and it seemed that both my face and body were covered with it: it also appeared to be warm, as if our Lord had just then shed it. The sweetness I found was excessive. (Me parece estava caliente, como que entonces acabara de derramarla el Señor, y era excesiva la suavidad que entonces sentia, &c.) Our Lord said to me: 'Daughter, I wish my blood to benefit thee, and fear not lest my mercy should fail thee. I shed it with great pain, and thou enjoyest it with great delight. Thou seest I abundantly reward the pleasure which thou hast given me this day.' These words He spoke, because for above thirty years I was accustomed to communicate on Palm-Sunday, if I could, and I endeavoured to prepare my soul to entertain my Lord, for I thought the Jews had shown Him great cruelty, after so solemn a reception.

"I had read in a book, that it was an imperfection to keep curious pictures, upon which I desired to part with one that I had in my cell; and even before I read this, I thought it more becoming religious poverty to have none but those which were made of paper. Our Lord spoke to me on this subject and said: 'This is no good mortification; which was better, poverty or the love of God? Since then love was lost, whatever helped to excite love, I was neither to remove from myself, nor forbid it to my nuns; that the book only spoke of superfluous pictures, not against pictures themselves; that the devil laboured with the followers of Luther, to deprive them of all means of exciting affections, and so they went on to destruction. My faithful ones, daughter, ought now more than ever, to practise the contrary to what they do. (Que lo que el demonio hazia con los Luteranos, era quitarles todos los medios para mas despertar, y asi iban perdidos.')

"Being one day in fear whether I were in a state of grace or no, our Lord said to me: 'Daughter, light is widely different from darkness: none shall perish without knowing it. He will deceive himself that presumes on spiritual favours: true security is the testimony of a good conscience. But let no one think that he can of Himself remain in light; this depends on my grace. The best remedy for keeping in the light is to know that the soul of herself can do nothing, and that all comes from me; for though she be in the light, yet the moment that I depart, night comes on. This is true humility, for a soul to know what she can do, and what I can do. Do not omit to write down the admonitions which I give you, lest they be forgotten.'

"On St. Sebastian's Eve, the first year that I was prioress in the monastery of the Incarnation, as the choir was beginning the 'Salve Regina,' I saw the Mother of God descending with a great multitude of angels, and placing herself in the seat of the prioress. I thought I saw not the picture which was over the seat, but our Lady herself. She seemed to me somewhat to resemble the picture given to me by the Countess (of Osma,) though I had but little time to compare them, being in a great ecstasy. She continued thus all the time of the 'Salve,' and said to me: 'Thou didst well to place me here. I will be present at the praises which are given to my Son, and will present them to Him (Yo estarè presente à las alabanzas que hizieren à mi Hijo, y se las presentarè.')

"One day after receiving the most B. Sacrament, I thought I saw most clearly that our Lord placed Himself near me, and began to comfort me with great kindness. Among other things He said: 'Seest thou here, daughter, that it is I? Show me thy hands.' Methought He took them and put them to His side, and said: 'Behold my wounds: thou art nothing without me.' By some things which He told me, I understood that after He ascended into heaven, He never descended on earth to converse with any one, except in the holy Sacrament. He told me that at His Resurrection He visited His Mother, because she had great need of Him, for her grief had so deeply pierced her heart that for some time she was not in her senses; He remained a long time with her, because it was necessary.

"After I had once communicated on the second day in Lent, in St. Joseph's monastery at Malagon, our Lord appeared to me in a vision represented to the imagination; and while I was looking on Him, I saw that instead of the crown of thorns on His head, He had a crown of excessive splendour. Being much devoted to this mystery (the crowning with thorns), I was exceedingly comforted with the sight; and I began to think what a grievous torment that must have been, which had so many wounds. Our Lord told me, 'not to grieve for these wounds, but for the many which men now gave Him.' I asked what I could do to remedy these insults? I was resolved to do anything. He answered: 'It was now no time for rest, but that I should hasten the erection of these houses because He took repose in the souls of those who were in those monasteries. That I should receive as many as offered themselves, for there were several persons who did not serve Him, because they had no monastery to enter.' He commanded me to write the 'Foundation of these Houses, &c.'"

There are several other "Relations" of the saint, which I have translated and published. (See "Select Translations from St. Teresa." Duffy, Dublin, 1850.)

No. IV.

THE following details connected with an authentic likeness of St. Teresa, kindly furnished me by the Rev. John Wyse, will be found interesting.

"I believe there are two or three authentic portraits of the Saint, taken at different periods of her Life. I am well acquainted with one, existing in a monastery of the Order where I once spent several months. The place is about fifteen miles from Rome, and is called Monte Compatri.

"The picture is considered to be very valuable. St. Teresa is represented in her habit, and at the age of sixty-three, and is strikingly unlike any of the ideal portraits of her. The likeness, however, is known to be very exact, as it gives every trait with precision, even to the moles which the Saint had on her face. Great care of course is taken of it, and the monks tell you even of certain wonders performed by its means. On the whole, it is most interesting, as being the only one taken at that time of her life," &c.

I wish my reverend friend could inform me in what year the likeness was taken. Mr. Digby has also seen the same picture. I may add here, that there is a very fine likeness of the Saint at Princethorpe Convent, belonging to the Rev. C. Comberbach. It is however only a copy, the original being now in the possession of a community at Brussels. An original portrait is said to exist in a convent of the Order at Vienna; and the Bollandists, in their last magnificent volume, give what appears to be a good likeness of the Saint. The two fervent communities of Teresians in England possess likenesses of their seraphic mother, but they cannot vouch for their being authentic.

The following interesting description of St. Teresa's person is taken from Ribera's Life of the Saint: –

"As among the angels, the one who is endowed with greater gifts of nature surpasses his fellows in the order of grace; so it often happens among creatures, that those whom the Almighty favours with more especial spiritual gifts, are at the same time possessed of great bodily attractions. Such was the case with the blessed Teresa, for the love our Lord bore her was manifested in her natural acquirements.

"In her younger days she was of good stature and pleasing form, and of this traces remained, even till the period of her death. Her body was stout and fair; her face round and full, and of an agreeable expression; her complexion was somewhat ruddy, which during prayer was often illuminated, and shone with resplendent brightness. The whole countenance had a sweetness of expression far above nature.

"Her hair was black and curly, and the forehead high, regular, and beautiful. Her eyes were round and black, and slightly protruded, but not immoderately; they were well set, and of a soft and lively expression. When she laughed, they glistened and bore a disarming sweetness, though when she wished to assume a grave appearance her eyes spoke her thoughts.

"Her nose was small, out the extremity was round and somewhat prominent. It cannot be said that her mouth was either large or small; the upper lip was regular and delicately formed, but the lower a little thick and slightly bent; still there was on them a something very sweet and beautiful. Her teeth were also exceedingly beautiful; and her chin was remarkably fine. Her neck was large, though rather short. Her hands were small and delicately formed.

"On the left side of her face were three small moles, which added greatly to the natural beauty of her countenance. One was a little below the middle of her nose, another between the mouth and nose, and a third below the mouth.

"These particulars of her person I received from those who for a long time enjoyed her friendship. During the Saint's lifetime, John of Miseria took her likeness, by the command of his Provincial, Father Gratian. By ordering this likeness to be made, he conferred a great favour on posterity; though, considering who the Saint was, he ought to have had the best painter in Spain." (Book iv. chap, i.) See the Bollandist (p. 345), where a likeness of the Saint is given, according to the description above.

FINIS.

NOTES.

1 See Chapters xxxii, xxxiii, and xxxiv.

2 Chapter xxxvi. (page 342).

3 See the last vol. of the Bollandists.

4 See Yepez, "Vida de Santa Teresa" (lib. ii.); also "History of the Carmelite Order," written in Spanish by Francis de Sainte Marie, and translated into French by Gabriel de la Croix. (Paris, 1655.)

5 The whole of the "Primitive Rule "may be seen in Woodhead's Translation (Part ii).

6 "Cinco años despues de la fundacion de S. Joseph de Avila, estuve en el; que à lo que ahora me parece, entiendo seràn los mas descansados de mi vida, cuyo sosiego y quietud hecha harto menos muchas vezes mi alma." (Fundacion de Medina del Campo, cap. i.)

7 "Yo me estaba deleitando entre almas tan Santas y limpias, adonde solo era su cuidado, servir y alabar à nuestro Señor." (Cap. i.)

8 "Camino de Perfeccion," is the Spanish title.

9 "Libro che può dirse e piano, e sublime, e in vero dignessimo d'esser letto quotidianamente da chiunque fa profession di virtù." (S. Antonio, "Vita di Santa Teresa," lib. iv. cap. x.)

10 Speaking of the Saint, Palafox uses these remarkable words: "No he visto hombre devoto de Santa Teresa, que no sea espiritual. No he visto hombre espiritual, que si lee sus obras, no sea devotissimo de Santa Teresa." (Carta al Reverendissimo Padre Fr. Diego de la Visitacion.)

"I have not known any one who was devoted to St. Teresa, that did not become a spiritual man; nor have I met with any one who has read her works, that was not exceedingly devoted to her."

11 In her Life, now translated into English.

12 "Quieren poner su Iglesia por el suelo," &c.

13 Not in the original.

14 "Es un señorio grande."

15 "En lo interior procuremos tenerla."

16 Literally, "Dos horas son de vida" – we have only two hours of life.

17 "Habedla desta pecadorcilla, gusanillo, que ansi se os atreve."

18 That is, they will be holy; like their superior.

19 "Que tratan groseramente de contentar á Dios."

20 "El desear tener para regarlarla," &c.

21 "Por espiritu que uno les parezca tenga," &c.

22 "Gente de espiritu y letras."

23 Avila.

24 I have ventured to make a slight alteration here: the original is, "Que cosa es amar al Creador, ó á la creatura" – what it is to love the Creator or the creature.

25 "Venido á adelgazar, no me parece se sufre aqui," &c.

26 That is, at the fault.

27 "Sino varones fuertes."

28 "Y la entendiere alborota." "Alborota" is one who makes a noise or tumult in the community.

29 These words in brackets are not in the original, but I have added them to make the sense more complete.

30 "Ninguno dexamos de llorar, y algunas vezes mas que los mesmos."

31 That is, pious people.

32 Since our nature is always the same.

33 O soberanas virtudes, señoras de todo criado, emperadoras del mundo, libradoras de todos lazos y enredos que pone el demonio, tan amadas de nuestro Enseñador Jesu Cristo! Quien las treviere, bien puede salir y pelear con todo el infierno junto, &c.

34 By taking good care of their body, they prolong their life. This the saint blames in the nuns.

35 This is a good specimen of the saint's playfulness and wit, for which she was so remarkable.

36 In the way of eating more than the rule allows.

37 That is, one who complains without cause.

38 Literally, "Sé que no ha de volver las espaldas."

39 The words within brackets I have ventured to add, in order to make the sense clearer.

40 That is, must not on any account say, "I had reason," &c.

41 Mas unas condiciones, que hay de suyo, amigas de ser estimadas y tenidas.

42 Para qué quiere hacer daño á este colegio de Cristo?

43 "Cuando no proveche para mucho espiritu," &c.

44 "Bien que hay unas simplicidades santas."

45 Literally, "Pensando que es lo que es, y que es lo que no es."

46 "Que voy entablando el juego." What I have been saying is only preparatory to other more important things.

47 That is, to gain the victory.

48 "Que no quede por él." I do not clearly see the meaning of these words.

49 "Una determinacioncilla." This word is a diminutive.

50 In her Life, now translated into English. – (Dolman.)

51 "Gentíl humildad será querer vosotras eacoger," &c. D'Audilly thus translates the words: "Le serait ce pas une plaisante humilité que de vouloir passer à un autre?"

52 "El Señor le sacará á puerto de luz."

53 That is, in the prayer of union.

54 The Saint, no doubt, alludes to herself.

55 "Sino con suavidad cortar el hèlo con otra consideracion," &c.

56 That is, drinking of this Living Water.

57 "No es ya tiempo, Hermanas, de huego de Niños," &c.

58 "Que no sabe Algarabia," &c.

59 "Este viaje divino, que es camino real para el cielo."

60 These words I have added, to make the sense clearer.

61 These words are not in the original.

62 "Pues qué es esto, Señor mio? Qué es esto, mi Emperador? Como se puedo suffrir? Rey sois, Dios mio, sin fin, que no es reino prestado el que teneis."

63 This sentence is very difficult in the Spanish.

64 "O Emperador nuestro, sumo Poder, suma Bondad, la mesma Sabiduria sin principio, sin fin, sin haber terminos en vuestras Perfeciones, son infinitas sin poderse comprehender, un piélago sin suelo de maravillas, una hermosa que tiene en si todas las hermosuras, la mesma fortaleza!"

65 "Que no es delicado mi Dios."

66 These words I have added.

67 That is, the relation of her Life.

68 "Que seais vos la Señora."

69 The Saint alludes to the "Our father," which she commences explaining in the next chapter.

70 St. Teresa has likewise written some beautiful "Meditations on the Lord's Prayer," which I have lately translated into English. (Duffy, Dublin, 1850). It is disputed, however, whether these "Meditations" were really written by the Saint.

71 The Saint seems to be mistaken here. (See Butler, Aug. 24.)

72 Literally, "de mejor tierra."

73 "Porque recoge el alma todas las potencias."

74 "Toma alli bastimento," &c.

75 "De gente baga y de baratijas."

76 I am not quite sure if I have translated this sentence correctly. The Spanish is obscure.

77 "Aunque no en esta perfecion, ni en un ser," &c.

78 "Es como un amortecimiento interior, y exteriormente," &c.

79 Love.

80 "Que era muy posible." It was very possible she did not understand it. The subject is treated at length in the Saint's Life. (See "Translation:" Dolman, 1851.)

81 This sentence I am unable to understand.

82 This long sentence is very obscure.

83 That is, have arrived at this degree of prayer.

84 "Y despues tan escasos," &c.

85 "Cúmplase, Señor, en mi vuestra voluntad: si quereis con trabajos, dadme esfuerzo, y vengan: si con persecuciones, y enfermedades, y deshonoras, y necesiades, aqui estoy: no volveré, Padre mio, el rostro, ni es razon vuelva las espaldas."

86 "Que manden á veces, como dicen," &c.

87 "Panem nostrum quotidianum da nobis hodie."

88 "Maná de la humanidad."

89 "Desventurados destos herejes, que han perdido por su culpa esta consolacion con otras!"

90 That is, in this world.

91 Here the Saint shows the same wonderful humility that appears in her "Life."

92 "Ya, Señor, ya, Señor, haced que sosiegue este mar."

93 "No ande siempre en tanta tempestad esta nave de la Iglesia."

94 Receiving our Lord's body.

95 This Sentence is much longer in the original, and hence I was obliged to divide it.

96 "Haced vos esto, Señor, y harán mis hermanos estotro."

97 "Sono como los soldados, que están mas contentos, cuando hay mas guerra," &c.

98 "Que nos desjarreta las piernas para no andar este camino," &c.

99 "Tiénelo por cosa accessoria, y no principal."

100 "Despedazada irá al infierno!"

101 "Embebida en juego de Niños."

102 "Mas pacado muy de advertencia, por muy chico que sea, Dios nos libre dél, que yo no sé como tenemos tanto atrevimiento, como es ir contra un tan Gran Señor, aunque sea en muy poca cosa," &c.

103 That is, the fear of God.

104 This sentence is very long and obscure in the Spanish, and hence the translation also must be obscure.

105 "Y lo que no se puede suffrir, Señor, es no poder saber cierto que os ama," &c.

106 That is, the "Way of Perfection."

107 The Saint mentions this holy man in her Life.

108 "Conceptos del Amor de Dios sobre algunas Palabras de los Cantares" is the Spanish title.

109 St. Teresa would never mention the name of the confessor.

110 Ribera says of him: "Illius qui tam temerè imprudenterque id mandare est ausus – quod non intelligebat." (Lib. iv. cap. iii.)

111 That is, the style of the book of Canticles.

112 "Porque tengo muy mala memoria, y asi no podrè dezir sino lo que el Señor me eñsare," &c. These words show us, that the Saint was divinely assisted in her writings. She says the same in her "Life."

113 That is, those souls whom I have known.

114 "Una obra virtuosa sea principio de mucho mal," &c.

115 That is, in the religious life.

116 The Saint evidently alludes to the "Book of the Foundations," in which the subject is treated. I have translated this work, but it is not yet published.

117 St. Paulinus was Bishop of Nola, but Alban Butler does not mention the circumstance of his having gone among the Moors.

118 "Que hijos de obras heroïcae podràn nacer de alli!"

119 The "Interior Castle." Castillo Interior, o Las Moradas, is the Spanish title of the books.

120 "Con una manera de borrachez divina," &c.

121 "Da quod jubes, et jube quod vis."

Printed in Great Britain
by Amazon.co.uk, Ltd.,
Marston Gate.